FAST TRACK TO A 5

Preparing for the **AP***
United States Government & Politics Examination

To Accompany
American Government
by James Q. Wilson and John J. DiIulio, Jr.

David G. Benson
Cherry Creek High School, Greenwood Village, Colorado

Karen K. Waples
Cherry Creek High School, Greenwood Village, Colorado

McDougal Littell A Houghton Mifflin Company
Evanston, Illinois   Boston   New York

Printed in the U.S.A.

ISBN: 0-618-57319-4

123456789-QUD-09 08 07 06 05

CONTENTS

About the Authors   vii

Preface   ix

Part I: Strategies for the AP Examination   1

Preparing for the AP Exam   3
What's in This Book   3
Setting Up a Review Schedule   4
Before the Examination   4

Taking the AP U.S. Government & Politics Exam   6
Strategies for the Multiple-Choice Section   6
Types of Multiple-Choice Questions   7
Free-Response Questions   10
Scoring for Free-Response Questions   12

A Diagnostic Test   15
United States Government and Politics Examination   15
Answer Key   33
Calculating Your Score on the AP Exam   43

Part II: A Review of AP U.S. Government & Politics   45

Chapter 1. The Constitution   47
The Path to Independence   48
The Articles of Confederation   49
The Constitutional Convention   50
James Madison as Architect   51
Ratification of the Constitution   52
Changing the Constitution   53
Multiple-Choice and Free-Response Questions   54

Chapter 2. Federalism   58
Sharing Power   59
Federalism's Historical Trail   59
Federalism and State Monies   62
Mandates   62
Multiple-Choice and Free-Response Questions   64

Chapter 3. Theories of Democratic Government   69
Power and Authority   70
The Meaning of Democracy   70
Distribution of Political Power   71
Political Change   73
Multiple-Choice and Free-Response Questions   74

Chapter 4. American Political Culture   79
Politics, Economics, and Religion   80
Sources of Political Culture   81
Mistrust of Government   83
Political Efficacy   83
Political Tolerance   84
Multiple-Choice and Free-Response Questions   84

Chapter 5. Public Opinion and Political Beliefs   89
The Problem of Defining Public Opinion   90
Sources of Public Attitudes   90
Cleavages in Public Opinion   91
Political Ideology   92
Political Elites and Public Opinion   93
Multiple-Choice and Free-Response Questions   94

Chapter 6. Political Participation   100
The American Electorate   101
Voter Turnout   102
Participation   103
Multiple-Choice and Free-Response Questions   105

Chapter 7. Elections and Campaigns   111
Comparing Presidential and Congressional Campaigns   112
How Campaigns Are Conducted   113
Money and Campaigning   114
Elections and Party Alignments   116
Multiple-Choice and Free-Response Questions   116

Chapter 8. Political Parties   122
The Rise and Decline of Political Parties   123
Parties at the National, State, and Local Levels   124
The Two-Party System and Minor Parties   126
Delegates and Voters   127
Multiple-Choice and Free-Response Questions   127

Chapter 9. Interest Groups   133
The Growth of Interest Groups   133
Kinds of Interest Groups   134
Interest Groups in Action   136
Multiple-Choice and Free-Response Questions   138

Chapter 10. Mass Media   144
The Background and Structure of the Media   145
Government Influence on the Media   147
Effects of the Media on Politics   147
Interpreting Political News   148
Multiple-Choice and Free-Response Questions   149

Chapter 11. Congress   155
The Evolution and Composition of Congress   156
Types of Representation   158
The Organization of Congress   158
How a Bill Becomes a Law   160
Power and Ethics in Congress   162
Multiple-Choice and Free-Response Questions   163

Chapter 12. The Presidency 169
Divided Government and the Powers of the Presidency 170
The Executive Branch 171
Presidential Power in Action 172
The President's Program 173
Vice Presidents and Presidential Succession 174
Multiple-Choice and Free-Response Questions 175

Chapter 13. The Bureaucracy 182
Growth of the Bureaucracy 183
Activities of Agencies 183
Bureaucrats 184
Congressional Oversight 185
Reforming the Bureaucracy 186
Multiple-Choice and Free-Response Questions 187

Chapter 14. The Federal Courts 192
The Development of the Federal Courts 193
The Selection of Judges 194
The Jurisdiction of the Federal Courts 194
The Powers of the Supreme Court 195
Checks on Judicial Power 196
Multiple-Choice and Free-Response Questions 197

Chapter 15. Policy-Making in the Federal System 202
Setting the Political Agenda 203
Costs, Benefits, and Policy 204
Business Regulation: A Case Study 205
Perceptions, Beliefs, Interests, and Values 206
Multiple-Choice and Free-Response Questions 207

Chapter 16. Economic Policy and the Budget 212
Economic Health 213
The Politics of Taxing and Spending 214
The Machinery of Economic Policy-Making 215
The Budget 216
Multiple-Choice and Free-Response Questions 217

Chapter 17. Domestic Policy: Social Welfare and the Environment 223
Social Welfare Politics and Policy 224
The Politics of Environmental Protection 226
Multiple-Choice and Free-Response Questions 229

Chapter 18. Foreign and Military Policy 235
The Constitutional and Legal Context 236
Foreign Policy Making Since World War II 237
The Foreign Policy Elite 238
The Defense Budget 239
The Structure of Military Decision-Making 240
Multiple-Choice and Free-Response Questions 241

Chapter 19. Civil Rights   247

The Background of the Civil Rights Movement   248
The Civil Rights Movement in the Courts   248
The Civil Rights Movement in Congress   250
Women and Equal Rights   251
Affirmative Action   252
Multiple-Choice and Free-Response Questions   253

Chapter 20. Civil Liberties   259

Background of Civil Liberties Issues   260
First Amendment Rights   260
Rights of the Accused   262
Terrorism and Civil Liberties   263
Multiple-Choice and Free-Response Questions   264

Part III: Practice Tests   271

Practice Test 1

United States Government and Politics Examination   273
Answer Key   286
Calculating Your Score   295

Practice Test 2

United States Government and Politics Examination   296
Answer Key   310
Calculating Your Score   318

ABOUT THE AUTHORS

DAVID G. BENSON has been teaching for twenty-six years. A member of the Cherry Creek High School Social Studies Department, he comes to AP U.S. Government and Politics by way of U.S. History, Humanities, Law, World History, International Government, World Geography, and AP Comparative Government. For the past three years he has been an AP examination grader for the College Board.

KAREN K. WAPLES has taught for sixteen years. Coordinator of the Social Studies Department at Cherry Creek High School, she has graded AP U.S. History examinations and now grades AP U.S. Government and Politics examinations. In addition, she conducts one-day workshops and one-week institutes in the western region for the College Board, and she is a College Board "trainer of trainers."

PREFACE

It is our hope that you will find this review book helpful in brushing up on the extensive material covered in an AP U.S. Government and Politics course. Years of teaching our own AP students have taught us that some of the best learning goes on in the process of review rather than in the original presentation of the material, for review affords you the opportunity to see the broad outlines of the subject. The content in this book is condensed, but we are confident that you will encounter on the examination little, if anything, that does not appear in these pages.

We are indebted to two fine teachers who critiqued our work. They brought enormous brainpower to the project. Ken Wedding must be the preeminent AP Government and Politics teacher in the nation. Further, he has graded AP exams, written his own review book for AP Comparative Government and Politics, and now serves as a national consultant to the College Board. Ken's editorial suggestions not only were invaluable for our writing but often extended our own knowledge of American government. A born historian, Charles Robinson teaches on the college level, and his astute comments showed him to be a commanding teacher of history and government and a master at turning a phrase. Margot Mabie is perhaps the most supportive project manager anywhere, and her gift of language in writing and editing shows up even in mundane e-mails. Finally, we would like to thank our students, whose intelligence, energy, and enthusiasm inspire us. We learn from them every day.

David G. Benson
Karen K. Waples
Cherry Creek High School
Greenwood Village, Colorado
November 2004

Part I

Strategies for the AP Examination

PREPARING FOR THE AP* EXAM

Advanced Placement can be exhilarating. Whether you are taking an AP course at your school or you are working on AP independently, the stage is set for a great intellectual experience. As the school year progresses and you burrow deeper and deeper into the course work, you can see the broad concepts that undergird government and politics in the United States. Fleshing out those concepts with a growing collection of nuances is exciting. More exciting still is recognizing examples of these concepts in the media.

But sometime after New Year's day, when the examination begins to loom on a very real horizon, Advanced Placement can seem downright intimidating—in fact, offered the opportunity to take the examination for a lark, even adults long out of high school refuse. If you dread taking the test, you are in good company.

The best way to deal with an AP examination is to master it, not let it master you. If you can think of these examinations as a way to show off how your mind works, you have a leg up: attitude *does* help. If you are not one of those students, there is still a lot you can do to sideline your anxiety. This book is designed to put you on a fast track. Focused review and practice time will help you master the examination so that you can walk in with confidence and get a 5.

WHAT'S IN THIS BOOK

This book is keyed to *American Government*, by James Q. Wilson and John J. DiIulio, Jr.; but because it follows the College Board Topic Outline, it is compatible with all textbooks. It is divided into three sections. Part I offers suggestions for getting yourself ready, from signing up to take the test and sharpening your pencils to organizing a free-response essay. At the end of Part I you will find a Diagnostic Test. This test has all of the elements of the U.S. Government and Politics examination, but the sixty multiple-choice questions are organized according to the College Board Topic Outline. When you go through the answers at the end of the Diagnostic Test, you will see how the examination is weighted for each content area; a cluster of wrong answers in one area will show you where you are weak. Page references at the end of each answer indicate where you will find the discussion on that particular point in both the 8th and 9th editions of *American Government*. Scoring is explained, so you will have some idea of how well you can do.

Part II, made up of twenty chapters—again following the College Board Topic Outline—is especially valuable for those who took the course in the fall semester and are taking the examination months later, in the spring. These chapters are not a substitute for your textbook and class discussion; they simply review the U.S. Government and Politics course. At the end of each chapter you will find ten multiple-choice questions and two free-response questions based on the material in that chapter. Again, you will find page references at the end of each answer directing you to the discussion on that particular point in *American Government.*

Part III has two complete AP U.S. Government and Politics examinations. At the end of each test you will find the answers, explanations, and references to *American Government* for the sixty multiple-choice questions and the four free-response questions. Following the answers and explanations is a work sheet that you can fill in to calculate your score and see how you scored compared with students who took the test in 2002.

SETTING UP A REVIEW SCHEDULE

If you have been steadily doing your homework and keeping up with the coursework, you are in good shape. But even if you've done all that—or if it's too late to do all that—there are some more ways to get it all together.

To begin, read Part I of this book. You will be much more comfortable going into the test if you understand how the test questions are designed and how best to approach them. Then take the Diagnostic Test and see where you are right now.

Take out a calendar and set up a schedule for yourself. If you begin studying early, you can chip away at the review chapters in Part II. You'll be surprised—and pleased—by how much material you can cover with half an hour a day study for a month or so before the test. Look carefully at the sections of the Diagnostic Test; if you missed a number of questions in one particular area, allow more time for the chapters that cover that area of the course. The practice tests in Part III will give you more experience with different kinds of multiple-choice questions and the wide range of free-response questions.

If time is short, skip reading the review chapters. Look at the Key Terms listed at the beginning of each chapter to be sure that you have a working knowledge of the vocabulary that will be used in the examination, and work on the multiple-choice and free-response questions at the end of each review. This will give you a good idea of your understanding of that particular topic. Then take the tests in Part III.

If time is *really* short, go straight from Part I to Part III. Taking practice tests over and over again is the fastest, most practical way to prepare.

BEFORE THE EXAMINATION

By February, long before the exam, you need to make sure that you are registered to take the test. Many schools take care of the paperwork and handle the fees for their AP students, but check with your teacher or the AP coordinator to make sure that you are on the list. This is especially important if you have a documented disability and need test accommodations. If you are studying AP independently, call AP Services at the College Board for the name of the local AP coordinator, who will help you through the registration process.

The evening before the exam is not a great time for partying. Nor is it a great time for cramming. If you like, look over class notes or drift through your textbook, concentrating on the broad outlines, not the small details, of the course. You might also want to skim through this book and read the AP tips.

The evening before the exam *is* a great time to get your things together for the next day. Sharpen a fistful of no. 2 pencils with good erasers for the multiple-choice section; set out several black or dark-blue ballpoint pens for the free-response questions; wind your watch and turn off the alarm if it has one; get a piece of fruit or a power bar and a bottle of water for the break; make sure you have your Social Security number and whatever photo identification and admission ticket are required. Then relax. And get a good night's sleep.

On the day of the examination it is wise not to skip breakfast—studies show that students who eat a hot breakfast before testing get higher grades. Be careful not to drink a lot of liquids, necessitating a trip to the bathroom during the test. Breakfast will give you the energy you need to power you through the test—and more. You will spend some time waiting while everyone is seated in the right room for the right test. That's before the test has even begun. With a short break between Section I and Section II, the U.S. Government and Politics exam lasts for over two and a half hours. So be prepared for a long morning. You do not want to be distracted by a growling stomach or hunger pangs.

Be sure to wear comfortable clothes, taking along a sweater in case the heating or air-conditioning is erratic. Be sure, too, to wear clothes you like—everyone performs better when they think they look better—and by all means wear your lucky socks.

You have been on the fast track. Now go get a 5.

TAKING THE AP U.S. GOVERNMENT & POLITICS EXAM

The AP U.S. Government and Politics examination consists of two sections: Section I has sixty multiple-choice questions; Section II has four free-response questions. You will have 45 minutes for the multiple-choice portion. The questions are collected, and you will be given a short break. You then have 100 minutes for the free-response portion. You must write an essay for each of the four questions—some AP examinations allow you to choose among the free-response questions, but this is not one of them. Keep an eye on your watch and devote 25 minutes to each free-response question. Watch alarms are not allowed.

STRATEGIES FOR THE MULTIPLE-CHOICE SECTION

Here are some rules of thumb to help you work your way through the multiple-choice questions:

- **Guessing penalty** There are five possible answers for each question. Each correct answer is worth 1 point, and there is a 1/4-point guessing penalty for each incorrect answer. If you cannot narrow down the answers at all, it is against the odds to guess, so leave the answer sheet blank. However, if you can narrow down the answers even by eliminating one response, it is advantageous to guess. If you skip a question, be very careful to skip down that line on the answer sheet.

- **Read the question carefully** Pressured for time, many students make the mistake of reading the questions too quickly or merely skimming them. By reading a question carefully, you may already have some idea about the correct answer. You can then look for it in the responses. Careful reading is especially important in EXCEPT questions.

- **Eliminate any answer you know is wrong** You can write on the multiple-choice questions in the test book. As you read through the responses, draw a line through any answer you know is wrong.

- **Read all of the possible answers, then chose the most accurate response** AP examinations are written to test your precise knowledge of a subject. Sometimes there are a few probable answers but one of them is more specific. For example, the Fifteenth Amendment gave the vote to African

Americans, but only men could vote at that time. An answer that referred to black men would be more correct than an answer that referred to all African Americans.

- **Avoid absolute responses** These answers often include the words "always" or "never." For example, the statement "Voter turnout in presidential elections is always slightly above 50 percent" is incorrect because in the 1996 presidential election, turnout was a little below 50 percent.
- **Mark and skip tough questions** If you are hung up on a question, mark it in the margin of the question book. You can come back to it later if you have time. Make sure you skip that question on your answer sheet too.

TYPES OF MULTIPLE-CHOICE QUESTIONS

There are various kinds of multiple-choice questions. Here are some suggestions for how to approach each kind:

CLASSIC/BEST ANSWER QUESTIONS

This is the most common type of multiple-choice question. It simply requires you to read the question and select the most correct answer. For example:

1. How is the president of the United States usually selected?
   (A) by direct vote of the populace
   (B) by the House of Representatives
   (C) by the Senate
   (D) in a runoff election between the top two vote getters
   (E) by the electoral college

ANSWER: E.   The electoral college usually selects the president, although the House of Representatives decides on the rare occasion when no candidate receives a majority of electoral college votes. The word "usually" is very important in this question. This is a standard question that has one correct answer.

EXCEPT QUESTIONS

In the EXCEPT question, all of the answers are correct but one. The best way to approach these questions is as true/false. Mark a T or F in the margin next to each possible answer. There should be only one false answer, and that is the one you should select. For example:

1. Congress the express power to do all of the following EXCEPT
   (A) lay and collect taxes
   (B) regulate interstate commerce
   (C) establish uniform standards for weights and measures
   (D) declare war
   (E) regulate intrastate commerce

ANSWER: E. Congress does not have the power to regulate intrastate commerce, so that is a false statement. You should have put an "F" next to it. All of the other statements are true.

LIST AND GROUP QUESTIONS

In this type of question, there is a list of possible answers, and you must select the answer that contains the correct group of responses. These questions look hard, but you can simplify them by crossing out items from the list and then eliminating them in the answers below. For example:

1. According to the Constitution, as amended, which of the following is elected directly?

To approach the question, draw a line through choice I, because the president and vice president are not elected directly but are chosen by the electoral college. Then cross out any response that contains choice I.

   I.   The president and vice-president
   II. members of the House of Representatives
   III. justices of the Supreme Court
   IV. senators

   (A) I and II
   (B) II and III
   (C) I, II, and III
   (D) I and IV
   (E) II and IV

Continue to cross out items that are wrong and the responses that contain them. Justices of the Supreme Court are appointed, not elected. Draw a line through III and answer (B), which contains choice III. Now you have narrowed down the possible responses.

ANSWER: E.   Under the Constitution, including the Seventeenth Amendment, which provides for the direct election of senators, members of the House of Representatives and Senate are elected directly.

CHART/GRAPH QUESTIONS

These questions require you to examine the data on a chart or graph. While these questions are not difficult, spending too much time interpreting a chart or graph may slow you down. To avoid this, first read the question and all of the possible answers so that you know what you are looking for. Before you look at the chart, you may be able to eliminate some obviously incorrect responses. For example:

Table 13.2	Minority Employment in the Federal Bureaucracy by Rank, 2000			
			Percentage of Total	
Grade	Black	Hispanic	Black	Hispanic
GS 1–4	26,895	8,526	29.7%	9.4%
GS 5–8	99,937	31,703	27.0	8.6
GS 9–12	82,809	36,813	16.0	7.0
GS 13–15	31,494	12,869	10.3	4.2
SES	1,180	547	7.3	3.4
Total	298,701	115,247	17.0	6.7

Note: GS stands for "General Service." The higher the number, the higher the rank of people with that number.

Source: Statistical Abstract of the United States, 2001, 482.

1. Which of the following statements does the table above best support?
    (A) At all levels of the bureaucracy, blacks and Hispanics are represented according to their percentage in the general population.
    (B) At all levels of the bureaucracy, there are three times more blacks than Hispanics.
    (C) Because of race discrimination, very few blacks and Hispanics have been able to rise to high levels in the bureaucracy.
    (D) As GS rating rises, the percentage of blacks and Hispanics in the bureaucracy decreases at every level.
    (E) There are more black and Hispanics in the bureaucracy than in any other branch of the federal government.

After reading the question and the responses, you could eliminate answer (A) without even reading the table; there is no affirmative action program that requires all levels of the bureaucracy to reflect the population as a whole. After reading the table, eliminate choice (C) immediately—while discrimination may play a role, it is not addressed in the table, and the question requires you to find your answer from the table. You can eliminate answer (E) for the same reason—while there are more minorities in the bureaucracy than in any other branch of the federal government, the table does not contain information about the other branches, and you must answer the question using information from this table. Answer (B) is wrong because at the GS 13-15 level, there are not three times more Blacks than Hispanics.

ANSWER: **D.** As the table shows, as GS rating rises, the number of blacks and Hispanics in the bureaucracy decreases.

POLITICAL CARTOON QUESTIONS

These questions require you to interpret a political cartoon. Every political cartoon contains symbolism and a point of view. Examine the cartoon before you read the question and possible responses to determine what each part of the drawing represents and to identify the artist's viewpoint. For example:

1. What is the viewpoint expressed in the above cartoon?
   (A) One barrier to improving congressional control of the bureaucracy is the large number of federal agencies.
   (B) One barrier to improving presidential control of the federal bureaucracy is that even the White House has become a large bureaucracy.
   (C) The budget grows incrementally each year, and the result is a larger and larger bureaucracy.
   (D) Although the bureaucracy has become very large, there are many people on the White House staff who would approve of cutting the bureaucracy.
   (E) Neither the president nor his staff has any meaningful incentive to control the size of the federal bureaucracy.

ANSWER: **B.** The box on the left symbolizes the presidency (the president is speaking from the White House). The box on the right symbolizes the federal employees who work at the White House (all of the reactions to his comments are also coming from the White House). The viewpoint of the cartoonist is that although White House employees may claim to agree that the bureaucracy is hard to control, they are part of the problem.

FREE-RESPONSE QUESTIONS

There are four mandatory free-response questions on the U.S. Government and Politics examination. At least one of the questions will require interpretation of a chart, graph, or cartoon. Essays for free-response questions can be written in any order. Whether you write the essays in or out of order, make sure you put the number of the question in the corner of each page of your essay booklet. In addition, questions are sometimes broken into parts, such as (a) and (b). When this is the case, label each part of your response.

Usually these are not traditional essay questions. Most free-response questions do not require an introduction or conclusion. Most do not even require a thesis. Many of these questions may be written in a bulleted or short-answer format. Although this may sound easier than writing a traditional essay, it is important that you know the material very well because these are targeted questions. Examination readers want specifics. They are looking for accurate information presented in clear, concise prose. You cannot mask vague information with elegant prose.

You will have a 100-minute block of time for this section, so watch your time. Allow 25 minutes for each question. Spend 5 minutes reading the question and jotting down a few words on each point you want to cover in your answer. Then spend 15 minutes writing your response. Save the last 5 minutes to read over your response to make sure you have covered each point with enough detail. If 25 minutes have passed and you are not finished with a question, leave some space, and start a new question on the next page. You can come back later if you have time.

VOCABULARY

In answering the free-response questions, carefully read the question, and do exactly what it asks. It is important to note the word choices used in the questions:

- **Define** to state the meaning of a word or phrase or to give a specific example. For instance, if a question asks you to define "iron triangle," the response is "An iron triangle is a close, advantageous relationship between an interest group, a congressional committee, and an administrative agency." Definitions are usually just one sentence.
- **Identify** to select a factor, person, or idea and give it a name. For instance, if a question asks you to identify one advantage of incumbency, one possible response is "One advantage of incumbency is the opportunity to do *casework* for constituents."
- **Explain why/explain how** to give a cause or reason. Explanations usually include the world *because*. For instance, if a question asks you why the ability to do casework gives incumbents an advantage, one possible response is "By doing casework, such as helping a constituent get her Social Security check, members of Congress are able to leave a favorable impression on members of their district. This increases their chances of reelection *because* they are able to get positive results for their constituents, who will vote for them in the next election."

SCORING FOR FREE-RESPONSE QUESTIONS

These questions are scored using a rubric that assigns points for each part of the answer. For example, if Part (a) requires you to identify and explain two factors, that part of the response will be worth 4 points (1 point for each identification and 1 point for each explanation). If Part (b) requires you to identify and explain one factor, that part of the response will be worth 2 points (1 point for the identification and 1 point for the explanation), for a total of 6 points possible on the question.

For the following free-response question you will find three sample responses—one excellent, one mediocre, and one poor—and an explanation of how the responses were scored.

QUESTION Congress has several ways of checking the power of the executive branch.
    a.   Identify and explain TWO formal powers that Congress may use to limit executive authority.
    b.   Identify and explain ONE informal power that Congress may use to limit executive authority.

SAMPLE ESSAY 1

Part (a): The Constitution provides several formal, expressed powers that Congress can use to limit executive authority. One is by overriding a veto. When the president vetoes a bill passed by Congress, that bill does not usually become law. However, Congress may override a presidential veto by a two-thirds vote in each house. This limits presidential power because the president does not have the final say over legislation. If enough members of Congress feel strongly enough about the legislation, it can still become law. Sometimes presidents are aware that their vetoes will be overridden and will sign bills they do not support in order to avoid the negative press that may come later with a defeat in Congress.

Another formal power that Congress has to limit executive authority is that Congress has the power to declare war. The president is commander in chief and has substantial authority in foreign affairs. He may commit troops for sixty days without congressional approval under the War Powers Act. However, for prolonged conflict, the president must turn to Congress to get an official declaration of war.

Part (b): An informal power that Congress has to limit executive authority is legislative oversight. Congress can conduct investigations and hold hearings to supervise the activities of the executive branch. This may pressure the executive to make changes in those agencies. For example, after the terrorist attacks of September 11, 2001, Congress held hearings to investigate the effectiveness of the nation's intelligence-gathering agencies.

SCORING 6/6. In Part (a) the response identifies overriding a veto as a formal power of Congress (1 point for identification). The essay explains that by overriding a veto, presidential power is limited because the president does not have the final say over legislation (1 point for explanation).

The student also identifies the power to declare war as a check on the presidency (1 point for identification). The essay explains that presidential power is limited because the president must turn to Congress in prolonged conflicts (1 point for explanation). Part (a) earns all 4 points.

In Part (b) the essay identifies legislative oversight as an informal limit on the power of the executive (1 point for identification). The essay explains that this limits the power of executive agencies because their activities are investigated and their effectiveness may be challenged (1 point for explanation). Part (b) earns 2 points.

SAMPLE ESSAY 2

Part (a): Under the Constitution, all appropriations bills must originate in the House. This means that the House has the power of the purse over executive proposals. This limits executive authority because Congress may reduce or eliminate funding altogether for presidential initiatives. Likewise, Congress must approve the budget. This limits executive authority because the president may not get everything he wants in his budget. This happened in 2004, when Congress cut President Bush's budget before it passed.

In addition Congress may limit executive authority because the Senate must ratify treaties. Although the executive branch negotiates treaties, often through the State Department, the Senate must ratify them in order to become law.

Part (b): One informal power that Congress has over the executive branch is the ability to go to the press. If Congress does not like a presidential proposal, a press conference can be held to get the public to oppose the president's policies.

SCORING 3/6. In Part (a) the student is awarded 3 points. The essay identifies the power of the purse as a limitation on the executive (1 point for identification). The response explains that Congress can limit executive power by refusing to fund presidential initiatives by cutting the budget proposed by the president (1 point for explanation).

The student also identifies Senate ratification of treaties as a limit on executive power (1 point for identification), but there is no meaningful explanation of how this limits presidential power.

In Part (b) the student does not receive any points. While congressional leaders may call press conferences as a way to put public pressure on the president, Congress is made up of 535 members. Congress as a whole cannot appeal to the press.

SAMPLE ESSAY 3

Part (a): One formal power of Congress that limits the executive branch is the power to declare war. However, the president is the commander in chief. As a result, he is able to commit troops to foreign conflicts without a formal declaration of war. This is what Lyndon Johnson did during the Vietnam conflict.

Another formal power of Congress is the power to regulate interstate commerce. This gives Congress the power to enact laws affecting the economy. Such laws have been used to provide civil rights to African Americans, as well as to provide consumer protection nationwide.

Part (b): One informal power of Congress is the ability to support a president's reelection campaign. If the president does not do what Congress wants, it can oppose his reelection.

SCORING 1/6. The student identifies the power to declare war as a limit on the executive (1 point for identification). However, the essay does not explain how this power limits the president. Instead, it discusses how the president has not been limited by this power.

While the power to regulate interstate commerce is a power of Congress, it does not generally limit the power of the presidency. The student does not earn any points for the rest of Part (a).

In Part (b) the response indicates that Congress may not support a president's reelection. While this may be true of individual members of Congress, it is not true of Congress as a whole. The student earns no points for Part (b).

A DIAGNOSTIC TEST

This diagnostic test will you give some indication of how you might score on the multiple-choice portion of the AP U.S. Government and Politics exam. Of course, the exam changes every year, so it is never possible to predict a student's score with certainty. This test will also pinpoint strengths and weaknesses on the key content areas covered by the exam. Practice Tests

UNITED STATES GOVERNMENT AND POLITICS
Section I
Time: 45 minutes
60 Questions

MULTIPLE-CHOICE QUESTIONS

1. The Framers of the Constitution mistrusted direct democracy for all of the following reasons EXCEPT
   (A) they believed that direct democracy might lead to a tyrannical popular majority
   (B) they supposed that most citizens did not have the time, information, interest, and expertise to make reasonable choices
   (C) they suspected that direct democracy would be too slow and inefficient to make good policy
   (D) they thought the nation was too big for a direct democracy to be effective
   (E) they believed that basic rights, like freedom of speech, should not hinge on a popular vote

2. James Madison believed that various groups, or factions, would compete within our democratic system. The result would be effective policy-making. Madison's theory can best be described as
   (A) pluralism
   (B) Marxism
   (C) bureaucratic elitism
   (D) hyperpluralism
   (E) elitism

3. Which of the followings statements best describes most of the Founding Fathers?
   (A) They were older, wealthy, and very experienced politicians.
   (B) They were relatively young, wealthy, and well educated.
   (C) They were representative of the population as a whole.
   (D) They were radicals who favored states' rights and the protection of individual liberties.
   (E) They were young and inexperienced.

4. What is the result of the Great Compromise?
    (A) Both the House of Representatives and the Senate directly represent the population as a whole.
    (B) The House of Representatives represents the interests of the states, while the Senate represents individuals within a district.
    (C) The Senate represents state interests, while the House of Representatives mirrors the population proportionally.
    (D) The electoral college vote does not always mirror the popular vote.
    (E) Large states have more power in the Senate than small states.

5. The president nominates Supreme Court justices, who must be confirmed by the Senate. Once appointed, those justices usually serve for life terms. This is an example of
    I. separation of powers
    II. federalism
    III. checks and balances
    IV. judicial review

    (A) I and II
    (B) I and III
    (C) II and III
    (D) III and IV
    (E) I, II, and IV

6. The United States is characterized by cooperative federalism, whereby the national government shares money with the states through grants. Which of the following is most favored by the states?
    (A) categorical grants, because the states can spend the money on broad categories of projects
    (B) formula grants, because the states can use a precise equation to determine how to spend the money
    (C) categorical grants, because they rarely have any strings attached
    (D) block grants, because they give states considerable freedom in deciding how to spend the money
    (E) project grants, because the states can compete to build specific projects, such as libraries and airports

7. All of the following characterize American beliefs about the political system EXCEPT
    (A) Americans believe that, barring a disability, people should be responsible for their own actions and well-being
    (B) Americans believe government officials should be accountable to the people
    (C) Americans believe that they ought to engage in civic participation and help out their communities when they can
    (D) Americans believe that everybody should have an equal vote and an equal chance to participate and succeed
    (E) Americans believe that the government should try to equalize wealth so that there is less conflict among citizens

8. When citizens have a political culture that allows the discussion of ideas and the selection of rulers in an atmosphere reasonably free of oppression, there is a high degree of
    (A) political agreement
    (B) political socialization
    (C) political effectiveness
    (D) political tolerance
    (E) civic duty

9. Which of the following examples best illustrates the concept of political efficacy?
    (A) feminists organizing a march in favor of the Equal Rights Amendment
    (B) Protestants holding a revival meeting
    (C) atheists preaching against organized religion
    (D) a civic group collecting canned goods for the homeless
    (E) all of the above activities

"Yes, son, we're Republicans."

10. The cartoon above best illustrates which concept?
    - (A) Political parties play a role in family life.
    - (B) The family has an effect on political socialization
    - (C) Republicans socialize their children more than Democrats.
    - (D) Children tend to follow their parents' political ideology, but they tend to stray from those beliefs when they become young adults.
    - (E) Teen-agers are more likely to identify themselves as Republicans than as Democrats.

Table 5.2 The Gender Gap: Differences in Political Views of Men and Women		
Issue	**Men**	**Women**
Federal spending for welfare programs should be increased.	8%	14%
Abortion should be permitted by law.	57	60
Sexual harassment is a very serious problem in the workplace.	24	38
This country would be better off if we just stayed home and did not concern ourselves with problems in other parts of the world.	24	29
I voted for Clinton in 1996.	45	59
Generally speaking, I think of myself as a Democrat.	32	44
The United States should increase defense spending.	37	26
The United States should increase spending on solving the problems of the homeless.	51	63
Ban all handguns except for the police.	33	58

Source: ICPSR American National Election Survey, 1996. Pre- and Post-Election Surveys.

11. The table above supports which of the following conclusions?
    - (A) There is no significant difference between men and women about most issues.
    - (B) The biggest area of disagreement between men and women is international relations.
    - (C) More than half of all women surveyed have been sexually harassed in the workplace.
    - (D) Most men do not support spending more money to help the homeless.
    - (E) There is a gender gap in political views between men and women on issues such as the size of government, gun control, and social spending.

12. A person who holds a consistent conservative political ideology would support which of the following?
    - I. support for a market economy with few government regulations
    - II. keeping taxes low
    - III. cutting back on the welfare state
    - IV. locking up criminals to prevent recidivism

    - (A) I and II
    - (B) I, II, and III
    - (C) I, III, and IV
    - (D) III and IV
    - (E) I, II, III, and IV

GO ON TO NEXT PAGE

13. What was the impact of the Motor Voter law of 1993?
    (A) It increased voter turnout significantly, especially in the 18- to 21-year-old age group.
    (B) It increased voter registration but did not significantly increase voter turnout.
    (C) It was widely evaded, especially in southern states.
    (D) It had no significant impact on either voter registration or voter turnout.
    (E) It increased voter registration and voter turnout in all age categories.

14. Which of the following persons is most likely to vote?
    (A) an 18-year-old white high school graduate
    (B) a 65-year-old retired union member
    (C) a 40-year-old soccer mom with an associate's degree
    (D) a 55-year-old African American attorney who works for the federal government
    (E) a 21-year-old married father of two

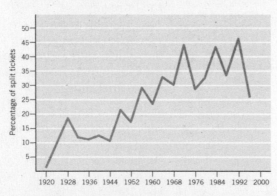

Figure 7.2 **Trends in Split-Ticket Voting for President and Congress, 1920–1996**

Note: The figure is the percentage of congressional districts carried by presidential and congressional candidates of different parties in each election year.

15. The chart above supports which of the following conclusions?
    (A) During nonpresidential congressional election years, split-ticket voting increases.

(B) Split-ticket voting rarely occurred prior to 1920.
(C) Because of split-ticket voting, policy gridlock occurs.
(D) From 1944 until 1996, there has been a steady increase in split-ticket voting.
(E) Split-ticket voting increases during periods of economic decline.

16. What is the impact of third parties on the American political system?
    (A) Minor parties develop ideas that the major parties later come to adopt.
    (B) Minor parties create new coalitions within the major parties, often resulting in party realignment.
    (C) Minor parties tend to develop around charismatic personalities, who are recruited as candidates by the major parties.
    (D) Minor parties usually get enough votes to prevent a majority vote in the electoral college.
    (E) Minor parties have had no significant impact on the American political system.

17. All of the following are examples of interest groups EXCEPT
    (A) Greenpeace
    (B) Right to Life
    (C) Christian Coalition
    (D) Libertarians
    (E) National Organization of Women

18. How do interest groups differ from PACs?
    (A) Interest groups donate money to candidates, while PACs hire lobbyists to influence policy-making.
    (B) Interest groups can hire PACs to help them conduct polls, create direct mail solicitations, and produce TV ads.
    (C) PACs are committees, often set up by interest groups, to raise and spend money on campaigns and causes.
    (D) Interest groups are required to register with the Federal Election Commission, but there are no registration requirements for PACs.
    (E) PACs run candidates for election, while interest groups do not.

19. Which of the following groups have led a social movement?
    I.   labor union members
    II. civil rights advocates
    III. environmentalists
    IV. tax protestors

    (A) I and II
    (B) I, II, and III
    (C) II and III
    (D) II, III, and IV
    (E) I, II, III, and IV

20. A primary in which voters must declare a political affiliation before the election is
    (A) a blanket primary
    (B) a closed primary
    (C) an open primary
    (D) a runoff primary
    (E) a party primary

21. How has broadcast journalism changed news coverage?
    (A) It has become more detailed, with more in-depth discussion of political issues.
    (B) It has become less sensationalized, with visual images replacing lurid written descriptions.
    (C) It has become more biased, with newscasters frequently giving their own viewpoints.
    (D) It has become more like a headline service, with the length of the average sound bite dropping to less than ten seconds.
    (E) It has resulted in more coverage of Congress and less coverage of the president, because large numbers of reporters can now cover the capitol.

22. The Watergate story, as originally reported by Woodward and Bernstein, is an example of
    (A) investigative journalism
    (B) beat reporting
    (C) a trial balloon
    (D) yellow journalism
    (E) broadcast journalism

23. How does regulation of radio and television broadcasts differ from the treatment of newspapers and magazines?
    (A) Newspapers are not subject to libel and slander laws, while broadcasters are.
    (B) The FCC regulates broadcasters but not newspapers.
    (C) Because of the First Amendment, broadcasters and newspapers have equal free-speech rights.
    (D) Newspapers do not need to be regulated because their content is rarely controversial; most papers simply report the news as it happens.
    (E) Both newspapers and television stations must be licensed.

GO ON TO NEXT PAGE

24. How do the rules governing conduct of the House of Representatives compare with the rules governing conduct of the Senate?
    (A) There are fewer rules governing the conduct of the House of Representatives because it is the lower house and has less power.
    (B) There are fewer rules governing the conduct of the House of Representatives because the House is so big that its individual members lack power.
    (C) There are fewer rules governing the conduct of the Senate because its smaller size makes it more manageable.
    (D) There are fewer rules governing the conduct of the Senate because of its strong leadership structure.
    (E) The same rules of conduct govern both the House and the Senate.

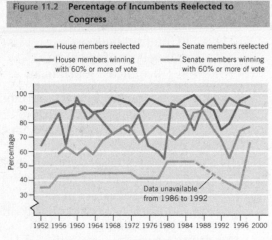

Figure 11.2 **Percentage of Incumbents Reelected to Congress**

Source: Harold W. Stanley and Richard G. Niemi, *Vital Statistics on American Politics, 1999–2000* (Washington, D.C.: Congressional Quarterly Press, 2000), table 1-18.

25. The graph above supports which of the following conclusions?
    (A) Incumbency is a more important factor for reelection in the House than in the Senate.
    (B) From 1952 to 1976, most incumbents in the Senate were reelected with more than 60 percent of the vote.
    (C) The percentage of incumbent senators reelected is very consistent over time.
    (D) A challenger would be more likely to win in the House than in the Senate.
    (E) Because members of the House run for reelection every two years, they have more name recognition with their constituents.

26. Which of the following advantages does the majority party have regarding committees?
    I.   Committees usually reflect the party affiliations of the House or Senate as a whole.
    II. Committee chairs are appointed by the majority party.
    III. The majority leadership decides which bills to assign to a particular committee.
    IV. The majority party often creates committees that have no members from the minority party.

    (A) I and II
    (B) II and III
    (C) I, II, and III
    (D) II, III, and IV
    (E) I, II, III, and IV

27. What is a congressional caucus?
    (A) members of Congress who meet in their individual states during primary season to help select the party's presidential nominee
    (B) a subcommittee created to oversee an executive agency
    (C) an informal meeting of members of Congress to "logroll" pending legislation
    (D) a meeting between members of the House and Senate to revise language when a bill passes both houses in different forms
    (E) an association of members of Congress with similar characteristics or ideology, which acts like an interest group within Congress

28. What happens to most bills?
    (A) They are passed by one house of Congress but not by the other.
    (B) They are passed by Congress but vetoed by the president.
    (C) They are passed through committees but are defeated in the House.
    (D) They are never sent to committee.
    (E) They die in committee.

29. The Foreign Investors Act, a bill designed to solve the balance-of-payments problem, had riders added to it giving assistance to hearse owners, the mineral ore business, importers of scotch whiskey, and presidential candidates. This is an example of a
    (A) Christmas tree bill
    (B) revenue bill
    (C) authorization bill
    (D) concurrent resolution
    (E) reconciliation bill

30. A party whip does all of the following EXCEPT
    (A) helps the party leader stay informed about what party members are thinking
    (B) rounds up members when important votes are to be taken
    (C) attempts to keep a nose count on likely votes on controversial issues
    (D) contacts wavering party members and pressures them to toe the party line
    (E) schedules bills for floor debate

31. The presidency in the United States differs from the executive in a parliamentary system in all of the following ways EXCEPT
    (A) in a parliamentary system, the prime minister's party (or coalition) is guaranteed a majority in the legislature, while the U.S. president often faces a Congress led by the opposing party
    (B) United States presidents are often political outsiders, while

prime ministers are members of parliament
    (C) United States presidents choose cabinet members from outside of Congress, while cabinet members are chosen from within parliament
    (D) the prime minister is chosen by parliament and not through a separate election
    (E) the United States president is the chief executive while the prime minister is not

32. Political scientist David Mayhew studied important laws and found that significant legislation was as likely to be enacted in times of divided government as in periods of unified government. What is the best explanation for this phenomenon?
    (A) The Constitution ensures that the president and Congress will be rivals for power. Divided government is simply an example of separation of powers in action.
    (B) Most presidents have so much political clout that they are able to convince members of the opposing party to support their key legislative proposals.
    (C) Legislation is passed during periods of divided government because Congress frequently overrides presidential vetoes.
    (D) Legislation is passed in times of divided government because presidents tend to present noncontroversial proposals to Congress.
    (E) Divided government occurs most frequently in wartime. Congress is forced to pass legislation in order to meet the needs of the nation.

GO ON TO NEXT PAGE

33. All of the following are features of the electoral college EXCEPT
    (A) small states are underrepresented as a percentage of their population
    (B) there is a winner-take-all system in forty-eight states
    (C) candidates have to worry about carrying states as well as popular votes
    (D) candidates have a strong incentive to campaign in large states they have a chance of winning
    (E) if there is no majority winner in the electoral college, the election is decided by the House of Representatives, with one vote per state

34. Under the Constitution, the president can
    I. grant reprieves and pardons in federal offenses
    II. call a special session of Congress
    III. declare war
    IV. serve as commander-in-chief of the armed forces

    (A) I an II
    (B) I, II, and III
    (C) I, II, and IV
    (D) III and IV
    (E) II, III, and IV

35. How is the Federal Reserve Board classified?
    (A) as an executive agency because the chairman can be removed by the president at any time
    (B) as an executive agency because the president appoints the chairman
    (C) as an independent agency because the chairman serves for a fixed term, subject to reappointment by the president
    (D) as a government corporation because it regulates banks
    (E) as an independent regulatory commission because its chairman is selected from its board

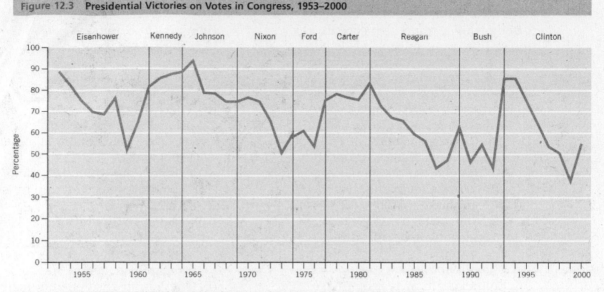

Figure 12.3   Presidential Victories on Votes in Congress, 1953–2000

Note: Percentages indicate number of congressional votes supporting the president divided by the total number of votes on which the president has taken a position.

Source: From Harold Stanley and Richard Niemi, *Vital Statistics on American Politics,* 2001–2002 (Washington, D.C.: Congressional Quarterly Press, 2001); and Gallup News Service, February 6, 2001. Reprinted with permission.

36. The chart above best supports which of the following conclusions?
   (A) No president since 1980 has had more than 80 percent victories on votes in Congress.
   (B) Eisenhower had more bills passed than any president since 1956.
   (C) Presidents start with a high percentage of victories, but that percentage drops throughout their term(s).
   (D) President Clinton had the worst percentage of victories on votes in Congress in a single year.
   (E) The percentage of presidential victories in Congress drops in time of economic crisis.

37. What was the intent of Congress in passing the Budget Reform Act of 1974?
   (A) to keep presidents from submitting budget proposals that contained deficits
   (B) to prevent presidents from presenting budgets that raise taxes greater than the rate of inflation
   (C) to require presidents to submit balanced budgets
   (D) to require across-the-board cuts in three categories of spending (discretionary, domestic, and military) in order to balance the budget
   (E) to require presidents to spend all appropriated funds unless Congress agrees to delete the items within forty-five days

GO ON TO NEXT PAGE

38. When candidates run for office, they often promise to present certain legislative programs once elected. Why is it difficult for presidents to get these promised programs passed?
    I. Unexpected crisis may divert attention from previous plans.
    II. Controversial aspects of a program may face adverse and well-publicized reactions.
    III. The presidency is characterized by long hours and hundreds of activities, which make it difficult to concentrate on specific programs.
    IV. The public rarely expects politicians to deliver on their promises, so they are frequently abandoned.

    (A) I and II
    (B) II and III
    (C) II, III, and IV
    (D) I, II, and IV
    (E) I, II, and III

39. What is the impact of the line-item veto on the federal government of the United States?
    (A) It allows the president to eliminate parts of budget bills before signing them.
    (B) It allows the president to eliminate parts of a bill, as long as he does not change the bill's basic intent, before signing it.
    (C) It allows the president to make significant changes to a bill before signing it into law.
    (D) It allows the president to make changes to a bill, sign the bill, and resubmit it to Congress for final approval.
    (E) It has no impact in the United States, because the Supreme Court has held that the line-item veto violates separation of powers.

40. What was the Supreme Court's ruling in *United States v. Nixon*?
    (A) There is not an absolute, unqualified, claim of executive privilege in criminal investigations.
    (B) There is not an absolute, unqualified, claim of executive privilege unless national security is involved.
    (C) Confidential communications between a president and his staff are privileged.
    (D) Written communications are privileged, but taped conversations are not protected from judicial subpoenas.
    (E) There is an absolute, unqualified, executive privilege for all written and oral communications in the White House between the president and his staff.

41. What is the process for impeachment and removal of the president?
    (A) The House must vote to impeach a president by a two-thirds vote, and the president is tried in the Senate, which must vote to convict by a three-fourths vote.
    (B) The House must vote to impeach a president by a majority vote, and the president is tried in the Senate, which must vote to convict by a two-thirds vote.
    (C) Both houses of Congress must vote on impeachment charges, and the Supreme Court has original jurisdiction to hear the case.
    (D) The House votes on articles of impeachment, a trial is held in the Senate, and then the case is sent back to the House for a final vote on conviction.
    (E) The House and Senate appoint members to a joint committee on impeachment, which then holds hearings and makes a final recommendation to the Congress as a whole.

42. What gives the American bureaucracy its distinctive character in comparison with most other nations?
    (A) Both Congress and the president exercise authority over the bureaucracy.
    (B) Bureaucrats report to and take orders from the heads of their departments.
    (C) Most agencies of the federal government do not have to share authority with state or local agencies.
    (D) Bureaucratic agencies are able to operate with little public scrutiny.
    (E) The bureaucracy regulates large sectors of the economy.

43. How has the role of the bureaucracy changed since the New Deal and World War II?
    (A) The bureaucracy used to regulate the economy, but now its primary role is to provide services to the public.
    (B) The bureaucracy has less power to regulate the economy than it had prior to the New Deal.
    (C) The bureaucracy now provides a wide variety of programs and plays an active role in regulating economic activity.
    (D) The bureaucracy has fewer employees today because of the devolution of powers to state and local governments.
    (E) The role of the bureaucracy has become less controversial.

44. How are most members of the federal bureaucracy selected?
    (A) The president, often on the basis of party loyalty, appoints them.
    (B) They are selected by the Congressional Committee on Hiring and usually reflect the political affiliations of Congress.
    (C) They are appointed after they have passed a written exam or have met certain selection criteria.
    (D) Federal positions are filled using strict affirmative action guidelines that require the bureaucracy to mirror the population as a whole.
    (E) They are interviewed by the OPM, and the top three candidates are sent to the agency head, who makes the final selection.

45. How can Congress supervise the bureaucracy?
    I.   No agency may exist without congressional approval.
    II. No money can be spent unless it has been authorized by Congress.
    III. Congressional committees may fire agency heads.
    IV. Congressional committees may hold oversight hearings.

    (A) I and II
    (B) I, II, and III
    (C) II and III
    (D) II, III, and IV
    (E) I, II, and IV

46. What is judicial review?
    (A) the right of the Supreme Court to rewrite a federal law to make it constitutional
    (B) the right of the Supreme Court to review the evidence in a trial and hear new testimony
    (C) the right of the Supreme Court to hear appeals in cases involving constitutional issues
    (D) the right of the Supreme Court to declare a state or federal law void if it violates the Constitution
    (E) the right of the Supreme Court to reduce a defendant's criminal sentence upon review if that sentence is excessive

47. The Supreme Court has ruled that the Fourth Amendment contains a right of privacy, even though the amendment does not contain the word "privacy." This is an example of which judicial approach?
    (A) strict construction
    (B) restraint
    (C) activism
    (D) statutory construction
    (E) discretionary construction

GO ON TO NEXT PAGE

48. Partisanship affects judicial selection in all of the following ways EXCEPT
    (A) the president usually nominates candidates who are members of his political party
    (B) senatorial courtesy allows the senior senator from the state where the district is located to object to a nominee
    (C) the opposing party in the Senate often delays judicial confirmations
    (D) during confirmation hearings, prospective judges can be asked how they would rule in specific cases
    (E) during confirmation hearings, prospective judges can be asked about their judicial philosophy

49. Those who dramatize issues, galvanize public opinion, and mobilize congressional support can best be described as
    (A) policy entrepreneurs
    (B) policy specialists
    (C) interest groups
    (D) issue networks
    (E) PACs

50. Some laws both regulate and help business. Antitrust laws are one example. They prevent businesses from becoming so large that they can control the market. This may hinder the growth of large businesses, but at the same time, it protects businesses from unfair competition. This is an example of
    (A) majoritarian politics
    (B) interest-group politics
    (C) client politics
    (D) entrepreneurial politics
    (E) party politics

51. What is the difference between monetary policy and fiscal policy?
    (A) Monetary policy involves taxing, and fiscal policy involves spending.
    (B) Fiscal policy occurs when there is a deficit, and monetary policy is used when there is a surplus.
    (C) Fiscal policy uses tax cuts to stimulate the economy, while monetary policy uses government spending to stimulate the economy.
    (D) Fiscal policy involves the budget, and monetary policy involves interest rates and the money supply.
    (E) There is no difference; these terms are synonymous.

52. The economic theory that emphasizes deregulation and tax cuts is
    (A) Keynesianism
    (B) supply-side economics
    (C) monetarism
    (D) fiscal federalism
    (E) New Deal activism

53. What is the difference between a means-tested social welfare program and an entitlement?
    (A) Means-tested programs, like Medicaid, are available to everyone, regardless of income.
    (B) Entitlement programs, like Social Security, are available regardless of income.
    (C) Entitlement programs, like Social Security, are available only to people who fall below certain income levels.
    (D) Means-tested programs, like food stamps, are available only to people who do not work full-time.
    (E) Means-tested programs were eliminated in the Welfare Reform Act.

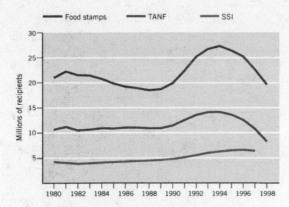

54. According to the above graph, what is the relationship between Supplemental Security Income (SSI), Temporary Assistance for Needy Families (TANF), and Food Stamps?
    (A) Since 1992, the number of recipients of all three programs has dropped.
    (B) For all years shown, the number of recipients of Food Stamps was at least double the number of recipients of TANF.
    (C) While the number of people receiving SSI rose after 1994, the number of recipients of Food Stamps and TANF declined.
    (D) There were fewer poor people in 1998 than there were in 1980.
    (E) There has been a steady decline in all three programs since the Reagan administration.

55. All of the following are restraints on free speech EXCEPT
    (A) libel
    (B) clear and present danger
    (C) prior restraint
    (D) obscenity
    (E) slander

56. A state decides to provide funding for math textbooks. This law will provide tax dollars for both public and private schools. What would be the most likely result if this law were challenged in court on grounds that it violates the Establishment Clause?
    (A) It will be overturned because it fosters an excessive government entanglement with religion.
    (B) It will be overturned because it violates the principle of separation of church and state by using tax dollars to benefit private schools.
    (C) It will be overturned because it advances religious beliefs.
    (D) It will be upheld because tax dollars can be spent for primary or secondary educational purpose.
    (E) It will be upheld because it has a secular purpose, does not advance religion, and will not cause excessive government entanglement with religion.

57. What is required for a search warrant to be valid?
    I. probable cause
    II. a description of the place to be searched
    III. a description of the things to be seized
    IV. a lawful arrest

    (A) I and II
    (B) I, II, and III
    (C) I, II, and IV
    (D) II, III, and IV
    (E) I, II, III, and IV

58. What was the Court's decision in *Bakke v. University of California*?
    (A) Affirmative action programs are reverse discrimination and violate the Fourteenth Amendment.
    (B) Affirmative actions programs were designed to provide racial equality and are required by the Fourteenth Amendment.
    (C) Schools can take race into account in making admissions decisions, but the use of quotas will be viewed with strict scrutiny.
    (D) Schools can take race into account in making admissions decisions, and using quotas is the best way to accomplish this.
    (E) Affirmative action programs are permissible but not required; states may abolish them if they wish.

GO ON TO NEXT PAGE

59. What is the result of *Roe v. Wade* and subsequent Supreme Court decisions about abortion?
    (A) There is an unlimited right of abortion throughout pregnancy.
    (B) Abortion is legal until a fetus is viable, and may be regulated, but not unduly restricted.
    (C) There is an unrestricted right to abortion before a fetus is viable, after which abortion may be regulated but not prohibited.
    (D) States may regulate, and even prohibit, abortion, but the national government may not restrict access to abortion.
    (E) Although abortion is legal until a fetus is viable, protests can occur at entrances to abortion clinics.

60. What is the standard for determining whether a racial classification violates the Constitution?
    (A) strict scrutiny
    (B) mid-level review
    (C) rational basis
    (D) absolute scrutiny
    (E) none because race-based classifications are unconstitutional

STOP

END OF SECTION I

IF YOU FINISH BEFORE TIME IS CALLED, YOU MAY CHECK YOUR WORK ON THIS SECTION. DO NOT GO ON TO SECTION II UNTIL YOU ARE TOLD TO DO SO.

UNITED STATES GOVERNMENT AND POLITICS
Section II
Time: 100 minutes

Directions You have 100 minutes to answer all four of the following questions. Unless the directions indicate otherwise, respond to all parts of each question. It is recommended that you take a few minutes to plan and outline each answer. Spend approximately 25 minutes on each question. Support your essay with specific examples where appropriate. Be sure to number each of your answers.

1   The due-process clause of the Fourteenth Amendment has been used by the Supreme Court to protect individuals from state actions that violate fundamental rights. For TWO of the following cases (a) identify the issue that the court was asked to resolve, (b) describe the Court's ruling, and (c) explain how the ruling expanded individual rights.

> *Mapp v. Ohio*
> *Miranda v. Arizona*
> *Roe v. Wade*

2. The United States has evolved from a system of dual federalism (in which the national and state governments are supreme in their own spheres) to a system of cooperative federalism (in which federal and state powers overlap). In the past two decades, some powers have devolved (been given by the national government to the states).
    a. Identify and explain one factor that led to the national government having significantly more power than the states.
    b. Identify and explain one factor that led to cooperative federalism.
    c. Identify and explain one factor that has led to devolution.

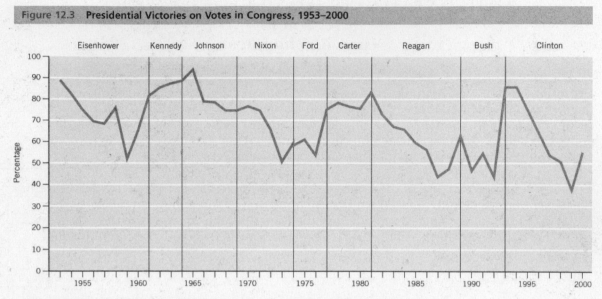

Figure 12.3 Presidential Victories on Votes in Congress, 1953–2000

Note: Percentages indicate number of congressional votes supporting the president divided by the total number of votes on which the president has taken a position.

Source: From Harold Stanley and Richard Niemi, *Vital Statistics on American Politics*, 2001–2002 (Washington, D.C.: Congressional Quarterly Press, 2001); and Gallup News Service, February 6, 2001. Reprinted with permission.

3. Using the information in the figure above and your knowledge of United States politics, complete the following tasks.
   a. Identify one trend with regard to presidential victories in Congress.
   b. Identify and explain two relevant factors that have affected presidential victories in Congress.

4. Congress is made up of the House of Representatives and Senate, both of which must approve the same legislation before it is sent to the president. Despite this similarity of purpose, each house functions differently.
   a. Identify and explain two differences in the way the House of Representatives and the Senate are run.
   b. Identify and explain one similarity in the way the House and the Senate are run.

END OF EXAMINATION

Scoring This Diagnostic Test

Using the table below, score your test. Determine how many you answered correctly and how many you answered incorrectly.

1. D	11. E	21. D	31. E	41. B	51. D
2. A	12. E	22. A	32. A	42. A	52. B
3. B	13. B	23. B	33. A	43. C	53. B
4. C	14. D	24. C	34. C	44. C	54. C
5. B	15. A	25. A	35. C	45. E	55. C
6. D	16. A	26. C	36. D	46. D	56. E
7. E	17. D	27. E	37. E	47. C	57. B
8. D	18. C	28. E	38. E	48. D	58. C
9. A	19. B	29. A	39. E	49. A	59. B
10. B	20. B	30. E	40. A	50. A	60. A

CALCULATE YOUR SCORE

Number answered correctly _____

ADJUST FOR THE 1/4 POINT GUESSING PENALTY This applies to questions you answered incorrectly. Do not count questions you skipped in determining the guessing penalty.

Less the number answered incorrectly multiplied by .25 - _____

Determine your adjusted score = _____

WHAT YOUR SCORE MEANS

Your adjusted score will give you some idea of how well you might do on the AP exam. Keep in mind that your essays will count for 50 percent and will also determine your score. The following percentages are based on the results of the 2003 exam:

Adjusted Score	AP Exam Score	Percentage of Students Receiving That Score
51 to 60	5	64.7
	4	33.5
	3	1.8
41 to 50	5	12.4
	4	57.3
	3	29.4
	2	0.9
31 to 40	5	0.1
	4	13.1
	3	64.3
	2	22.0
	1	0.2
21 to 30	4	0.2
	3	19.2
	2	76.1
	1	4.6
11 to 20	3	0.5
	2	49.8
	1	49.8
0 to 10	2	03.5
	1	96.5

Answer Key

The AP exam covers key content areas in certain percentages. This answer key will give you an indication of how much weight each area is given and your knowledge of each of the important content areas. Page numbers at the end of each answer refer to the pages in *American Government*, 8th ed. and 9th ed., where that issue is discussed.

ANSWERS FOR MULTIPLE-CHOICE QUESTIONS

Questions 1-6 are about Constitutional Underpinnings (covered in American Government, *8th ed., Chapters 1-3 / 9th ed., Chapters 1-3), which will be 5-15 percent of the multiple-choice portion of the AP exam.*

1. **(D)** The Framers mistrusted direct democracy because they did not trust the average citizen to make reasonable choices and were worried about tyranny of the majority and abuses of power by officeholders. They also wanted to protect basic rights from the whims of the majority. Although representative democracy proceeds slowly, the Framers believed it would result in good government (*American Government*, 8th ed., page 8 / 9th ed., page 8).

2. **(A)** Pluralism is the belief that groups compete within a democratic system. Because no single group can dominate the policy-making process, the result is that all relevant interests can affect policy-making outcomes (*American Government*, 8th ed., pages 9-10 / 9th ed., pages 9-10).

3. **(B)** The Founding Fathers were relatively young but politically experienced. They were wealthier and more educated than the general population (*American Government*, 8th ed., page 24 / 9th ed., page 24).

4. **(C)** There are two senators per state. Thus states are represented equally in the Senate. Seats in the House are awarded based on a state's population, as determined by the census. Thus the number of members in the House of Representatives reflects a state's population (*American Government*, 8th ed., page 27 / 9th ed., page 27).

5. **(B)** The appointment process for the Supreme Court is an example of both separation of powers and checks and balances. The executive and legislative branches have distinct roles. By confirming presidential nominees, Congress has a check on the presidency. Lifetime tenure is a check on both the executive and the legislature, because justices cannot be removed for political reasons (*American Government*, 8th ed., page 29 / 9th ed., page 29).

6. **(D)** States prefer block grants because, in theory, they allow states more freedom in deciding how to spend the money. However, in practice, the federal government has been increasing the number of strings attached to supposedly unrestricted money (*American Government*, 8th ed., pages 62-64 / 9th ed., pages 62-63).

Questions 7-14 are about Political Beliefs and Behavior (covered in American Government, *8th ed., Chapters 4-6 / 9th ed., Chapters 4-6), which will be 10-20 percent of the multiple-choice portion of the AP exam.*

7. **(E)** Americans believe in equality, personal responsibility, and civic participation. They also believe government officials should be held accountable for their actions. Equalizing income is not a goal of most Americans, who believe that those who work hard or are better educated should receive higher salaries (*American Government,* 8th ed., pages 80-81 / 9th ed., pages 78-79).

8. **(D)** Not all behavior is acceptable. However, political tolerance requires that citizens be able to discuss and disagree about controversial issues in an atmosphere that is fairly free of oppression (*American Government,* 8th ed., pages 95-94 / 9th ed., page 94).

9. **(A)** Political efficacy is the belief that a citizen has the capacity to understand and influence political events. The feminists who are protesting believe that they can influence the passage of the Equal Right Amendment. The other examples do not involve an attempt to influence the government's policy-making processes (*American Government,* 8th ed., pages 93-94 / 9th ed., page 93).

10. **(B)** The majority of young people identify with their parents' political party. This is a result of political socialization (*American Government,* 8th ed., pages 106-107 / 9th ed., pages 106-107).

11. **(E)** There is a gender gap, with more women than men voting for the Democratic party. This is caused by differences in beliefs about the size of government, gun control, and spending programs (*American Government,* 8th ed., pages 109-110 / 9th ed., page 109).

12. **(E)** Pure conservatives support the free market and tax cuts. They want to reduce the welfare state and lock up criminals to prevent them from committing other crimes (*American Government,* 8th ed., page 122-123 / 9th ed., page 121).

13. **(B)** The Motor Voter Act of 1993 increased voter registration but not voter turnout. For example, in the 1996 presidential election (the first presidential election following the enactment), voter turnout fell to slightly below 50 percent (*American Government,* 8th ed., page 130 / 9th ed., page 132).

14. **(D)** This person has the most demographic factors that favor voting. He is older, well educated, and works for the government. While African Americans vote at lower rates than whites, this is probably more a result of socioeconomic status than of race (*American Government,* 8th ed., pages 137-141 / 9th ed., pages 140-144).

Questions 15-23 are about Political Parties, Interest Groups, and the Media (covered in American Government, 8th ed., Chapters 7-10 / 9th ed., Chapters 7-10), which will be 10-20 percent of the multiple-choice portion of the AP exam.

15. **(A)** Split-ticket voting increases during nonpresidential congressional election years, when the president's party usually loses seats in Congress (*American Government,* 8th ed., pages 211-212 / 9th ed., page 162).

16. **(A)** The conventional wisdom is that minor parties develop ideas that the major parties later adopt. For example, in 1996, Ross Perot emphasized campaign finance reform, an issue later adopted by both the Republicans and the Democrats (*American Government,* 8th ed., pages 170-171 / 9th ed., page 177).

17. **(D)** An interest group is any organization that seeks to influence public policy. In America, these groups do not usually run candidates for office. The Libertarians are best described as a political party, rather than an interest group, because they hold positions on a variety of issues and frequently run candidates for office (*American Government,* 8th ed., pages 221-222 / 9th ed., page 227).

18. **(C)** Political Action Committees are set up by and represent a corporation, labor union, or special-interest group. They raise and spend campaign contributions on behalf of candidates or causes (*American Government,* 8th ed., pages 236-238 / 9th ed., pages 241-243).

19. **(B)** Civil rights leaders, labor union members, and environmentalists have all led social movements—widely shared demands for change in some aspect of the social or political order. While there are people and groups who protest taxes, this movement is not widespread (*American Government,* 8th ed., pages 225-229 / 9th ed., pages 231-235).

20. **(B)** In a closed primary, a voter must declare in advance (sometimes several weeks in advance) that he or she is a member of a specific political party. Voters may vote only in the primary of the party to which they have registered (*American Government,* 8th ed., page 186 / 9th ed., page 196).

21. **(D)** Broadcast journalism has changed the way politicians get their message across. Because viewers can easily turn off the TV set, speeches must be boiled down to very interesting, short catchphrases that can be captured in sound bites (*American Government,* 8th ed., pages 249-250 / 9th ed., page 255-256).

22. **(A)** The original Watergate story, run in the *Washington Post,* is an example of investigative journalism, in which reporters use detectivelike tactics to uncover a story (*American Government,* 8th ed., page 255 / 9th ed., page 260).

23. **(B)** The FCC regulates broadcasters, because the content of their programs is available to the general public, including children, over the airwaves (*American Government,* 8th ed., page 258 / 9th ed., page 262).

Questions 24-48 are about Institutions, including Congress, the Presidency, the Courts, the Bureaucracy, and the Budget (covered in American Government, *8th ed., Chapters 11-14 / 9th ed., Chapters 11-14), which will be 35-45 percent of the multiple-choice portion of the AP exam.*

24. **(C)** There are fewer rules governing the conduct of the Senate because it has only 100 members, compared to 435 members in the House of Representatives. As a result, it is easier to manage (*American Government,* 8th ed., page 283 / 9th ed., page 287).

25. **(A)** A greater percentage of incumbents in the House is reelected than in the Senate (*American Government,* 8th ed., page 287 / 9th ed., page 291).

26. **(C)** Committees usually reflect party membership in the chamber as a whole. Chairs are appointed by the majority party, which also decides which bills will be sent to particular committees. Although there have been occasions when the majority takes extra seats on a committee, they do not take all of the seats (*American Government,* 8th ed., pages 306-307 / 9th ed., page 305).

27. **(E)** A congressional caucus is made up of members of Congress who share certain characteristics (for example, there is a women's caucus) or ideology. They advocate for their interests within Congress (*American Government,* 8th ed., pages 304-306 / 9th ed., pages 303-304).

28. **(E)** Most bills die in committee. They are often introduced only to get publicity for a member of Congress or to enable a member to say that he or she "did something" on a particular matter (*American Government,* 8th ed., page 314 / 9th ed., page 314).

29. **(A)** A bill with a large number of unrelated riders attached, many of which provide "pork," is known as a Christmas tree bill (*American Government,* 8th ed., page 316 / 9th ed., page 316).

30. **(E)** A whip tries to "whip party members into shape" by determining their views, reporting to other party leaders, rounding up members for votes, keeping vote counts, and putting pressure on party members (*American Government,* 8th ed., page 299 / 9th ed., page 298).

31. **(E)** Both the president and the prime minister are chief executives, although the prime minister is also a member of parliament (*American Government,* 8th ed., pages 334-335 / 9th ed., pages 330-331).

32. **(A)** Divided government is separation of powers and checks and balances in action. Opposing parties must compromise to pass legislation (*American Government,* 8th ed., page 336 / 9th ed., page 332).

33. **(A)** As a percentage of their population, small states, although they may not get much attention from the candidates, are overrepresented in the electoral college (*American Government,* 8th ed., pages 340-341 / 9th ed., pages 336-337).

34. **(C)** The president is the commander in chief, may grant reprieves and pardons for federal offenses, and can call Congress into special session. Congress has the power to declare war (*American Government,* 8th ed., page 344 / 9th ed., page 340).

35. **(C)** The chairman of the Federal Reserve Board is appointed by the president and serves for a fourteen-year term. During this time, the chairman is not generally subject to removal. The Federal Reserve Board is an independent federal agency (*American Government,* 8th ed., page 351 / 9th ed., page 347).

36. **(D)** In 1999, President Clinton had fewer than 40 percent victories on votes in Congress. This is the lowest percentage for any president since 1953 (*American Government,* 8th ed., page 359 / 9th ed., page 355).

37. **(E)** The Budget Reform Act was a response to presidents who refused to spend money appropriated by Congress. It requires that the money be spent unless notice is given to Congress within forty-five days and the items are deleted from the budget (*American Government,* 8th ed., page 362 / 9th ed., page 358).

38. **(E)** People expect presidents to deliver on their promises. However, presidential programs may face negative reactions, crises may erupt, and a president's hectic schedule may impair his ability to deliver a program (*American Government,* 8th ed., pages 362-364 / 9th ed., pages 359-360).

39. **(E)** The line-item veto has been ruled unconstitutional because it violates separation of powers by giving the president the power to legislate (*American Government,* 8th ed., page 360 / 9th ed., page 357).

40. **(A)** In *United States v. Nixon,* the Supreme Court ruled that taped conservations were not protected by a broad executive privilege because such a privilege would block the function of the federal courts in criminal cases (*American Government,* 8th ed., page 361 / 9th ed., page 358).

41. **(B)** The House votes, by a simple majority, on impeachment charges. The Senate holds an impeachment trial. A conviction requires a two-thirds vote in the Senate (*American Government,* 8th ed., page 369 / 9th ed., page 365).

42. **(A)** One distinctly American feature of the bureaucracy is that both Congress and the president exercise authority over it. In parliamentary systems, bureaucrats do not report directly to the legislature (*American Government,* 8th ed., page 376 / 9th ed., page 374).

43. **(C)** Following the New Deal and World War II, the government was expected to play a more active role in dealing with economic and social problems. The bureaucracy provides a wide variety of government programs and plays an active role in regulating the economy (*American Government,* 8th ed., pages 379-380 / 9th ed., pages 377-378).

44. **(C)** Most bureaucrats serve in the competitive service, in which positions are filled through written examinations or are based upon certain selection criteria (*American Government,* 8th ed., page 381 / 9th ed., page 379).

45. **(E)** Congress must approve the creation of agencies, and no money may be spent until Congress authorizes it. In addition, congressional committees hold hearings to investigate the efficiency and effectiveness of agencies (*American Government,* 8th ed., pages 393-394 / 9th ed., pages 391-392).

46. **(D)** In *Marbury v. Madison,* the Supreme Court asserted its authority to invalidate state and federal laws that violate the Constitution (*American Government,* 8th ed., pages 405-407 / 9th ed., pages 405-407).

47. **(C)** When the Supreme Court held that the Fourth Amendment contains a right to privacy, this was an example of judicial activism, by which the Supreme Court discovers the general principles underlying the Constitution and its often-vague language and, based on some moral or economic philosophy, applies them to cases (*American Government*, 8th ed., page 404 / 9th ed., page 404).

48. **(D)** During confirmation hearings, prospective judges can be asked about their judicial philosophy but cannot be asked how they would rule on specific cases (*American Government*, 8th ed., pages 412-414 / 9th ed., pages 412-414).

Questions 49-54 are about Public Policy (covered in American Government, *8th ed., Chapters 15-21 / 9th ed., Chapters 15-21), which will be 5-15 percent of the multiple-choice portion of the AP exam.*

49. **(A)** Policy entrepreneurs are those, both in and out of government, who find ways of pulling together a legislative majority on behalf of interests that are not well represented in government (*American Government*, 8th ed., page 445 / 9th ed., page 444).

50. **(A)** Majoritarian politics occurs when laws are passed that reflect the views of a majority of voters. This neither imposes on a hostile business community nor accedes to the desires of a privileged industry (*American Government*, 8th ed., pages 446-448 / 9th ed., pages 446-447).

51. **(D)** Monetary policy involves government decisions that control interest rates and the money supply. Fiscal policy concerns the budget (*American Government*, 8th ed., pages 463-466 / 9th ed., pages 464-466).

52. **(B)** Supply-side economists favor less government planning, more deregulation, and tax cuts to stimulate economic growth. (*American Government*, 8th ed., pages 464-465 / 9th ed., page 464).

53. **(B)** Entitlement programs are available to everyone who meets certain requirements, such as the age requirement for receiving Social Security retirement benefits, regardless of income (*American Government*, 8th ed., pages 479-480 / 9th ed., pages 479-480).

54. **(C)** Since the Welfare Reform Act of 1994, the number of recipients of TANF and Food Stamps has declined. There was an increase in the number of recipients of SSI during the same time period (*American Government*, 8th ed., page 483 / 9th ed., page 483).

Questions 55-60 are about Civil Rights and Civil Liberties (covered in American Government, *8th ed., Chapters 18-19 / 9th ed., Chapters 18-19), which will be 5-15 percent of the multiple-choice portion of the AP exam.*

55. **(C)** Although the First Amendment protects freedom of speech, there are prohibitions against defamation (libel and slander), speech that presents a clear and present danger to the public, and obscenity. However, as a general rule, speech may not be restrained prior to its publication (*American Government*, 8th ed., pages 500-506 / 9th ed., pages 503-508).

56. **(E)** This funding for math books will probably be upheld. It has a secular purpose (improve math skills), does not advance religion, and will not cause excessive government entanglement in religion (*American Government*, 8th ed., page 510 / 9th ed., page 512).

57. **(B)** A judge, upon a finding of probable cause, issues a valid search warrant. It requires a description of the place to be searched and the items to be seized. Searches without warrants may be made when a person is being arrested (*American Government*, 8th ed., page 512 / 9th ed., page 514).

58. **(C)** In the *Bakke* case, the University of California's racial quota system was found to violate the prohibition against race discrimination in the Fourteenth Amendment. The Court did not abolish affirmative action, stating that race can be a factor in admissions decisions (*American Government*, 8th ed., pages 541-543 / 9th ed., pages 544-545).

59. **(B)** Abortion is legal before a fetus is viable. States may pass regulations, such as a mandatory waiting period, as long as they do not unduly restrict abortion (*American Government*, 8th ed., pages 540-541 / 9th ed., page 543).

60. **(A)** The standard for reviewing race-based classifications is strict scrutiny. Race-based classifications are inherently suspect, because of the long history of race discrimination (*American Government*, 8th ed., page 538 / 9th ed., page 540).

ANSWERS FOR FREE-RESPONSE QUESTIONS

QUESTION 1 This question required you to write about TWO of the following three cases:

In *Mapp v. Ohio*, the Supreme Court was asked to consider whether evidence obtained in an illegal search could be used against a defendant at trial. Police broke into Mapp's home in search of drugs. They did not find any drugs, but they found pornography. The police had plenty of time to obtain a search warrant, but they did not get one. The Supreme Court held that the evidence could not be used in Mapp's trial. This established the exclusionary rule. This rule protects defendants from having illegally obtained evidence used against them in court. The right being protected is provided in the Fourth Amendment, which prohibits unreasonable searches and seizures. This right is protected to make sure police will be diligent in getting proper warrants (*American Government*, 8th ed., page 512 / 9th ed., page 514).

In *Miranda v. Arizona*, the Supreme Court considered whether a suspect's confession could be used in court if he was not informed of his rights. Miranda was arrested for kidnapping and rape. Police did not inform him that he had the right to remain silent, that his statements could be used against him, or that he had a right to have an attorney present during questioning. Miranda confessed. The Supreme Court threw out the confession because defendants have a right to be protected against self-incrimination. This right is meaningful only when suspects are fully aware of their rights. As a result of this ruling, it is now standard police procedure to read from a "Miranda card" when taking suspects into custody (*American Government,* 8th ed., pages 516-517 / 9th ed., pages 517-518).

The *Roe v. Wade* case is one of the most controversial decisions of the Supreme Court. A Texas law outlawed abortion, except when the woman's life is threatened. Roe, a pregnant woman, challenged the law. The issue was whether laws prohibiting abortion were a violation of the right of privacy implied in the Fourth Amendment. The Court overturned the Texas law and ruled that states may not outlaw abortion during the first two trimesters of pregnancy. The impact of the ruling was to expand the right of privacy by legalizing abortion (before the fetus is viable) nationwide. Women can make individual decisions about their pregnancies. Later Court decisions allow states to regulate the procedure, as long as those regulations do not impose an undue burden on the woman (*American Government,* 8th ed., pages 540-541 / 9th ed., pages 542-543).

SCORING This essay is worth 8 points. The discussion of each of the two cases you choose is worth 4 points.

Part (a) is worth 1 point for identifying the issue. The issue in *Mapp v. Ohio* was whether illegally obtained evidence can be use in Court. In *Miranda v. Arizona,* the issue was whether the use in court of a confession made when the suspect has not been read his rights violates the prohibition against self-incrimination. *In Roe v. Wade,* the issue was whether state laws prohibiting abortion violate the right of privacy.

Part (b) is worth 1 point for explaining the Court's decision. In *Mapp,* the Court established the exclusionary rule. In *Miranda,* the Court held that confessions cannot be used in court if the suspect has not been read his rights. In *Roe,* the Court held that state laws banning abortion during the first two trimesters violate the Fourth Amendment.

Part (c) is worth 2 points for explaining how the decision expands rights. An incomplete but correct explanation would receive 1 point. In *Mapp,* the exclusionary rule protects people from illegal searches (1 point) because police will be more diligent (1 point). In *Miranda,* suspects will be protected from self-incrimination (1 point) because police now read Miranda cards when taking suspects into custody (1 point). In *Roe,* women have a right to privacy (1 point), because they can make decisions about a pregnancy without substantial state interference (1 point).

QUESTION 2 Part (a): One way the federal government became significantly more powerful than the states is through rulings of the Supreme Court. For example, in *McCulloch v. Maryland,* the Court held that the national government could establish a bank even though this power is not expressly granted in the Constitution. The Court interpreted the elastic clause (also known as the "necessary and proper" clause) broadly. Because the national government has the expressed power to regulate commerce and currency, establishing a bank was necessary to carry out those powers. In addition, the Court held that Maryland could not tax the bank because "the power to tax is the power to destroy." This gave the federal government significant economic powers not specifically in the Constitution and paved the way for broad federal powers in comparison to the states (*American Government,* 8th ed., pages 54-56 / 9th ed., pages 55-56).

Part (b): Grants-in-aid have encouraged cooperative federalism. These grants of money allow states to build projects, like airports and universities. Programs like Medicaid are also funded with grant money. Although states enjoy receiving federal money, the money comes with strings attached, known as conditions-of-aid. This means that in order to receive funding, the states must comply with certain requirements, such as nondiscrimination requirements. The state and federal governments often jointly manage federally funded projects. This means they have to cooperate in building projects and administering services (*American Government,* 8th ed., pages 59-61, 68-70 / 9th ed., pages 59-61, 67-68).

Part (c): Devolution is the renewed effort by the national government to shift functions back to the states. One example of this is funding for Temporary Assistance for Needy

Families. This welfare program used to be administered as a categorical grant with federal requirements about how welfare money must be spent. It is now partially paid for by the federal government as a block grant, which gives states substantially more control over how the money is spent and how the programs are administered (*American Government,* 8th ed., pages 70-72 / 9th ed., pages 68-70).

SCORING This essay is worth 6 points.

Part (a) is worth 2 points—1 point is awarded for identifying a reason for more federal power (court cases), and 1 point is awarded for an explanation (the elastic clause was interpreted in a manner that gives the national government power beyond its expressed powers). Other factors could be discussed, including the use of the Commerce Clause by the federal government to regulate private businesses.

Part (b) is worth 2 points—1 point is awarded for identifying a factor that results in cooperative federalism (grants-in-aid), and 1 point is awarded for explaining the influence of that factor (shared administration requires levels of government to work together). Other factors could be discussed, such as budget surpluses and the federal income tax, which provided funds that could be given by the federal government to the states.

Part (c) is worth 2 points—1 point is awarded for identifying a reason for devolution (block grants), and 1 point is awarded for explaining how this causes devolution (states have more control over AFDC policies). Other factors could be discussed, like the desire by conservatives in the 1990s to scale back the functions of the federal government.

QUESTION 3 Part (a): The figure demonstrates that most presidents are more successful in Congress at the beginning of their terms (*American Government,* 8th ed., page 359 / 9th ed., page 359).

Part (b): One factor that impacts presidential victories in Congress is the honeymoon period immediately following an election. Presidents are often most popular right after an election, and they can use the public's optimism to persuade Congress to enact legislation. This is called a honeymoon period. Franklin Roosevelt took advantage of this period to get much of his first New Deal programs enacted. Because times were hard, it would have been political suicide for Congress to reject his plans. Another factor affecting presidential victories in Congress is divided government—when one or both houses of Congress are controlled by the political party opposite the president's. An example of this occurred during President Clinton's first term in office. In 1994, Congress became Republican and thereafter blocked much of his proposed legislation. The federal government even "shut down" because the president and Congress could not agree on a budget (*American Government,* 8th ed., pages 354-358 / 9th ed., pages 351-356).

SCORING This essay is worth 5 points.

Part (a) is worth 1 point for describing what the figure demonstrates (presidents are more successful in the beginning of their terms). Points would be awarded for other trends, such as a decline in victories over time.

Part (b) is worth 4 points, with 1 point awarded for identifying each factor affecting presidential victories in Congress (honeymoon period, divided government), and 1 point awarded for each explanation (Congress supports the president because he has popular approval and divided government makes it difficult for the president to get his program enacted). Points would be awarded for other factors, such as a crisis, that would cause Congress to support the president's program.

QUESTION 4 Part (a): The House of Representatives, with 435 members, is much larger than the Senate, with 100 members. Because of its size, the House has more rules to keep it organized. One difference between the House of Representatives and the Senate is that the Senate is run more informally. In the House, the Rules Committee sets the limits for debate on a bill. This can include time limits, as well as limits on the kinds of amendments that may be proposed. In the Senate, there is no rule limiting debate, and senators can speak for as long as they want.

Another difference between the House and Senate is that senators can filibuster legislation, and filibusters are not allowed in the House of Representatives. A filibuster allows senators to talk a bill to death. This allows senators who are in the minority to block actions favored by the majority. During the fifties and sixties, southern senators used it to block civil right legislation. More recently, it has been used to block appointments to the federal bench. Filibusters give senators more power than representatives, because one determined senator can block legislation (*American Government,* 8th ed., pages 283, 298-302, 306-318 / 9th ed., pages 288, 297-299, 304-317).

Part (b): One similarity between the way the House of Representatives and Senate are run is committees. Both houses have standing and select committees. These committees review legislation, make changes, and give recommendations to the House and Senate as a whole. In addition, a conference committee irons out legislation when it has been passed in different versions. Joint committees have members from both houses. Committees allow members of Congress to develop expertise in certain policy areas. Committees also create a division of labor that makes the legislative process more efficient (*American Government,* 8th ed., pages 283, 298-302, 306-318 / 9th ed., pages 288, 297-299, 304-317).

Scoring This essay is worth 6 points.

Part (a) is worth 4 points; 1 point is awarded for identifying each difference between the House and Senate (the House has a Rules Committee; senators can filibuster) and 1 point is awarded for explaining each difference (the Rules Committee can limit the time for debate; the filibuster allows senators to block legislation favored by the majority). Points would be awarded for other differences, such as different leaders (the Speaker of the House and the President Pro Tempore of the Senate).

Part (b) is worth 2 points, with 1 point awarded for identifying a similarity between the House and Senate (both have committees) and 1 point awarded for the explanation (committees allow members to develop expertise and make the legislative process more efficient). Points would be awarded for other similarities, such as majority and minority leaders and whips.

Calculating your score on the AP Exam

SECTION 1: MULTIPLE-CHOICE QUESTIONS

_____ Minus (1/4 X _____) Equals _____
correct   wrong   score

Rounded to nearest whole number _____
                                   adjusted score

SECTION II: FREE-RESPONSE QUESTIONS

Question 1 _____ X 1.875 equals _____
Out of 8   do not round

Question 2 _____ X 2.5 equals _____
Out of 6   do not round

Question 3 _____ X 3.0 equals _____
Out of 5   do not round

Question 4 _____ X 2.5 equals _____
Out of 6   do not round

TOTAL FOR SECTION II   _____

COMPOSITE SCORE:

_____ + _____ = _____
Section I   Section II   Composite Score

Student scores are weighted a differently each year to determine the final AP score. The conversion chart below is according to the weighing on the 2002 exam:

COMPOSITE SCORE RANGE	AP GRADE
94-120	5
79-93	4
61-78	3
35-60	2
0-34	1

Part II

A Review of AP U.S.
Government & Politics

1

THE CONSTITUTION

When delegates reached Philadelphia in 1787 with the charge of revising the Articles of Confederation, none could have imagined the momentous outcomes their meetings would have. While the Articles had established a government for the new nation, their failings were apparent to most. The delegates brought with them a host of historical and philosophical concerns that would shape a new constitution.

KEY TERMS

amendment process	Great Compromise
Antifederalists	judicial review
bicameral	natural rights
Bill of Rights	New Jersey Plan
checks and balances	ratification
constitution	republic
Declaration of Independence	separation of powers
factions	Shays's Rebellion
federalism	Virginia Plan
Federalist Papers	Unalienable
Federalists	unicameral

KEY CONCEPTS

- The path to independence accelerated with Britain's difficulty in administering and financing territory gained in the French and Indian War.

- The Articles of Confederation were the nation's first constitution and created a number of problems for the new nation.
- Called to revise the Articles of Confederation, the Constitutional Convention scrapped them and drafted the Constitution, which we live under today.
- There were many talented delegates to the Constitutional Convention, but it was James Madison who most profoundly shaped the Constitution.
- Proponents of the Constitution argued that it provided for a much needed and stronger national government; opponents preferred that state governments remain stronger.
- The Constitution has two amendment processes, which account in large measure for its endurance.

For a full discussion of the Constitution, see *American Government*, 8th ed., Chapter 2 / 9th ed., Chapter 2.

THE PATH TO INDEPENDENCE

Life for most colonial Americans was good by most measures of the day. Colonists enjoyed more liberty, wealth, and even equality than most of the rest of world. The king and Parliament generally ventured only into matters of trade and foreign relations. This benign relationship changed abruptly when Britain gained extensive new North American territory by winning the French and Indian War (also known as the Seven Years' War) in 1763. The expense of defending the newly won territory was overwhelming. Britain reasoned that the colonists should share in the burden of paying for the administration and defense of the new land through taxes on items such as newspapers, glass, paint, official documents, paper, and tea.

Colonial resentment towards the new taxes crystallized political and philosophical values in the colonies that had been evolving for some time. Colonial leaders, including Benjamin Franklin, John Adams, Thomas Jefferson, James Madison, Robert Morris, and Alexander Hamilton, were heavily influenced by European political philosophies of the Enlightenment. Perhaps the most widely read of the European philosophers was John Locke, an Englishman who wrote *The Second Treatise of Civil Government* (1689). Locke outlined his belief in natural rights—rights that are inherent in all human beings apart from any form of government and can be neither taken away nor given up. Locke's natural rights included life, liberty, and property. Government, Locke argued, exists for the securing of these rights and must therefore be built upon the consent of the governed. Furthermore, government must be limited. Locke believed that laws should be written, and government should not take any part of a man's property without his consent.

As colonial unhappiness with various British taxes escalated, war broke out. Colonial leaders met almost continuously during 1775 and 1776 as the Continental Congress. By May of 1776, resolutions concerning independence were being openly debated, resulting in the Declaration of Independence being formally adopted on July 4, 1776. Written primarily by Thomas Jefferson, the document is both political and philosophical, emphasizing many of Locke's ideas. It announces and rationalizes a revolution, listing twenty-seven specific ways that King George III had abused the Americans. Its philosophical statements, however, set forth many of the underlying assumptions of American government, then and now.

The colonists seemed badly outmatched by the mighty British army, and at several points during the Revolution the Americans appeared to be beaten. Nevertheless, in 1783, after a variety of unlikely twists and turns and with international aid from the Spanish and especially the French, the Americans won their independence.

THE ARTICLES OF CONFEDERATION

The Declaration of Independence merely created a voluntary union of the former colonies. The Continental Congress appointed a committee to devise a more formal and permanent union. The result of the committee's work was the Articles of Confederation, the nation's first constitution. The Articles created a national legislature that was unicameral. Several delegates could be sent to the new Congress by a particular state, but each state had only one vote. Passing a new law required nine of the thirteen states to vote in favor. There was only a powerless executive and no judicial branch included in the national government, and legislative powers were severely limited. Most power was reserved for the state legislatures. The Continental Congress adopted the Articles in 1777, but they did not go into effect until 1781, when Maryland ratified them, because unanimous consent was required for them to become operative.

From the beginning, the Articles appeared to create more problems than they solved. Among the notable weaknesses were the following:

- Congress had no power to tax. To obtain money, Congress had to request funds from the states, which often refused.
- Congress had no power to regulate commerce. This severely hindered efforts to create a national economy.
- The national government had no court system to deal with disputes between states.
- Congress *did* have the power to maintain an army and navy, yet it lacked the resources to adequately do even that.

The ineffectiveness of the Articles was further revealed in 1786, when a band of farmers in western Massachusetts staged a rebellion to protest the loss of their land to creditors. Led by a Revolutionary War captain, Shays's Rebellion was a series of attacks on courthouses to keep judges from foreclosing on farms. Neither the national government nor the state of Massachusetts was able to raise a militia to put down the rebellion. A privately funded force was hastily organized to do the job. National leaders cringed at the seeming chaos.

Shays's Rebellion and the perceived weaknesses of the Articles of Confederation convinced many that bold solutions were needed to mend the country's post-Revolutionary War problems. A handful of leaders met in Annapolis, Maryland, in September of 1786 to offer suggestions for putting the country on better footing. Because only five states were represented, the meeting had little effect. The Annapolis delegates petitioned Congress for a meeting of all the states the following year. Congress agreed, and in May of 1787, delegates convened in Philadelphia for the Constitutional Convention.

THE CONSTITUTIONAL CONVENTION

Although the fifty-five delegates to the convention were commissioned only to revise the Articles of Confederation, they dismissed this as impossible because it would have required the unanimous consent of the states. Instead, they set about writing a new constitution.

Of the fifty-five delegates, only about thirty participated consistently. Rhode Island refused to send any delegates. Most were relatively young, though Benjamin Franklin was already past eighty. They were mostly wealthy planters, lawyers, or merchants. Some famous names were notable for their absence: Thomas Jefferson and John Adams were serving abroad; Sam Adams was too ill to attend; Patrick Henry refused to attend, fearing the convention would create a government tending towards monarchy.

Some of the most contentious and difficult issues were the following:

- **Representation** The composition of the new Congress was hotly contested. The Virginia Plan called for representation to be based on a state's proportion of the total American population. The New Jersey Plan insisted on equal representation for each state. The solution is known as the Connecticut Compromise or the Great Compromise. The Senate would have two members from each state. The House of Representatives would be based on population.

> ### AP Tip
>
> Delegates to the Constitutional Convention wrangled over the question of representation for some six weeks. The Great Compromise, which provided the basis for our federal system, also served to keep the Convention together. Delegates spent another two months working on the Constitution, but no issue proved as contentious as that of representation. The Great Compromise is sure to appear on the exam.

- **Slavery** The contradictions between the Declaration of Independence and slavery were evident. Slaves were allowed to count three-fifths in the population census, a compromise between southern delegates, who wanted slaves counted in their entirety, and northern delegates, who wanted slaves not counted at all. Congress was given the power to end the importation of slaves, though not slavery itself, after 1808.

- **Voting** The delegates ultimately evaded the difficult question of who should be permitted to vote by leaving the issue to the individual states.
- **Economic Issues** The extent to which their own economic interests influenced the delegates has been debated ever since the Constitution was ratified. Many features were designed to empower the national government to make economic policy and protect property. Congress was given the power to tax and borrow, to regulate foreign and interstate commerce, and to create currency.
- **Individual Rights** The delegates assumed that state constitutions would continue to assure individual rights. As a result, the Constitution says little about personal freedoms (which would create a major issue during the ratification process). The Constitution does prohibit the suspension of the writ of habeas corpus (which enables persons detained by authorities to receive immediate justification for the cause of their detention). It also prohibits bills of attainder (which punish people without trial), ex post facto laws (which punish people for acts not illegal when they were committed), and religious qualifications for holding national office. Treason is defined, and conviction for treason is carefully described. Lastly, the right to trial by jury in criminal cases is explicitly stated.

The Constitution was finally finished and signed on the 109th day of the meetings. Not all the remaining delegates were willing to add their name to the document, however, foreshadowing the difficult process of ratification ahead.

JAMES MADISON AS ARCHITECT

More than any other individual figure, James Madison was the principal visionary of the government's structure. Madison feared factions of self-interested individuals banding together to create tyranny. To prevent the possible evils of powerful factions, Madison drew on examples from state constitutions and proposed (and eventually saw instituted within the Constitution) the following:

- **Separation of powers** Each of the three branches of government—executive, legislative, and judicial—would be given independent powers so that no one branch could control the others, yet no branch could operate with total independence. Power would not be divided absolutely but would be shared among the various branches.
- **Checks and balances** Because the three branches would share power, each could check the powers of the other two branches to a certain extent. For instance, the president could veto legislation passed by Congress. Congress could confirm or deny certain presidential appointments. The Supreme Court could interpret laws.
- **Limits on the majority** Madison feared the power of the masses and worked to keep most of the government beyond

their control. Only the House of Representatives had members directly elected by the majority. State legislatures selected senators, and an electoral college chose the president. Judges were to be nominated by the president and serve for life.

■ **Federalism** Political authority was divided between the national government and the various state governments. Madison assumed that this would check any tyranny by the national government.

The delegates knew that it is impractical to have the citizenry make all decisions. Instead, the Constitution created a republic, in which representatives of the public make policy and exercise power. Representation ensures that the principle of the consent of the governed will prevail. The American system is moderate and prone to compromise.

RATIFICATION OF THE CONSTITUTION

The proposed Constitution called for nine of the thirteen states to approve the document at special state ratifying conventions. This was technically illegal because the Articles of Confederation, which were still in effect, called for the approval of all thirteen state legislatures in order for there to be any amendments. The Framers of the Constitution wanted to evade this requirement because they feared that the legislatures would resist the new document, thus retaining their extensive powers.

Advocates of the Constitution called themselves Federalists, though they might have more accurately called themselves "nationalists." Their opponents, those wanting to thwart the ratification of the Constitution, became known as Antifederalists, though they might well have been called "states' righters."

To help persuade the public of the merits of the Constitution, Alexander Hamilton published a series of articles in the New York newspapers. Soon he recruited John Jay and James Madison to help him, and the trio wrote eighty-five articles from late 1787 through 1788. Known as the *Federalist* papers, they provide rare glimpses into the Philadelphia meetings and important elaborations regarding the Constitution itself. Although Hamilton wrote fifty-one of the articles, Madison penned the two most famous: *Federalist* 10 offers Madison's warning about factions and strategies to deal with them; *Federalist* 51 elaborates on checks and balances as the solution to factions.

The Antifederalists countered with articles of their own that made scathing and insightful attacks on the proposed Constitution. Antifederalists argued that a strong national government would be too distant from the people and would abuse its powers by absorbing functions that appropriately belonged to the states. They feared that Congress would tax far too heavily and that the Supreme Court would overrule state courts. They also feared that the president would become the head of a large standing army.

If a strong national government was to be created, argued the Antifederalists, it should be restrained by much more explicit guarantees of individual liberties than those found in this Constitution. Leading Federalists were persuaded by this argument and promised to add amendments to the document with explicit protections of individual liberties. Later James Madison, at the First Congress in 1789, proposed twelve constitutional amendments that restrained the national government from limiting civil liberties. Ten of these were ratified by the states by 1791. Collectively they have become known as the Bill of Rights. Another of Madison's original amendments, regarding congressional salaries, was ratified 201 years later as the Twenty-Seventh Amendment.

Using special conventions for ratification (which met independently of the state legislatures for the express purpose of examining the Constitution) proved to be a winning formula for the Federalists. State legislatures would have likely voted down the new Constitution. Delaware became the first state to approve, on December 7, 1787. Though bitter opposition continued in Virginia and New York that seemed to threaten ratification, within six months New Hampshire became the ninth to approve, and the Constitution was ratified. Virginia and New York joined shortly thereafter, seeing that further resistance was futile. North Carolina and Rhode Island waited for the Bill of Rights to be ratified before they joined in 1791.

CHANGING THE CONSTITUTION

The Framers of the Constitution wisely allowed for changes to be made in accord with the needs of later times. Constitutional changes can be made either through a formal amendment process or through informal processes.

- **The formal process** Article V of the Constitution sets forth procedures for formal amendments. For an amendment to pass, it must survive two stages of the process—proposal and ratification. In turn, each of these stages has two possible courses of action. An amendment may be proposed by either a two-thirds vote of both houses of Congress or by a national convention called by Congress at the request of two-thirds of the state legislatures. An amendment may be ratified by either the legislatures of three-fourths of the states or by special state conventions in three-fourths of the states. All but one of the amendments to pass (the Twenty-First) was the result of being proposed by Congress and ratified by the state legislatures. Formal amendments have tended to emphasize equality and expand voting rights.
- **Informal processes** There are several ways that the Constitution can change informally. Judicial interpretation is one. Though the Constitution only implies the power of the Supreme Court to consider the constitutionality of a case, the Court has exercised such power since the *Marbury v. Madison* case of 1803. The power of judicial review enables the Court to settle disputes regarding interpretations of the Constitution. Changing political practices also change the Constitution. Many Americans would be surprised to know that the Constitution mentions nothing of political parties, much less a two-party system. The electoral college system as outlined in the Constitution does not include any provisions that require

an elector to vote for the winner of the popular vote in a particular state, yet this is now a firm tradition and even the law in most states. Technology has affected the role of the media in politics, the ability of the civil service to provide services, and the power of the military in ways the Framers could never have imagined. The president now commands a position in the world that has significantly increased presidential powers far beyond the powers described in the Constitution.

The flexibility of the Constitution has served the nation well for over two hundred years. Ongoing issues—for example, the line-item veto that would allow the president to veto only part of a bill—continue to be debated and might well become part of the Constitution in the future. Though the United States is a young country in relation to much of the world, it has the oldest functioning constitution. By way of comparison, France had seven constitutions within a generation of its own revolution. Despite the enormous changes and the diversity and size of the nation, it continues to operate effectively and legitimately.

Multiple-Choice Questions

1. All of the following were weaknesses of the Articles of Confederation EXCEPT
   (A) the national government could not resolve state boundary disputes
   (B) currency was not accepted outside of local areas
   (C) the military could not put down even small rebellions
   (D) the national government had too much power
   (E) there was no national judicial system

ANSWER: **D**. Most of the power under the Articles of Confederation was given to the states (*American Government,* 8th ed., pages 21-22 / 9th ed., pages 21-22).

2. What was the result of the Great Compromise?
   (A) States were represented in the upper house, and individuals were represented in the lower house.
   (B) Individuals were represented in the upper house, and states were represented in the lower house.
   (C) Individuals were given proportional representation in both the House of Representatives and the Senate.
   (D) All members of Congress were selected by direct election.
   (E) Slaves were not counted in the census.

ANSWER: **A**. Under the Great Compromise, the House of Representatives is proportional and elected directly; and there are two senators per state. Senators were originally chosen by state legislators; they are now chosen by direct election (*American Government,* 8th ed., page 27 / 9th ed., page 27).

3. Under the original Constitution, which branch or branches of government were selected directly by the citizens?
   I.   the president and vice president
   II. the Supreme Court
   III. the Senate
   IV. the House of Representatives

   (A) I and II
   (B) I, III, and IV
   (C) III and IV
   (D) III only
   (E) IV only

ANSWER: E. Under the original Constitution, only members of the House of Representatives were elected directly. Senators were not elected directly until ratification of the Seventeenth Amendment in 1913. The president is chosen through the electoral college, and the Supreme Court is appointed (*American Government*, 8th ed., page 28 / 9th ed., page 28).

4. What is the main result of judicial review?
   (A) The Supreme Court is protected from interference by the executive.
   (B) The Supreme Court has the power to revise state laws.
   (C) The Constitution is safeguarded from popular passions.
   (D) The Supreme Court has the power to advise Congress in drafting bills.
   (E) The Supreme Court provides supervision of the lower courts.

ANSWER: C. Because Supreme Court justices are not popularly elected and are appointed for life, they can exercise independence and, through judicial review, protect the Constitution from the passions of the majority (*American Government*, 8th ed., page 28 / 9th ed., page 28).

5. All of the following are part of the amendment process EXCEPT
   (A) a proposal accepted by a two-thirds vote of Congress
   (B) a proposal accepted at a national convention called by Congress as requested by two-thirds of the states
   (C) a national referendum (by popular vote) with two-thirds voter approval
   (D) ratification by three-fourths of state legislatures
   (E) ratification by three-fourths of states in special conventions

ANSWER: C. A proposed amendment must receive a two-thirds vote in Congress or in a specially held national convention. It must then be approved by a three-fourths vote in state legislatures or through special state ratifying conventions (*American Government*, 8th ed., page 28 / 9th ed., page 28).

6. How does the Constitution provide an executive check on the judicial branch?
   (A) by allowing the president to remove Supreme Court justices from office
   (B) by permitting bureaucrats to ignore a decision of the Supreme Court
   (C) by allowing the president to propose a bill to Congress to overturn a decision by the Supreme Court
   (D) by nominating federal judges, subject to Senate confirmation
   (E) by appointing federal judges

ANSWER: **D**. The president nominates federal judges. Judges must be confirmed by the Senate (*American Government*, 8th ed., page 29 / 9th ed., page 29).

7. How did the Antifederalists differ from the Federalists?
   (A) The Antifederalists wanted a stronger central government.
   (B) The Federalists wanted to protect state sovereignty.
   (C) The Antifederalists had a more positive view of human nature.
   (D) The Antifederalists believed that a strong central government would be too distant from the people.
   (E) The Antifederalists were opposed to representative democracy.

ANSWER: **D**. The Antifederalists argued that a strong national government would be too distant from the people and would take away powers that belong to the states (*American Government*, 8th ed., page 31 / 9th ed., page 31).

8. Which of the following guarantees of individual liberties is found in the original Constitution?
   (A) freedom of speech, press, and assembly
   (B) no official state religion
   (C) a prohibition against double jeopardy
   (D) no unreasonable searches and seizures
   (E) no religious tests to hold office

ANSWER: **E**. Under the original Constitution, there may be no religious qualification or test to hold office. The rest of the protections are contained in the Bill of Rights (*American Government*, 8th ed., pages 34-35 / 9th ed., pages 34-35).

9. Which of the following is NOT a criticism of separation of powers?
   (A) It creates gridlock in policy-making.
   (B) It makes it difficult for the government to act decisively in times of crisis.
   (C) It results in prompt, but hasty, decision-making.
   (D) It makes it difficult to stimulate economic growth.
   (E) It damages our position of international leadership.

ANSWER: **C**. Separation of powers results in slow and deliberate decision- making. This can make it difficulty to act quickly regarding foreign affairs, crises, and the economy (*American Government*, 8th ed., pages 42-43 / 9th ed., page 42).

10. What would be the impact of the line-item veto on the separation of powers?
    (A) It would weaken the presidency and strengthen Congress.
    (B) It would strengthen the presidency in relation to Congress.
    (C) It would prevent the Supreme Court from using judicial review.
    (D) It would strengthen the power of the states.
    (E) It is not clear how the line-item veto would affect the separation of powers.

ANSWER: **B.** The line-item veto would strengthen the president by allowing him to veto a part of a bill. The president does not have line-item veto power (*American Government,* 8th ed., page 43 / 9th ed., page 43).

Free-Response Questions

1. It has been said, "The Constitution reflects a basic distrust of direct popular government." Identify two features of the Constitution and explain how they show this distrust of popular government.

RESPONSE: There are several features of the Constitution that indicate distrust of popular government. These include the election of the president by the electoral college, the fact that judges are appointed for life, and the selection of senators by state legislatures. Voting requirements were left to the states, which imposed property requirements. These requirements reflect a distrust of popular government, because citizens could vote directly only for members of the House of Representatives—the lower house, which has a two-year term of office. In addition, property requirements prevented many citizens from voting at all (*American Government,* 8th ed., pages 28-29 / 9th ed., pages 28-29).

2. Identify and explain two arguments made by the Federalists and explain how the Antifederalists countered each of these two arguments.

RESPONSE: The Federalists argued that large republics were more capable of protecting against factions. They contended that separation of powers, checks and balances, and federalism would prevent tyranny by any group or individual. Antifederalists argued that a strong national government would be too distant from the people. They wanted to narrow the jurisdiction of the Supreme Court and enlarge the House of Representatives. Most of all, the Antifederalists wanted a Bill of Rights to protect states and individuals from overreaching by the national government (*American Government,* 8th ed., pages 30-35 / 9th ed., pages 30-35).

2

FEDERALISM

Federalism is a philosophy of government based on the division of power between the state and federal government. In the United States, it has been a persistent source of political conflict.

KEY TERMS

block grants	grants in aid
categorical grants	initiative
conditions of aid	mandates
cooperative federalism	*McCulloch v. Maryland*
devolution	nullification
dual federalism	referendum
federalism	revenue sharing
federal system	unfounded mandates
Gibbons v. Ogden	unitary system

KEY CONCEPTS

- Federalism is the sharing of power between local and national governments.
- Defining the relationship between the national government and state governments has been—and continues to be—a major issue in the nation's history.
- The cornerstone of federal and state government relations today is the system of grants-in-aid, or funds distributed by Congress to state and local governments.
- The federal government tells a state government what its activities and policies must be in the form of mandates and conditions of aid.

For a full discussion of federalism, see *American Government,* 8th ed., Chapter 3 / 9th ed., Chapter 3.

SHARING POWER

Federalism is a political system in which power is shared between local units of government—states—and a national government. Only a handful of the world's governments are federal. (The United States, Canada, Australia, India, Germany, and Switzerland are examples.) Most are unitary systems, in which the national government has final authority over all government activities.

In the United States, federalism has endured mainly because of the American commitment to local self-government and because Congress consists of people who are elected by and responsible to local constituencies. Even though the national government has taken on vast powers, it often exercises those powers through state governments. The national government often finds itself seeking state compliance through regulations, grants, and other forms of pressure.

Among Americans, federalism has its advocates and its opponents. To some, federalism has meant that state governments can block important national actions, prevent progress, upset national plans, and protect powerful local interests. Historically, federalism has allowed the perpetuation of slavery, segregation, and racism, particularly in the South. Advocates argue, however, that the federal system has created a unique and beneficial separation of power between national and state governments. It allows for political flexibility and assures individual rights. They note that local control in some places has led to ending segregation and regulating harmful economic practices long before these ideas gained national support or became national policy.

One advantage is undeniable: federalism facilitates political participation and activity. Average citizens are often likely to become involved in organized politics if they can have impact. This is far more likely within a relatively small constituency. Local politics can draw in more activists and voters. Whether this was one of the Framers' intentions in instituting federalism is impossible to say because they were unclear in their writings about how the system was supposed to work. Instead, questions about the jurisdiction and powers of the national and state governments had to be settled by many years of various, often bitter, conflicts.

FEDERALISM'S HISTORICAL TRAIL

The goal of the Founders in regard to a federal system seems clear enough: dividing power between the national and state governments was another way of hindering runaway power and assuring personal liberty. A federal system was a new idea in the eighteenth century; thus the delegates to the Constitutional Convention groped to define it. Because it was assumed that the federal government would have only those powers given to it, the Constitution does not spell out state powers. According to the Tenth Amendment, "The powers not delegated to the United States by the Constitution, nor prohibited by it to the States, are reserved to the States respectively, or to the people."

Interpretation of the Tenth Amendment has been inconsistent over the centuries. Early Supreme Court rulings attempted to give states powers beyond the domain of the federal government, but those rulings were later contradicted.

The relationship between the national government and the state governments is explained clearly in some clauses of the Constitution. For instance, states may not make treaties with foreign nations, coin money, or issue paper currency. Other clauses are far vaguer. Knowing that the Constitution could not provide an exhaustive list of all things that the federal government could do, the Founders added the so-called elastic clause in Article 1, which allows Congress "To make all Laws which shall be necessary and proper for carrying into Execution the foregoing Powers ..." This language meant different things to different Founders. Alexander Hamilton, for instance, viewed the national government as superior in political affairs with broadly defined and liberally constructed powers. Thomas Jefferson, while not a Founder, held the view that the powers of the national government were to be as narrowly construed and strictly limited as possible. Thus the Constitution alone is of limited use in defining relationships between the states and the national government.

The Supreme Court became the arbiter of what the Constitution means and the focal point of the federalism debate that has lasted throughout United States history. The evolution of federalism can be observed in several distinct cases and periods:

- The first important case to define federalism arose in 1819 when James McCulloch, the cashier of the Baltimore branch of the bank of the United States, refused to pay a tax levied on the bank by the state of Maryland. The Court's ruling on the case answered two questions that expanded the powers of Congress and confirmed the supremacy of the federal government. The first question was whether Congress even had the right to set up such a bank, since such a power is not explicit in the Constitution. Chief Justice John Marshall held that while the federal government possessed only those powers mentioned in the Constitution, the meaning of those powers required interpretation. Because the power to manage money is in the Constitution, Congress may reasonably charter a national bank as "necessary and proper" (referring to the elastic clause). The second question was whether a federal bank could be taxed by a state. Here Marshall urged the ideal that the government of the United States was not established by the states but by the people. The federal government was therefore supreme in those powers conferred upon it. The states could not challenge those powers and destroy them, as a tax might do. *McCulloch v. Maryland* was clearly a victory for those favoring the supremacy of the national government.
- On the heels of *McCulloch* came another case that furthered the supremacy of the national government. The Constitution gives Congress the power to regulate interstate and international commerce. An 1824 case, *Gibbons v. Ogden,* forced clarification of the difference between intrastate and interstate commerce. The Supreme Court defined commerce

very broadly in the case to include virtually any form of commercial activity, again strengthening federal power.

- Leaders of southern states attempted to settle the ongoing power struggle through the doctrine of nullification. Nullification first arose in 1798 when Congress passed laws punishing newspaper editors critical of the federal government. James Madison and Thomas Jefferson, in statements known as the Virginia and Kentucky Resolutions, suggested that the states had the right to declare null and void a federal law that a state considered unconstitutional. Later, southern leaders revived nullification in opposition to federal efforts to restrict slavery. This time the issue was settled by war. The northern victory in the Civil War settled the issue of nullification, establishing that states cannot declare acts of Congress unconstitutional.

- After the Civil War, the interpretation of federalism focused on economic issues and the commerce clause of the Constitution. Out of this emerged the idea of dual federalism: the idea that the national government is to be supreme in its own sphere and states are to be supreme in theirs. In the economic realm, interstate commerce was regulated by the federal government, and intrastate commerce was regulated by the states. As more modern transportation and communication techniques developed, however, this distinction blurred. The federal government was increasingly allowed to regulate a greater amount of commerce.

- In recent decades a certain measure of state sovereignty has been reestablished. This trend is known as devolution. A 1995 Supreme Court case, *United States v. Lopez,* held that Congress had exceeded its commerce clause power by prohibiting guns in schools. Other cases also reaffirmed the view that the commerce clause does not justify every federal action taken using its authority. The rise of deficits as a major issue and the deficit reduction programs led by Congresses with Republican majorities has also promoted devolution. Two of the federal government's biggest grant-in-aid programs, welfare and Medicaid, became block grant programs (grants given by the federal government to state and local authorities for general purposes) even though they had not been created to be administered by states. Currently, as a general rule, the most important activities of state and local governments involve public education, law enforcement and criminal justice, health and hospitals, roads and highways, public welfare, and control over the use of public land and water supplies. Many states also offer avenues to direct democracy through initiatives, which allow voters to place legislative measures directly on the ballot, and referendums, which enable voters to reject a measure adopted by the legislature. There is also some early evidence that the devolution of federal welfare programs has triggered second-order devolution, a flow of power and responsibility from the states to local governments, and third-order devolution, the increased role of nonprofit organizations and private groups in policy implementation.

FEDERALISM AND STATE MONIES

Most political scientists today argue that the concept of dual federalism is outdated, and cooperative federalism now prevails. Not only are powers and policy often shared between states and the national government; so too are costs and administration. Today the cornerstone of the federal and state government relationship is the provision of federal grants to the states. Grants-in-aid, or funds designated by Congress for distribution to state and local governments, are the main vehicle the national government uses to both help and influence the states and localities. There are three major forms of aid:

■ **Categorical grants:** These grants are for specific purposes defined by federal law—to build an airport or a college dormitory, for example. Such grants often require that the state or locality put up money to match some part of the grant. They also come with strings attached, such as provisions for nondiscrimination.

■ **Block grants:** Because many governors and mayors found categorical grants too narrow to adapt to their local needs, block grants were begun in the 1960s. They are given regularly to states and localities with few strings attached in order to support broad programs in areas such as community development and social needs.

■ **Revenue sharing:** As another response to dissatisfaction with categorical grants, revenue sharing became a common practice. Revenue sharing is federal aid with no requirement as to matching funds and freedom to spend the money on almost any governmental purpose. It occurs when there is a budget surplus.

With billions of dollars of federal grants at stake, states and cities often compete with each other for a larger share. Most states and some cities have full-time staffs in Washington to vie for federal grant money. More and more grants, however, are based on distributional formulas, which provide grants automatically and objectively. These make the census, taken every ten years, monumentally important in establishing the amount of monies available to a state or locality. The federal government continues to hold great power over the actions of the states through grants-in-aid, and other ways of exerting control over the states have arisen in the form of mandates.

MANDATES

There are two kinds of federal controls on state government activities. Sometimes the federal government tells a state government what its activities and policies must be in order to receive grant money. These stipulations are called conditions of aid. Conditions of aid can be attached to grants-in-aid. When the federal government imposes its will outside the context of grants, these requirements are called mandates.

AP Tip

Because conditions of aid and mandates are the primary ways that the federal government pressures state governments to do what it wants, they are a significant aspect of federalism and are likely to appear on the AP exam.

Most mandates concern civil rights and environmental protection. States may not discriminate in their programs. States must comply with federal standards for clean air, pure drinking water, and sewage treatment. On the surface these appear to be quite reasonable, and they often are. Yet some mandates are written in vague language that creates administrative and financial problems. They give federal administrative agencies the power to decide for themselves what states and localities are supposed to do.

Medicaid is a good example of the problems that mandates can create for state governments. Medicaid provides health care for the poor and is administered by the states. It is widely supported by both political parties. Beginning in 1984, Congress moved to expand Medicaid, requiring states to cover certain children, pregnant women, and the elderly poor. By 1989, states could not keep up with the expanded coverage, and all but one governor called for a two-year moratorium on the mandated expansions of Medicaid.

At times Congress passes laws that create expenses for the states but provide no funds to meet the expenses. These are known as unfunded mandates. In 1990 Congress passed the Americans with Disabilities Act. Accessible facilities (such as government offices, courtrooms, colleges, and universities) for individuals with disabilities were mandated. No money, however, was allocated to implement the new law. The Clean Air Act of 1970 is another law that created an unfunded mandate. National air quality standards were established, but states were required to pay for the administration and implementation of the policy. Gun buyers have also received unfunded mandates. They must bear the cost of background checks.

Federalism was built into the Constitution to prevent concentration of power and threats to liberty. It no doubt expands democracy in many ways. However, the multitude of state and local governments has also created problems, such as inequalities among states in several vital areas. The inevitability of some policies being controlled by the national government because of global, technological, economic, and social changes has given the states a reduced role in American government. The states continue, nevertheless, to play a central role in American political life.

Multiple-Choice Questions

1. Which of the following is the best example of devolution?
   (A) the No Child Left Behind law, which provides states with monetary incentives for meeting national educational guidelines
   (B) the *McCullough v. Maryland* case, which allowed the federal government to maintain a national bank
   (C) civil rights legislation mandating that states not discriminate
   (D) block grants, by which money from the national government is given to the states for discretionary use with broad guidelines
   (E) the federal tax code, which provides deductions for local charities

ANSWER: **D.** Devolution is an effort by the national government to return some powers to the states. Block grants, which allow states to spend federal money using some discretion, are an example of devolution (*American Government,* 8th ed., pages 49-50 / 9th ed., pages 49-50).

2. The Founding Fathers devised a federal system for all of the following reasons EXCEPT
   (A) federalism is one method for checking government's power and protecting personal liberty
   (B) concentrating power in a single entity might create tyranny
   (C) under the Articles of Confederation, the national government was too dependent on the states for survival
   (D) a federal system provides balance of power between the state and national governments
   (E) federal systems were common throughout the world and were proven to be effective

ANSWER: **E.** Federal systems were uncommon when the Constitution was written and they are relatively rare today. There are only eleven countries with federal systems (*American Government,* 8th ed., pages 51-53 / 9th ed., pages 51-53).

3. Which of the following statements best describes the impact of the Tenth Amendment?
   (A) It has been effective in protecting and expanding the powers of the states.
   (B) It had little impact at first but has been expanded over time to protect state powers.
   (C) It has rarely had much practical significance.
   (D) The Supreme Court has interpreted it consistently over time.
   (E) It has protected the powers of the states, but not those of individual citizens.

ANSWER: **C.** The Supreme Court has tried to interpret the Tenth Amendment as giving the states certain powers beyond the reach of the federal government, but there is a pattern of contradictory decisions by the Supreme Court over time. As a result, the Tenth

Amendment has rarely had much practical significance (*American Government*, 8th ed., pages 53-54 / 9th ed., pages 53-54).

4. Which of the following Constitutional provisions has been interpreted as weakening the Tenth Amendment?
   (A) the full faith and credit clause
   (B) the supremacy clause
   (C) the Ninth Amendment
   (D) the necessary and proper clause
   (E) the extradition clause

ANSWER: **D**. The necessary and proper clause, also known as the elastic clause, gives to the national government any power important for carrying out its expressed powers. As a result, the power of the national government was expanded relative to state power (*American Government*, 8th ed., pages 54-55 / 9th ed., page 54).

5. What did the Supreme Court determine in *McCulloch v. Maryland*?
   I.   To carry out its economic powers, Congress may reasonably decide to create a national bank.
   II. The necessary and proper clause enables Congress to take actions not specifically listed in the Constitution.
   III. States have the right to tax all economic activity within their borders.
   IV. States may not tax any federal institution.

   (A) I and II
   (B) I, II, and III
   (C) I and IV
   (D) I, II, and IV
   (E) II and IV

ANSWER: **D**. In *McCulloch v. Maryland* the Supreme Court ruled that the necessary and proper clause enables Congress to take actions not specifically mentioned in the Constitution, including the creation of a national bank. Maryland could not tax the national bank, because "the power to tax is the power to destroy" (*American Government*, 8th ed., pages 55-56 / 9th ed., pages 55-56).

6. The concept that the national government is supreme in its own sphere while the states are equally supreme in theirs is known as
   (A) cooperative federalism.
   (B) balanced federalism.
   (C) home rule.
   (D) emerging federalism.
   (E) dual federalism.

ANSWER: **E**. Dual federalism is the idea that the national and state governments are supreme in their own respective spheres. This has been replaced with cooperative federalism, with each level of government sharing overlapping powers (*American Government*, 8th ed., pages 57-58 / 9th ed., pages 57-58).

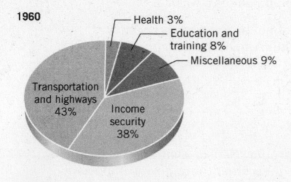

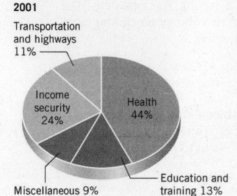

7. The pie charts above support which of the following conclusions?
    (A) The amount of federal grant money given to states more than doubled between 1960 and 2001.
    (B) The category in which federal grant money increased the most from 1960 until 2001 is health.
    (C) Because the interstate highway system was built by 2001, spending on transportation dropped.
    (D) Most of the money given to states for education and training comes in the form of block grants.
    (E) Devolution has taken place for all categories of federal grants.

ANSWER: **B**. While 3 percent of federal grant money to states went to health in 1960, spending on health represented 44 percent of the purpose of federal grants to states in 2001 (*American Government,* 8th ed., pages 61-62 / 9th ed., page 61).

8. States have found federal funding attractive for all of the following reasons EXCEPT
    (A) in the late nineteenth and early twentieth centuries, the national government had surplus money to spend on the states
    (B) in the late twentieth century, the income tax provided a flexible source of federal grant money
    (C) the federal government can print money when it is needed to fund programs
    (D) federal grants rarely come with strings attached
    (E) state politicians can get federal money without having to take the unpopular political position of supporting expanding government

Answer: **D.** While federal funding has historically provided states with significant resources, it often comes with provisions regarding how the money must be spent (*American Government,* 8th ed., pages 59-61 / 9th ed., pages 59-61).

9. Why do states prefer block grants to categorical grants?
   (A) Categorical grants require the states to spend matching funds.
   (B) Block grants allow states to spend funds on any governmental purpose.
   (C) Categorical grants are often rescinded.
   (D) The amounts given in block grants are stable from year to year.
   (E) Block grants allow local officials to satisfy the needs of interest groups.

Answer: **B.** Block grants allow states to spend federal money on any governmental purpose, although they are coming with more strings attached. Categorical grants require the states to spend the money on a specific purpose, like building an airport (*American Government,* 8th ed., pages 62-64 / 9th ed., pages 62-63).

10. The Americans with Disabilities Act (ADA) requires states and local governments to provide equal access for the disabled. This is an example of a(n)
   (A) categorical grant.
   (B) block grant.
   (C) revenue sharing.
   (D) mandate.
   (E) administrative regulation.

Answer: **D.** A mandate tells the state government what it must do. Under the ADA, states are required to make buildings accessible to the disabled. When federal funding does not accompany the requirement, this is known as an "unfunded mandate" (*American Government,* 8th ed., pages 66-68 / 9th ed., pages 65-66).

Free-Response Questions

1. Discuss the facts used by the Supreme Court's majority in the *McCulloch v. Maryland* decision, and explain how the case expands the power of the federal government in relation to the states.

Response: A national bank was established, and Maryland tried to tax it. The Supreme Court determined that the federal government had the power to create the bank, even though this power is never expressly mentioned in the Constitution. The establishment of a national bank was allowed under the necessary and proper clause, which gives Congress the authority to make all laws necessary for carrying out its express powers—in this case, the powers to control interstate commerce and the currency. The Court held that Maryland could not tax the bank because "the power to tax is the power to destroy." This decision expanded the power of the federal government to take actions not specifically mentioned in the Constitution and limited the states' authority over these actions (*American Government*, 8th ed., pages 55-56 / 9th ed., pages 55-56).

2. For TWO of the following (a) identify the term, (b) give a specific example, and (c) explain how it affects policy-making within the states:

> categorical grants
> revenue sharing
> block grants
> mandates

RESPONSE: Categorical grants are given to the states to be used for a specific purpose defined by federal law, such as building a college dormitory. This affects policy-making within the states because it restricts the states' ability to make new policy. States must spend the money in relatively narrowly defined ways, as prescribed by the federal government.

Revenue sharing occurs when there is a surplus. States are given funds, usually in accordance with their populations, to spend as they please on government functions. This enables the states to make creative and innovative policies and address their own unique needs with little federal control.

Block grants are devoted to some general programs with few restrictions on their use. Welfare money, for example, is given to states in a block grant. This enables states to create policies to address issues identified by the national government in ways that will most benefit their unique circumstances.

Mandates are laws enacted by the national government that the states must follow. Sometimes mandates require the states to spend money, and when the federal government does not accompany the requirement with funding, this is called an "unfunded mandate." Mandates make states act in a certain way. Often they cost money, which could be spent on other programs, and this limits policy-making by the states (*American Government*, 8th ed., pages 62-69 / 9th ed., pages 62-67).

3

THEORIES OF DEMOCRATIC GOVERNMENT

Americans regularly use terms such as *democracy, power,* and *authority.* Few take the time, however, to analyze the shades of meaning behind these critical words and their implications for understanding government. Political scientists devote their careers to considering two basic questions drawn largely from these concepts: Who governs? To what ends?

KEY TERMS

authority

bureaucratic theory

democracy

direct democracy

initiative

legitimacy

Marxist theory

nongovernmental elitist theory

pluralist theory

political elite

power

referendum

representative democracy

KEY CONCEPTS

- Power and authority are concepts at the heart of an understanding of government.
- Democracy has shades of meaning that must be understood in order to examine American government.
- Distribution of political power among a nation's political elite is viewed in various ways.
- Institutions and policies change as a nation evolves.

For a full discussion of theories of democratic government, see *American Government,* 8th ed., Chapter 1 / 9th ed., Chapter 1.

POWER AND AUTHORITY

In its simplest sense, power is the ability to get another to act in accord with one's intentions. Power is found in all human relationships, of course, but examining political power specifically involves a close look at those who hold government offices and how government officials behave in using power. A president telling the air force that it can or cannot build the B-1 bomber is an obvious example of political power. Exercising political power can also be subtle, as when an advisor informally convinces the president to alter even a minor policy.

Authority is the legal right to use power. We accept decisions from the government if we believe they come from those who have the right to make them. In most countries, including the United States, the right to exercise authority comes from legal or constitutional sources. A valid question, therefore, is what makes a law or constitution a source of authority. This is a question of legitimacy. In the United States, the Constitution is almost universally accepted as a source of legitimacy, yet this was not always the case. The Constitutional Convention was an attempt to legitimize a more powerful national government. The early presidential administrations were dominated by conflict over the kinds of decisions that the federal government could legitimately make. The legitimacy of a federal union as opposed to a confederation of states was at the heart of the Civil War. The New Deal was constantly scrutinized as to its legitimacy regarding the government's intrusion into the private sector of the economy. Today the legitimacy of activist judges is often questioned. As these tests on the legitimacy of the Constitution have played out over the course of American history, that legitimacy has become increasingly more established.

In the minds of Americans today, the legitimacy of the government is also based on the concept of democracy. Because democracy has become so ingrained in the American conscience, many have even extended its tenets to other institutions of public life, such as schools, universities, corporations, trade unions, and churches. These are often judged by the degree of democracy they practice. Democracy has different meanings, however, and a core knowledge of these is fundamental to finding the one that best describes the government of the United States.

THE MEANING OF DEMOCRACY

Democracy has at least two widely used meanings. The ancient Greek philosopher Aristotle put forth one of the most basic. To Aristotle, democracy was simply "the rule of the many." He believed that a government was democratic if all, or at least most, citizens participated directly by holding office and making policy. This is often called direct, or participatory, democracy. Such a government was possible in Aristotle's Greece, where the city-state was quite small. (Even there, slaves, women, minors, and those without property were kept from participating.) Colonial New England town meetings also practiced direct democracy.

A second meaning of democracy is what most democratic nations practice today: representative democracy. In this, leaders gain office and power by means of a competitive contest for the votes of the people. Because of limits on time, information, energy, interest, and expertise, it is impractical for the people to decide on all public issues, so representatives must be elected to formulate policy.

Representative government has many inherent problems. It prospers only when certain conditions are met. The opportunity for leadership competition (most often in the form of elections) must be present. Communication (through speeches or media) must be free and untainted so that voters can make meaningful choices. Political parties must be allowed to compete. Even if these requirements are met, another persistent problem is deciding which offices should be elected and which appointed. Yet another involves the number of candidates allowed to compete before choices become hopelessly confused. Finally, the problem of who should pay for campaigns— candidates, parties, or the government—is often an issue. Many Americans argue that some of the virtues of direct democracy could still be had even in our modern and complex society. In the spirit of direct democracy, many states have referendums and initiatives—that is, policy choices that appear on the ballot, either at the suggestion of citizens themselves or of the state legislature.

The Framers of the Constitution clearly favored representative democracy. Most did not think that the will of the people was synonymous with the public good or even the common interest. Their philosophy was that government should mediate, not mirror, popular opinion. They assumed that most citizens do not have the time or knowledge to make good policy choices. Although representative democracy often proceeds slowly, a government capable of quickly doing great good would also be capable of quickly doing great harm. Representative democracy, they believed, is a way of controlling both a tyrannical majority and self-interested officeholders, thus assuring civil rights and liberties. As our representative democracy has evolved, so too have various theories about the distribution of power in government.

DISTRIBUTION OF POLITICAL POWER

Even in a democracy, policy will reflect the views of those people who are sufficiently motivated to participate actively in policy-making. Usually small and perhaps even unrepresentative of the overall electorate, this group, called the political elite, represents the actual distribution of power in making and implementing policy. Political elites are identifiable groups that possess a disproportionate share of power, and political scientists have at least four theories to explain their actions:

- **Marxist theory** To most Marxists, government—whatever its outward form might appear to be—is a mere reflection of underlying economic forces, especially those concerning the ownership of the means of production. Marxists believe that all societies are divided into economic classes based on their relationship to the economy. Over the centuries, these groups generally have included capitalists (the bourgeoisie, according to Marxists), workers, farmers, and intellectuals. In modern life two major classes contend for power—capitalists and workers. The class dominating the economy also controls the government, which is nothing more than a vehicle to express and give legitimacy to the interests of the ruling class. Marxists believe that the U.S. government is "but a committee for managing the common affairs of the whole bourgeoisie." In other words, the government represents the rich.

- **Nongovernmental elitist theory** Closely related to Marxist theory, nongovernmental elitist theory argues that an elite primarily outside of the government makes most of the major decisions. However, this elite is not composed exclusively, or even primarily, of corporate heads. A loose coalition of three groups—corporate leaders, top military officers, and a handful of key political leaders—sets the most important policies, along with leaders of the major communications media, major labor leaders, and the heads of various special-interest groups. Regardless of the scope of this elite, the central argument is the same: Government is dominated by a few top leaders, most of whom are outside the government and enjoy great advantages in wealth, status, or position. Their actions are coordinated, and their policies serve the interests of the elites.

- **Bureaucratic theory** According to this theory, most political power belongs to bureaucrats—those who operate government agencies. Max Weber, a German historian and sociologist who wrote in the early twentieth century, popularized this theory as a criticism of Marxism. The Marxist position, thought Weber, made an error in assigning exclusive significance to economic power. Dominant social and political realities are vital as well. All institutions, governmental or nongovernmental, have fallen under the control of large bureaucracies whose expertise and specialized competence are essential to the management of contemporary affairs. Capitalists or workers might come to power, but those who operate them daily will dominate the government agencies they create. Weber saw this as both positive and negative. Decisions would be made more effectively because of the expertise of the bureaucrats, but bureaucratic power could be potentially overwhelming and dangerous. Today Weber's theory is given even more credence by the emergence of "technocrats." These technical experts are needed more and more as policy decisions become more complex. The programming of electronic voting machines, the specifications for satellites, and the defining of legal encryption for data privacy, all are matters that can pertain to policy questions and give more potential power to expert government and industry bureaucrats.

- **Pluralist theory** Pluralists argue that political resources like money, prestige, expertise, organizational position, and access to the mass media are so widely distributed in our society that no single elite has a monopoly on them. Furthermore, there are so many levels of government that no single group, even if it had vast resources, could dominate the political process. While pluralists do not argue that political resources are distributed equally, they believe that resources are sufficiently divided among various groups to assure that almost all relevant interests have an opportunity to participate in the political process.

While these theories emphasize that politics is always an expression of self-interest, this is not always the case. Though political elites are often motivated by self-interest, they can also transcend it and act quite selflessly, as was the case in responding to the events of September 11, 2001. In addition, many of the most important events in American history—the Revolution of the 1770s and 1780s and the civil rights movement, for instance—were led by people who risked much while knowing that they might not succeed and might not live to see the benefits of their efforts.

POLITICAL CHANGE

Who governs and how government behaves are two questions answered differently with changing circumstances. Of course, what government does today is heavily influenced by what it did yesterday, Clearly, the evolution of our institutions and policies has not stopped but is continuing. For example:

- In the 1920s the general view was that the federal government should play a minimal role in people's lives. From the 1930s through the 1970s, the general view was that the federal government should attempt to solve many economic and social problems, indeed creating a "safety net" for all Americans. The administration of Ronald Reagan, from 1981 to 1988, began to reverse this trend by cutting taxes, spending less on social programs, and reducing federal regulations on businesses.

- In foreign affairs, American policy has seen monumental changes. At the time the nation was founded, policy was a response to the actions of France and England, who seemed to control the destiny of the United States. By the 1840s, the United States sought to expand the nation into areas where Mexico and Canada had claims. In the late 1090s, many leaders believed we had an obligation to acquire an overseas empire in the Caribbean and the Pacific. Isolation, at least from European affairs, largely dominated policy until World War II. After that, the nation seemed to eagerly embrace its role as an international leader. Not only have American attitudes changed; economic, industrial, and transportation changes have created a new role for the United States to come to terms with.

Political change is not always accompanied by changes in policy and law, but the policy process is one of the best guides to who governs and how they govern.

Multiple-Choice Questions

1. For representative democracy to work, all of the following must be present EXCEPT
   (A) the opportunity for individuals to run for office
   (B) freedom of expression
   (C) voter turnout above 60 percent
   (D) competition among political parties
   (E) voter perception that there is a meaningful choice

ANSWER: **C.** For representative democracy to work, there must be meaningful political competition among individuals and parties who are able to freely express themselves (*American Government,* 8ᵗʰ ed., pages 6-7 / 9ᵗʰ ed., page 7).

2. All of the following statements about the beliefs of the framers of the Constitution are true EXCEPT
   (A) they favored representative democracy over direct democracy
   (B) they believed that most citizens did not have the time, information, and expertise to make informed choices
   (C) they believed that government decisions should mirror popular viewpoints
   (D) they recognized that representative democracy would proceed slowly
   (E) they insisted on the protection of civil rights and civil liberties

ANSWER: **C.** The framers believed that government should mediate, not mirror, popular views (*American Government,* 8ᵗʰ ed., pages 7-8 / 9ᵗʰ ed., page 8).

3. Which of the following statements best represents pluralist theory?
    (A) The class that dominates the economy also controls the government.
    (B) The most important policies are set by a loose coalition of three groups—corporate leaders, top military officers, and key political leaders.
    (C) Leaders outside of the government structure dominate government.
    (D) Unelected bureaucrats who run agencies dominate the government.
    (E) There are so many groups that none of them can dominate the political process.

ANSWER: E. Pluralism is the belief that competition among all affected interests shapes public policy (*American Government*, 8th ed., page 10 / 9th ed., pages 9-10).

4. In the past couple of decades, several events have challenged traditional theories of policy-making. Which of the following examples demonstrate that Americans do not always act in their own self-interest?
    I.   the response of police and firefighters to the attacks of September 11, 2001
    II. leaders of the AFL-CIO working for the passage of civil rights laws
    III. the Civil Aeronautics Board (CAB) working to have their agency abolished
    IV. the tobacco industry lobbying to prevent tobacco from being put under the authority of the Food and Drug Administration

    (A) I and II
    (B) I, II, and III
    (C) II and III
    (D) II, III, and IV
    (E) III and IV

ANSWER: B. The actions of the AFL-CIO, CAB, and the reaction to the September 11 attacks all demonstrate that people do not always act in self-interest (*American Government*, 8th ed., page 10 / 9th ed., page 10).

5. Which of the following is an example of political beliefs changing over time?
    (A) Americans have come to believe that the federal government should play a bigger role in our lives.
    (B) Americans have come to believe that the federal government should play less of a role in regulating the economy than it did when the country was founded.
    (C) Americans wanted the federal government to play a bigger role in our lives until the 1980s, when this trend was reversed.
    (D) Americans have held relatively consistent views about the role of the federal government over time.
    (E) Americans have become more convinced of the importance of political participation over the last fifty years.

ANSWER: **C**. During the 1980s taxes were cut, along with government services, as many citizens thought government had grown too big (*American Government,* 8th ed., page 11 / 9th ed., page 11).

6. What is one of the best barometers for measuring changes in who governs?
   (A) public opinion polls
   (B) an analysis of the topics covered in campaign speeches
   (C) an examination of the amount of coverage given by the media
   (D) an analysis of the policy process and changes in the laws
   (E) there is no real way of measuring political change

ANSWER: **D**. The authors of *American Government,* Wilson and DiIulio, contend that one of the best barometers of changes in who governs is the policy-making process (*American Government,* [not available in 8th ed.] / 9th ed., page 14).

7. Which of the following is the best evidence that direct democracy is expanding in America today?
   (A) more frequent use of ballot initiatives
   (B) increased voter turnout
   (C) a movement to lower the drinking age
   (D) a movement to directly elect federal judges
   (E) continued support for the electoral college

ANSWER: **A**. Initiatives allow citizens, by petition, to put issues directly on the ballot. This is an example of direct democracy (*American Government,* 8th ed., pages 7, 12 / 9th ed., pages 8, 12).

8. What is the most basic definition of democracy?
   (A) rule by the many
   (B) rule by representatives who are directly elected
   (C) any system of government with elections
   (D) any system of government with a written constitution
   (E) any system where citizenship is widely extended by most adults

ANSWER: **A**. Aristotle's basic definition of democracy is "rule of the many" (*American Government,* 8th ed., pages 5-6 / 9th ed., page 6).

9. All of the following are criticisms of direct democracy EXCEPT
   (A) people have limited time and energy to consider the issues
   (B) people don't have enough expertise in many policy areas
   (C) people make decisions based on fleeting passions
   (D) people will respond to popular demagogues
   (E) direct democracies have never been successful

ANSWER: **E**. Direct democracy was successful in New England town meetings, but the rest of the factors listed may make it impractical or unwise in a larger setting (*American Government,* 8th ed., pages 5-6 / 9th ed., page 6).

10. How are power and authority related?
   (A) A government can have power without having authority.
   (B) Power includes the right to rule.
   (C) Authority can exist without power.
   (D) Neither requires popular support.
   (E) The terms are synonymous.

ANSWER: A. Power is the ability to get another person to act, even by force. Authority means the right to use power (*American Government,* 8th ed., pages 4-5 / 9th ed., pages 4-5).

Free-Response Questions

1. The legitimacy of the United States government has increased over time. Identify and explain how legitimacy was increased by TWO of the following:

   the Constitutional Convention
   the Civil War
   the New Deal

RESPONSE: The Constitutional Convention was an effort to create a more powerful federal government by giving each branch of government enough power to provide strength and security for the nation, while preventing tyranny. George Washington's administration was tested by internal and foreign disputes, and his responses increased the legitimacy of the government. Thomas Jefferson also used the Constitution to expand the territory of the nation. This gave even more legitimacy to the government.

The Civil War was a bloody struggle over slavery and whether states could secede from the federal government. After the war, the issue of states' rights was more settled. The national government's authority was greater than the power of the states: although the war resulted in acrimony, it did prove the federal government's strength in holding the nation together.

The New Deal was a test of the federal government's authority to control the economy. Many of Franklin Roosevelt's proposals to increase the federal government's reach into new areas of the economy were challenged. Eventually, most were found to be constitutional, and the federal government expanded its ability to control economic forces. These attempts to prevent economic downturns have increased legitimacy (*American Government,* 8th ed., page 5 / 9th ed., page 5).

2. Identify and explain TWO of the following theories about how the elite rules government:

   Marxism
   rule by a nongovernmental elite
   bureaucratic theory
   pluralism

RESPONSE: Marxism is the theory that government is a reflection of economic forces and that class struggle between workers and capitalists dominates the economy. According to Marx, in a capitalist system, the elite property owners dominate government.

Rule by a nongovernmental elite is the theory that corporate leaders, top military officers, and a handful of key political leaders control government. These leaders dominate a country and are not representative of the population as a whole.

Bureaucratic theory contends that those who operate governmental agencies from day to day actually control policy-making. Unlike Marx, this theory, proposed by Max Weber, emphasizes social and political factors. The specialization and expertise of bureaucrats enables them to control key government functions.

Pluralism is the theory that political resources, such as money, prestige, expertise, organizational position, and access to the mass media are widely dispersed in our society. Therefore, one group cannot control policy. Groups compete for power. Pluralists acknowledge that political resources are not distributed evenly (*American Government,* 8th ed., pages 8-10 / 9th ed., pages 8-10).

4

AMERICAN POLITICAL CULTURE

Many Third World nations have adopted the American constitutional model, hoping to institute features such as federalism, an elected president, a bicameral legislature, and separation of powers. Most of these have experienced brief periods of democracy interrupted by military takeovers, the rise of demagogues, and wholesale corruption. It is the American political culture that has allowed the American model to endure in the United States.

KEY TERMS

civic duty

culture war

external efficacy

internal efficacy

political culture

political efficacy

political ideology

political subculture

work ethic

KEY CONCEPTS

- In addition to political values, economic and religious values shape political culture. Taken together, all of these values clarify the significance of American political culture.
- Americans increasingly mistrust government.
- Political efficacy is a citizen's capacity to understand and influence political events.
- Americans practice enough political tolerance to allow civil discourse.

For a full discussion of American political culture, see *American Government,* 8th ed., Chapter 4 / 9th ed., Chapter 4.

POLITICS, ECONOMICS, AND RELIGION

Political culture is a distinctive and patterned way of thinking about how political and economic life ought to be carried out. A political culture consists of fundamental assumptions about how the political process should operate. For example, Americans assume that when an election is lost, the loser will accept the results and not hinder the winner from taking office. The election of 2000 is a prime example. Likewise, Americans assume that social or family background should not keep potential candidates from running for office. In both of these cases the opposite is assumed in many countries. Furthermore, most countries, including the United States, have political subcultures— groups within a country made up of distinctive regions, religions, and ethnic groups that have different political assumptions. *Political culture* is not to be confused with *political ideology,* which is a consistent set of views an individual might have concerning the policies government ought to pursue.

Though there are many individual exceptions to the basic American political culture that have often caused serious conflict, Americans tend to believe the following about the political system:

- **Liberty** Americans are more fiercely protective of their rights. They believe they should be free to do as they please, with some exceptions, as long as they do not hurt other people.
- **Equality** Americans believe everyone should have an equal vote and an equal chance to participate and succeed.
- **Democracy** Americans think government officials should be accountable to the people.
- **Civic duty** Americans believe that people should take community affairs seriously and contribute when they can.
- **Individual responsibility** Americans believe that individuals are responsible for their own actions and well-being.

A comparison with other countries reveals that Americans are often more contentious than citizens in other countries, who tend to value harmony and emphasize obligations over rights. While voter turnout is lower in the United States than in most other democracies, Americans participate in government in other ways (for example, campaigning, attending political meetings, contacting government officials) to a far greater extent. Though Americans increasingly mistrust government, they still have greater confidence in their government than do people in many places abroad.

Americans believe that everyone should be equal politically but not necessarily economically. Americans tend to make these assumptions about the economy:

- **Liberty** Americans support the idea of a free-enterprise system within certain boundaries. People support government regulation of business to keep firms from becoming too powerful and to correct specific abuses.
- **Equality** Americans are more willing to tolerate economic inequality than political inequality. They believe in maintaining "equality of opportunity" but not "equality of results." Americans will support education and training programs to help disadvantaged people, but they are opposed to anything that looks like preferential treatment.
- **Individualism** Americans believe individuals have personal responsibility. They will support people truly in need but are skeptical of aid given to those who can take care of themselves.

These values are quite different than those of many other nations. Foreign governments often support programs that stress economic equality of results over opportunity among citizens. Americans are more likely to think that freedom is more important than equality and less likely to think that hard work goes unrewarded.

American political culture is also influenced by religion. There is some evidence that Americans are becoming more religious, and a recent Gallup poll showed that 54 percent of Americans attend worship services more than once a month. Eighty-two percent of Americans consider themselves a "religious person," more than in any European country. Churches, synagogues, mosques, and other religious organizations are the country's major source of volunteer and community services. Recent religious movements—for example, the Moral Majority of the 1980s and the Christian Coalition of the 1990s—have overlapped political movements. They saw how the civil rights movement was furthered by the Reverend Dr. Martin Luther King, Jr. Candidates for national office are well advised to stress the virtue of religion in their campaigns.

SOURCES OF POLITICAL CULTURE

Because the United States was founded through a war fought over liberty, the American emphasis on rights is understandable. The ongoing friction between liberty and social control has created an adversarial spirit unusual among the countries of the world.

Americans have a seeming preoccupation with rights and a long-standing mistrust of authority and power. This is rooted in the colonial experience with Britain but even more so in an older religious belief that saw human nature as fundamentally flawed. Since no one is born innocent, no one can be trusted with power. Thus the Constitution was designed to curb the darker side of human nature.

Political parties are one historical source of political culture. When John Adams had to give up his presidential seat to Thomas Jefferson, a political opponent, the nation had its first great test of peaceful transfer of power. Jefferson took the presidency, and soon the role of the opposition party became legitimate and a part of American political culture.

Another key to our political culture is religious diversity. The Constitution protects religious freedom. Puritan and later Protestant traditions have existed alongside other views since colonial days. Despite the lack of an established church, one Puritan idea—the work ethic—has transcended American history. This stresses that an individual has an obligation to work, save money, obey the secular law, and do good works. This work ethic goes far in explaining the rise of capitalism in the United States.

All aspects of culture, including the political, are transmitted primarily through the family. The family shapes in subtle ways how we think and act on political matters, including political party affiliation. Early on, Americans often learn from family that every person has rights deserving protection and that a variety of interests have a legitimate claim to consideration when decisions are made. This has created a relatively low degree of class consciousness among Americans.

If almost all Americans share some elements of a political culture, why is there so much cultural conflict in American politics? It is simplistic to say that there are two cultural classes in the United States, but to say that there is a culture war is not an exaggeration. Areas of disagreement include abortion, gay rights, drug use, school prayer, and pornography. This culture war differs from other political disputes in several ways. For the most part, money is not at stake. Compromise is virtually impossible. Emotions tend to run much higher than on topics such as taxes or foreign policy. A simple model divides the culture war into two camps. This is a conflict that fights over the boundary between liberty and social control:

- **The orthodox** On this side are people who believe that morality is more important than self-expression. They hold that moral rules are derived from the commands of God or the laws of nature and thus cannot be altered. The orthodox include fundamentalist Protestants and evangelical Christians, though many who are orthodox do not hold deep religious views. The orthodox can also come from Catholic and Jewish traditions as well as a secular background. They support two-parent families, condemn pornography, denounce homosexuality, and believe the United States is generally a force for good in the world.

- **The progressives** People in this camp think that personal freedom is more important than traditional moral rules, which should be reevaluated constantly in the light of modern life. Progressives include liberal Protestant denominations and people with no religious beliefs. Progressives believe that the rules of proper behavior are contextual. They suppose that there are legitimate alternatives to the traditional two-parent family, that pornography and homosexuality are private matters protected by individual rights, and that the United States has been no better than a neutral force in world affairs.

Two characteristics differentiate the modern culture war from earlier conflicts of this sort. The first is that far more Americans now see themselves as progressives than earlier generations did. The second is the rise of popular media, which makes it easier to fight a culture war on a large scale. The tensions of the culture war affect our views of how well government can work, how much impact an individual can have, and how much freedom we should grant our opponents.

MISTRUST OF GOVERNMENT

Since the late 1950s the nation has seen a continual decline in the level of trust that Americans have for the government. For instance, between 1952 and 1992, the fraction of Americans who said public officials did not care what the public thought doubled from one-third to two-thirds. However, people are commenting on government officials, not the system of government. Some attribute the declining faith in government to the turbulence of the 1960s followed by Watergate and, in the 1990s, the scandals of the Clinton administration. Others speculate that the 1950s were simply a period of abnormal prosperity, world power, and unity. The country had conquered the Great Depression and won World War II. A monopoly on the atomic bomb existed prior to 1950, and the United States dominated international trade. Perhaps such confidence in government never could have lasted.

The tragic events of September 11, 2001, created not only a wave of patriotism but also a unified spirit not felt in the country for decades. However, recent polls have shown another decline in confidence in the government, perhaps because of mistrust over the war in Iraq. High levels of sustained trust for the government as seen in the 1950s are not likely in the foreseeable future, yet high levels of patriotism still exist, and most Americans never question their system of government.

POLITICAL EFFICACY

Perhaps an even greater problem than the issue of mistrust is the sense Americans now have that the government will not *respond* to their needs and beliefs. A citizen's capacity to understand and influence political events is a concept called political efficacy. Efficacy has two parts—internal efficacy, which is the ability to understand and take part in politics, and external efficacy, which is the ability to make the system respond to the citizenry. Since the 1960s there has been a fairly sharp drop in the sense of external efficacy, though not much change in internal efficacy. Unlike the issue of mistrust, few specific events can be cited to account for the drop in efficacy. Americans may have gradually come to the conclusion that government is now too big and pervasive to respond to citizen preferences.

POLITICAL TOLERANCE

Democratic politics depends on civility in dealing with the opinions and actions of others. Democracy does not require perfect tolerance, but at a minimum, citizens must allow the discussion of ideas and the selection of leaders in an atmosphere free of oppression. Regarding the tolerance of the average American citizen:

- Most Americans are willing to let people they disagree with politically have great latitude in expressing their views.
- However, Americans as a whole have become more tolerant, but most think Americans tolerate too much.
- Most Americans believe that serious civic problems are rooted in a breakdown of moral values. Most citizens worry that the nation is becoming too tolerant of behaviors that harm society.

While there are many examples of political intolerance, Americans continue to practice enough civility in politics to permit a civil discourse.

American history and social organization have created a unique political culture in the United States. A preoccupation with rights and an adversarial style make the American political culture utterly unique, even among democracies of the world.

Multiple-Choice Questions

1. All of the following are important elements in the American view of the political system EXCEPT
   (A) Americans believe they should be able to do pretty much as they please
   (B) Americans think government officials should be accountable to the people
   (C) Americans believe that individuals are responsible for their own actions
   (D) Americans believe that government should try to equalize the property and living conditions of citizens
   (E) Americans feel people ought to help out in their communities

ANSWER: **D**. Americans believe everybody should have an equal chance to participate and succeed. Most Americans do not support equality of outcomes or living conditions (*American Government,* 8th ed., pages 80-81 / 9th ed., pages 78-79).

2. A person who has consistently supported a strong military and
    wanted to increase defense spending over the past twenty years
    has a well developed
    (A) political culture.
    (B) political subculture.
    (C) party identification.
    (D) party loyalty.
    (E) political ideology.

ANSWER: E. A political ideology is a more or less consistent set of
views concerning the politics the government ought to pursue. In
contrast, the term "political culture" refers to Americans' beliefs about
how the system should operate (*American Government*, 8th ed., page
81 / 9th ed., page 79).

3. One core American attitude about the economic system is
    (A) a widely held commitment to individualism and personal
        responsibility.
    (B) the belief that social welfare policies should be expanded.
    (C) the belief that women and minorities should have preferential
        treatment in hiring.
    (D) a commitment to help all citizens, whether or not they are truly
        in need.
    (E) the belief that wages should be based on economic need, as
        well as hard work.

ANSWER: A. There is a widely — but not universally — shared
commitment to economic individualism and personal responsibility as
the key determinants of economic success. (*American Government*, 8th
ed., page 83 / 9th ed., page 81).

4. In comparison to most other nations,
    (A) Americans have less confidence in public and private
        institutions.
    (B) Americans have less confidence in private institutions and
        more confidence in public institutions.
    (C) Americans have more confidence in both public and private
        institutions.
    (D) Americans have less confidence in public institutions and more
        confidence in private institutions.
    (E) This is impossible to measure because Americans' views are so
        diverse.

ANSWER: C. Today, people have less confidence in government than
they once did. However, compared to most countries, Americans have
more confidence in public and private institutions (*American
Government*, 8th ed., page 85 / 9th ed., page 83).

5. All of the following are true about religion in America EXCEPT
   (A) Americans are more likely than Europeans to believe in a higher power
   (B) Religiosity has increased in the past two decades
   (C) Religious institutions are the country's major source of volunteer and community service
   (D) Despite the high percentage of Americans who believe in a higher power, more than half of all Americans do attend church more than once per month
   (E) Americans are more likely than Europeans to pray every day

ANSWER: **D**. According to a Gallup poll conducted in 2000, 54 percent of Americans attend church more than once per month. By most measures, Americans are more religious than Europeans (*American Government*, 8th ed., pages 86-87 / 9th ed., pages 84-85).

6. What is the primary way culture is preserved over time and transmitted to a new generation?
   (A) through the public school system
   (B) through the media
   (C) through programs funded by the government
   (D) through the family
   (E) through churches and other civic organizations

ANSWER: **D**. Although culture is preserved and transmitted by schools, friends, the media, churches, and civic organizations, the family is the primary influence in the way we think about the world (*American Government*, 8th ed., pages 90-91 / 9th ed., page 89).

7. According to Wilson and DiIulio, the "culture war" in America "is about what kind of country we ought to live in, not just about what kinds of policies our government ought to adopt." Which of the following is NOT a major source of cultural disagreement in America?
   (A) abortion
   (B) legal rights of homosexuals
   (C) legalization or decriminalization of drugs
   (D) federal funding for the arts
   (E) socialism and communism

ANSWER: **E**. Americans disagree about abortion, legal rights of gays, legalization of drugs and federal funding for the arts. The vast majority of Americans is committed to a market system and does not support socialism or communism (*American Government*, 8th ed., pages 90-91 / 9th ed., page 89).

8. Which of the following statements best describes the trend in Americans' trust in government?
   (A) Americans have had a high level of trust in government officials since World War II.
   (B) Americans now trust government officials more than they did during the 1950s.
   (C) Beginning with the Watergate scandal, there has been a steady decline in Americans' trust in government officials.
   (D) Americans' trust in government officials has declined at a fairly steady rate since the 1950s.
   (E) Americans' trust in government officials drops in wartime and rises in peacetime.

ANSWER: **D**. Since the 1950s, there has been a more or less steady decline in the proportion of Americans who say they trust the government in Washington to do the right thing (*American Government,* 8th ed., page 92 / 9th ed., page 90).

9. Citizens who believe they can influence political events and trust the system to respond to their needs have a high sense of political
   (A) effectiveness
   (B) culture
   (C) efficacy
   (D) socialization
   (E) legitimacy

ANSWER: **C**. Political efficacy is the belief that a citizen can influence government and that the government will be responsive to peoples' needs. Since the mid-1960s, there has been a sharp drop in the sense of external efficacy (the ability to make the system respond to the citizenry) but not much change in the sense of internal efficacy (personal competence) (*American Government,* 8th ed., pages 93-94 / 9th ed., page 93).

10. All of the following are true about political tolerance in America EXCEPT
    (A) Americans are more tolerant of members of different religious groups than they are of atheists
    (B) Lawyers and judges are more tolerant of specific political activities than most citizens are
    (C) Americans are willing to allow many people with whom they disagree to participate in the political process
    (D) Americans have become more tolerant over the years
    (E) Americans will support liberties for all groups both in theory and in practice

ANSWER: **E**. Americans are generally tolerant. However, for most of us, there is some group or cause from which we are willing to withhold political liberties—even though we endorse those liberties in the abstract (*American Government,* 8th ed., pages 94-97 / 9th ed., pages 94-95).

Free-Response Questions

1. According to Wilson and DiIulio, "Since the 1950s, there has been a more or less steady decline in the proportion of Americans who say they trust the government in Washington to do the right thing."
   a. Identify and explain one example that supports this trend.
   b. Identify and explain one example that goes against their trend.

RESPONSE: Part (a): During the 1950s, patriotism and trust in government were high. This trust was reduced by several events. During the late 1960s and early 1970s, Americans were unhappy with the war in Vietnam. In addition, many Americans started to believe that the government was not giving them accurate information about the progress of that war. This led to a decline in the level of trust in government officials. The Watergate scandal in the early 1970s also decreased the public's confidence in government officials. The president was accused of lying to the public about his knowledge of the cover up of the burglary of Democratic party headquarters. President Nixon resigned before the House of Representatives voted on impeachment. Similarly, President Clinton was impeached for lying about his affair with Monica Lewinsky. Although he was not removed from office, trust and confidence in government officials declined.

Part (b) There have been times when trust and confidence in government officials have risen. This occurred at one point during the Reagan administration when his plan to lower taxes became law. Furthermore, after the attacks of September 11, 2001, there was a renewed sense of patriotism. Fire and police heroes were widely celebrated. By November 2001, about half of all Americans trusted Washington officials to do what is right most of the time—the highest level in many years. It is important to remember that although trust in government has declined in the United States, it is still relatively high compared with many European countries (*American Government,* 8th ed., pages 92-93 / 9th ed., pages 90-93).

2. How does American political culture differ with many West European nations—for example, Sweden—with respect to beliefs about the economic system?

RESPONSE: While many European leaders come from working class or blue-collar backgrounds, American leaders tend to come from the ranks of white-collar professionals and academia. This difference in backgrounds is reflected in policy-making. Americans do not support giving all workers in a particular industry equal pay. Furthermore, Americans are willing to accept a larger difference between the salaries of workers and those of managers. Americans value freedom over economic equality. They support higher pay for hard work. Americans are less likely to support a federal guarantee of a basic income. As a result of the policies that stem from these beliefs, the United States has a greater income gap than do most European countries (*American Government,* 8th ed., pages 85-86 / 9th ed., pages 83-84).

5

PUBLIC OPINION AND POLITICAL BELIEFS

Government action and inaction do not always match public opinion. This apparent contradiction to the animating principle of democratic government occurs for several reasons. First, the Framers of the Constitution set up a government that does not always give the majority what they want. Measuring public opinion is also very difficult. Finally, active participants in government are more apt to achieve their goals than is the uninvolved general public.

KEY TERMS

conservative

liberal

moderate

political cleavages

political elite

political ideology

political socialization

public opinion

KEY CONCEPTS

- Defining public opinion in the United States is a difficult task.
- Political attitudes are derived from many sources, among them family, religion, gender, and education.
- Social class, race and ethnicity, and region create cleavages in public opinion.
- Political ideology is a coherent and consistent set of beliefs.
- Political elites have great influence on American public opinion.

For a full discussion of public opinion and political beliefs, see *American Government,* 8th ed., Chapter 5 / 9th ed., Chapter 5.

THE PROBLEM OF DEFINING PUBLIC OPINION

Public opinion, or the collection of attitudes and views held by the general public, is very difficult to assess. The public is often uninformed about what the government is doing. A study that asked Americans about a fictitious piece of legislation found that over a quarter of those interviewed actually expressed opinions on the issue, fully thinking the legislation was real! The public also is quite capable of changing its mind. Another study that asked the same questions to the same respondents six months apart found that many people had changed their views.

An even greater problem exists in the polling techniques themselves. How a pollster *words* a question can dramatically affect the answer received. For instance, rates of agreement or disagreement with a one-sided statement can differ when two balanced statements on the same issue are offered. The order in which possible responses are listed can also have an effect on the poll. Accurate polling requires a random sample; there is a correlation between large samples and greater accuracy, but expense can prohibit large samples.

Americans are not ignorant, fickle, or gullible. However, for most Americans government and politics are not as big a priority as jobs, family, or friends. Democracy is not dependent on people investing major amounts of time on understanding government. In fact, it perhaps works best when people are given simple, clear-cut choices. Furthermore, attitudes towards specific issues are probably less important than larger values such as liberty, equality, individualism, and civic duty.

SOURCES OF POLITICAL ATTITUDES

Our political choices are based on our individual orientation. For adults, this is generally a combination of several factors and the result of a complex process known as political socialization:

AP Tip

The importance of family as an agent of political socialization is a widely known fact and would likely be part of any AP question regarding sources of political attitudes.

■ **Family** The most thoroughly researched aspect of opinion formation concerns party identification. The majority of young people identify with their parents' political party. This identification starts in elementary school. As people grow older, they naturally become independent of their parents in many ways, including their political outlook. Yet a strong correlation exists even between mature adults and their parents' political party preferences (probably around 60 percent).

- **Religion** Religious tradition often has an impact on political orientation, again most often through the family. For instance, studies have shown that Catholic families are somewhat more liberal on economic issues than white Protestant ones, while Jewish families are much more liberal on both economic and social issues than both Catholics or Protestants. Strong political movements associated with religious groups such as the Moral Majority and the Christian Coalition show that religious differences can certainly impact a person's politics.
- **Gender** A gender gap exists in American politics. The extent of that gap and its tendencies vary according to different time periods. Men have become increasingly Republican since the mid-1960s, while the voting behavior of women has changed little (they are about 58 percent Democrat). The biggest reason for this gap appears to be attitudes about the size of government, gun control, spending programs aimed at the poor, and gay rights.
- **Education** College students are more liberal than the general population, especially at the most selective colleges. Moreover, the longer students stay in college the more liberal they tend to be. Because Americans today are far more likely to be college graduates than a generation ago, college plays an increasingly important role in political socialization, most likely because of the ideas and movements encountered there.

Politics, like other aspects of life, is a learned behavior. Americans learn to vote, pick a party (or remain independent), and evaluate political events in the world around them. All of these factors help create public opinion.

CLEAVAGES IN PUBLIC OPINION

The process of political socialization helps explain why political cleavages exist among Americans. These cleavages overlap and crosscut in a bewildering array. Today there are cleavages based on social class, race and ethnicity, and region:

- **Social class** Though social class can be an ambiguous distinction, socioeconomic differences no doubt play a role in politics. They play less of a role in the United States, however, than they do in Europe, and in both, class has had a declining impact. Nevertheless, unskilled workers are more likely than affluent white-collar workers to be Democrats and have liberal views on economic policy. Class is playing a diminishing role because of the increasing importance of noneconomic factors in our ideologies. Political ideologies are now more likely to be framed by issues such as race relations, abortion, school prayer, arms control, and environmentalism.
- **Race and ethnicity** African Americans are overwhelmingly Democrats, while whites are more likely to be Republicans, but this traditionally strong cleavage seems to be weakening a little. More young African Americans are identifying themselves as Republicans. Latinos generally identify

themselves as Democrats, but to a less significant degree than African Americans. Asian Americans are more identified with the Republican party than are whites. However, all of these generalizations conceal important differences within these ethnic groups. For example, Japanese Americans tend to be more conservative than Korean Americans, and Cuban Americans tend to be more conservative than Mexican Americans.

- **Region** The most significant regional cleavage in American politics has been between southern and northern voters. The South has traditionally been more accommodating to business enterprise, and the Northeast supports labor unions. The biggest difference among white voters, however, has been on the issue of race. Today the political views of white southerners are less distinct from those of whites living in other parts of the country. The South, West, and Midwest continue to be conservative, while the Northeast and West Coast tend to be more liberal.

POLITICAL IDEOLOGY

When we refer to people as liberals or conservatives, we assume they have a coherent and consistent set of beliefs—a political ideology. A strong ideology implies consistency over time in patterns of voting and stances on issues. With some inevitable fluctuations, studies show that moderates are the largest group among American voters, conservatives the second largest, and liberals the smallest.

The definitions of *liberal* and *conservative* have changed over time. Originally, a liberal was a person who favored personal and economic liberty, free from the controls and powers of the government. The term "conservative" was first applied to those who opposed the excesses of the French Revolution. Beginning with the time of Franklin Roosevelt and the New Deal, liberal in the United States was used to describe someone who supported an active national government that would intervene in the economy and create social welfare programs. Conservative described those who opposed this activist national government. Conservatives supported a free market rather than a regulated one, states' rights over national supremacy, and greater reliance on individual choice in economic affairs. The meanings of these terms continue to evolve. For instance, liberals were once known for favoring laws guaranteeing equality of opportunity among the races, yet now many liberals would favor affirmative action plans that include racial quotas. Conservatives once opposed American intervention abroad, yet now many would support an active role internationally. The table below gives some indication of the contemporary views of modern liberals and conservatives.

Table 5.6 How Liberals and Conservatives Differ

Belief	Support Among Self-Declared Liberals	Support Among Self-Declared Conservatives
The government should provide "more services even if it means an increase in spending."	73%	32%
The government should guarantee "that every person has a job and a good standard of living."	55	21
Favor "government insurance plan which would cover all medical and hospital expenses for everyone."	82	27
The government "should make every effort to improve the social and economic position of blacks."	55	18
The U.S. "should spend less on defense."	85	65
"Aid to [Russia] should be increased."	36	32
"Women should have an equal role in running business, industry, and government."	96	81
The United States should always permit abortion "as a matter of personal choice."	72	36
"Homosexuals should be allowed to serve in U.S. Armed Forces."	70	45
"Oppose death penalty for persons convicted of murder."	35	15

Source: Robert S. Erikson and Kent L. Tedin, *American Public Opinion*, 5th ed. (Boston: Allyn and Bacon, 1995), 69. Copyright © 1995 by Addison-Wesley-Longman. Reprinted with permission.

In some respects, the categories of liberal and conservative seem too broad to be useful in understanding the ideologies of Americans. For instance, one can be liberal economically but not socially. Others might be quite conservative economically yet not agree with conservative positions on foreign policy. An ideology can be consistent and still contain liberal and conservative values. Overlapping values are so prevalent that liberal or conservative in their pure form describes relatively few people. Libertarians, for example, are conservative on economic matters and liberal on social ones.

POLITICAL ELITES AND PUBLIC OPINION

The political elite is likely to espouse a purely liberal or purely conservative ideology. The political elite is made up of those who have a disproportionate amount of power in policy-making. In the United States the political elites are activists. While an elite might be an officeholder, he or she might work for campaigns or newspapers, head interest groups or social movements, or have a wide audience in speaking out on public issues. The more a person is an activist, the more likely it is that he or she will show ideological consistency and take a position more extreme in its liberalism or conservatism. Congress, for instance, has a high degree of ideological consistency, as do delegates to national conventions.

Political elites and average voters see politics in different ways, making the power of the elites important for at least a couple of reasons. First, the political elite has more access to the media. This creates the power to raise and frame political issues. For instance, environmentalism at one time received little attention. Later it became an important concern of government. A major study found that elite views shape mass views by influencing both which issues capture the public's attention and how those issues are debated and decided.

Second, elites determine the range of acceptable and unacceptable policy options on an issue. For instance, civil rights leaders have said over and over again that racism and sexism are wrong. This repetition has created so much pressure that their opponents, even if not convinced that racism and sexism are wrong, must find ways to make their positions less obvious or less strident.

Elites do not have unlimited influence in American government. For instance, elites cannot *hide* unemployment from the general public. But by emphasizing—or not emphasizing—the problem and framing policy options, the elite can wield great power. The public needs to discriminate between public opinion and the opinions of the elites. Further, it is wrong to suppose that there is just one elite, unified in its interests and agendas. There are many elites, and hence many elite opinions. Whether there is enough difference among elites to consider the process for new and revised policy competitive is one of the major issues in the study of American government.

While a democracy must be sensitive to public opinion and the political beliefs of the citizens, discerning what the public thinks is a formidable task. Political scholars continue to consider the ever-changing views of the American political spectrum.

Multiple-Choice Questions

Table 5.1   Religious Orientation of White Voters, 1996

Political Opinion	Secular (36%)	In Between (39%)	Fundamentalist (25%)
Increase domestic spending	61%	76%	76%
For national health insurance	38	39	20
Guarantee good standard of living	23	24	11
Spend less on welfare	61	61	77
Always permit abortions	57	29	8
Allow gays in military	72	61	35
Punish criminals to cut crime	47	60	65
Favor gun control	44	46	29
Spend more on defense	48	69	76
Percentage Democratic (of party identifiers)	50	40	23
Percentage liberal (of ideological identifiers)	36	12	6
Percentage voted for Clinton (of 1996 two-party vote)	49	40	20

Source: From Robert S. Erikson and Kent L. Tedin, *American Public Opinion*, 6th ed., p. 196. Copyright © 2001 by Longman. Reprinted with permission.

1. The table above supports which of the following conclusions?
    (A) Very religious voters are less likely to support defense spending.
    (B) Twice as many secular voters as fundamentalist voters support national health insurance.
    (C) The largest percentage of voters is secular.
    (D) The more religious voters are, the more likely they are to support gun control.
    (E) Most voters agree the government should spend less on welfare, regardless of religious orientation.

ANSWER: **E**. According to the table, 61 percent of secular and "in between" voters support spending less on welfare, while the percentage increases to 77 percent for fundamentalist voters. This means that most voters support spending less on welfare (*American Government*, [not available in 8th ed.] / 9th ed., page 108).

2. The gender gap can be explained by major differences in policy views on all of the following issues EXCEPT
   (A) homelessness
   (B) gun control
   (C) abortion
   (D) the size of government
   (E) gay rights

ANSWER: **C**. Men and women are similar on their views regarding abortion, with 57 percent of men and 60 percent of women supporting it. On all of the other issues listed, the gender gap is more pronounced (*American Government*, 8th ed., pages 109-110 / 9th ed., page 109).

3. What is the effect of a college education on political attitudes?
   (A) People with college degrees tend to be more conservative, because they have higher than average incomes.
   (B) People who have attended college tend to vote more as independents because they think more ideologically.
   (C) People with college degrees are not as liberal as their parents.
   (D) People with college degrees describe themselves as liberal.
   (E) There is no correlation between a college education and political attitudes.

ANSWER: **D**. Although people who attend college are not as liberal as they used to be, they are still more likely to describe themselves as liberal (*American Government*, 8th ed., page 111 / 9th ed., page 111).

4. Which of the following voters will most likely prefer a Republican candidate?
   (A) a black woman with a college degree and high income
   (B) a middle-class Asian man who belongs to a labor union
   (C) a southern white male business owner
   (D) an Hispanic employee of the federal government
   (E) a white "soccer mom" who lives in the suburbs

ANSWER: **C**. While many of the voters mentioned have some factors that influence conservative voting, the southern white male business owner has the most. He is white and male. In addition, many business owners prefer to vote Republican, as do southerners (*American Government*, 8th ed., pages 112-118 / 9th ed., pages 111-115).

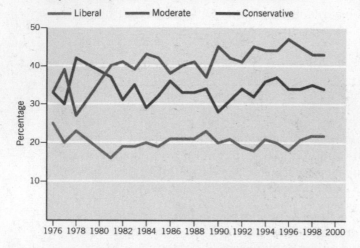

Figure 5.2 Ideological Self-Identification, 1976–1999

QUESTION

How would you describe your views on most political matters? Generally, do you think of yourself as a liberal, moderate, or conservative?

——— Liberal ——— Moderate ——— Conservative

Source: The American Enterprise (March/April 1993): 84, Robert S. Ericson and Kent L. Tedin, *American Public Opinion* (New York: Longman, 2001), 101, citing surveys by CBS/*New York Times*.

5. The chart above supports which of the following conclusions about the last half of the 1990s?
   (A) The country is evenly divided among liberals, conservatives, and moderates.
   (B) There are more liberals than moderates.
   (C) Both liberals and conservatives saw their percentages drop.
   (D) While most people identify themselves as moderate, there has been a slight decrease in this number and a corresponding increase in the percentage of liberals.
   (E) Most Americans are conservative.

ANSWER: **D**. About 43 percent of Americans describe themselves as moderate, with 34 percent conservative, and 21 percent liberal. However, in the last half of the 1990s, there was a slight drop in the percentages of conservatives and moderates and a slight increase in the number of liberals (*American Government*, 8th ed., page 120 / 9th ed., page 119).

6. A conservative would support which of the following measures?
   I. less government regulation of the economy
   II. affirmative action programs for underrepresented groups
   III. increased spending on social programs, such as welfare
   IV. the death penalty

   (A) I and II
   (B) I, II, and IV
   (C) II and IV
   (D) II, III, and IV
   (E) I and IV

Conservatives tend to oppose affirmative action and increased social spending. They tend to support the death penalty. They prefer less government regulation of the economy (*American Government*, 8th ed., pages 122-123 / 9th ed., pages 120-121).

7. All of the following are characteristics of an accurate random sample EXCEPT
   (A) the questions must be asked in clear, unemotional language
   (B) people must have some knowledge of the things they are asked about
   (C) the sample must include at least 10 percent of the population
   (D) each person must have an equal chance of being interviewed
   (E) even the most accurate polls have some sampling error

ANSWER: **C.** Accurate polling requires a random sample with clear questions about understandable topics. Although larger samples are more accurate, they are expensive. For any population over 500,000, at least 1,065 respondents are necessary to provide a 95 percent confidence, plus or minus 3 percent (*American Government*, 8th ed., pages 114-115 / 9th ed., pages 116-117).

8. According to Wilson and DiIulio, "the Framers of the Constitution did not try to create a government that would do from day to day 'what the people want'." Which of the following serve as checks on public opinion?
   I. federalism
   II. the House of Representatives
   III. an independent judiciary
   IV. separation of powers

   (A) I and IV
   (B) II and III
   (C) I, II, and III
   (D) I, III, and IV
   (E) I, II, III, and IV

ANSWER: **D.** Federalism, an independent judiciary, and separation of powers all serve as checks against popular rule. The House of Representatives, which is directly elected, most closely represents popular opinion (*American Government*, 8th ed., page 104 / 9th ed., page 104).

9. A public opinion poll asks whether or not people agree with the following statement: "The federal government should see to it that all people have adequate housing." Which of the following statements best describes the accuracy of the poll?
   (A) It will not be accurate because a random sample was not used.
   (B) It will not be accurate because the statement is loaded.
   (C) It will not be accurate because of sampling error.
   (D) It may be accurate depending upon how many people are polled.
   (E) There is no way to determine the accuracy of the poll.

ANSWER: **B.** The statement is one-sided. When people were asked this question, they agreed. However, when people were given a choice between a federal housing policy and individual responsibility, a slight majority favored the second choice (*American Government*, 8th ed., page 105 / 9th ed., page 105).

10. A voter who wants less government control over the economy as well as the personal lives of its citizens is
    (A) Republican
    (B) Democratic
    (C) Independent
    (D) Libertarian
    (E) Populist

ANSWER: **D**. Libertarians prefer a small, weak government that has little control over the economy or the personal lives of its citizens (*American Government*, 8th ed., page 123 / 9th ed., page 121).

Free-Response Questions

1. Specific political attitudes develop from a number of sources. Identify three of these sources, and explain how they affect political ideology.

RESPONSE: There are a number of sources you can discuss. One source of political opinion is the family. The vast majority of young people know their parents' political beliefs, and the majority share those beliefs. In some families, the dinner table is a political classroom where families discuss and share their values. However, on issues of civil liberties and race, young people tend to be more liberal than their parents.

Another source is religion. Catholics and Jews tended to support the Democratic party in the past, although that allegiance is weakening for Catholics. The Jewish religion has emphasized social justice, which may explain why many Jews vote Democratic. On the other hand, conservative Christians emphasize personal salvation and responsibility and have become a cornerstone of support for the Republican party.

Gender also influences political attitudes. A gender gap in voting signals that men and women see political issues differently. Men are more likely to support defense spending, while women are more likely to support social programs. As a result, more women than men vote for the Democratic party.

Education also has an impact on political attitudes. In general, the longer students stay in college, the more liberal they become. This could be because of the kind of people who are going to college, the information they are exposed to, or that colleges teach liberalism. Although college students may be more conservative today than they were in the past, the liberalizing effect of college remains (*American Government*, 8th ed., pages 106-111 / 9th ed., pages 106-111).

2. Liberals and conservatives differ in their view on the scope of government. Describe the differences in these views on both economic and social issues. Support your analysis with a discussion of one specific economic issue and one specific social issue.

RESPONSE: Liberals favor government regulation of the economy and support spending on social programs, but they do not want the government regulating personal lives. Conservatives want less economic regulation of business and want to cut back on the welfare state. However, conservatives favor regulations to curb personal conduct they view as against the best interests of society.

An example of an economic issue upon which liberals and conservatives disagree is tax policy. Conservatives favor cutting taxes on business and the wealthy, using the theory that the new investments and growth generated will benefit the economy as a whole. Liberals would prefer to tax corporations and the wealthy at a higher rate than the middle class under the theory that those who have the ability to pay more should do so.

An example of a social issue upon which liberals and conservatives disagree is the size of the welfare state. Liberals favor policies to give direct aid to the poor, such as welfare benefits, food stamps, and Medicaid. They believe that the social structure creates barriers for the poor that cannot be overcome without the government's help. Most conservatives favor reducing, but not eliminating, welfare programs. They believe that government programs have undercut personal responsibility and created a culture of poverty (*American Government*, 8th ed., pages 122-123 / 9th ed., pages 120-121).

6

POLITICAL PARTICIPATION

The low rate of participation in national elections in comparison with European democracies is a source of great embarrassment to the United States. However, the problem might be based less on apathy and more on problems of voter registration. Americans participate in ways other than voting to a much greater extent than other democracies.

KEY TERMS

activist

conventional participation

Fifteenth Amendment

grandfather clause

literacy test

motor-voter law

Nineteenth Amendment

poll tax

registered voters

Twenty-sixth Amendment

unconventional participation

Voting Rights Act of 1965

white primary

KEY CONCEPTS

- The American electorate has expanded through extended voting rights for minorities, women, and youth.
- Voter turnout in the United States is relatively low, and the relatively difficult process of voter registration probably accounts for it.
- There are many levels and forms of participation in the American political system.

For a full discussion of political participation, see *American Government,* 8th ed., Chapter 6 / 9th ed., Chapter 6.

THE AMERICAN ELECTORATE

The Framers of the Constitution, unable to reach a compromise on voter eligibility, left the matter mostly in the hands of the states. The Constitution does give Congress the right to alter state regulations regarding congressional elections. The only constitutional provision regarding a popular election was that "people of the several States" would choose members of the House of Representatives.

Control of the voting process has moved gradually from state to federal control. Early federal elections, under state management, varied greatly. Some states picked their representatives at large rather than by district. Others had districts but picked two per district. Still others had elections in odd-numbered years. Through law and constitutional amendment, Congress has required that all members of the House be elected by district and that all federal elections be held in even-numbered years on the Tuesday following the first Monday in November. The most important congressional changes over the years, however, have been those giving the vote to African Americans, women, and eighteen-year-olds.

The Fifteenth Amendment, adopted in 1870, stated that the right to vote would not be denied to any "on account of race, color, or previous condition of servitude." Though the language seems plain, several states passed laws to deny suffrage to African Americans—for example, literacy tests and poll taxes. To allow poor or illiterate whites to vote, a grandfather clause said that a person could vote while not meeting all the requirements if his ancestors voted before 1867. White primaries, in which African Americans were kept from voting in primary elections, emerged later. If none of these kept African Americans from the polls, they were intimidated, harassed, and threatened by government officials, law enforcement, and vigilantes.

Each of these restrictions has been challenged and overturned at the federal level. The grandfather clause was declared unconstitutional in 1915, and the white primary in 1944. Blatantly discriminatory literacy tests were also overturned. In 1965, the passage of the Voting Rights Act suspended all literacy tests and allowed the federal government to send registrars to states and counties where less than 50 percent of the voting-age public was registered or had voted in the previous presidential election. African American voting rose sharply, particularly in the South.

Suffrage for women was also slow in developing. Several states in the West had given women the vote by 1915. The Nineteenth Amendment, ratified in 1920, provided most women with their first opportunity to vote after decades of struggle. In one stroke the size of the voting population virtually doubled. Initially, women voted more or less in the same manner as men, squelching fears that dramatic changes would result from the amendment.

The Twenty-sixth Amendment, ratified in 1971, gave suffrage to eighteen-year-olds. The impact of this has also been less dramatic than expected. Voter turnout for people between the ages of eighteen and twenty-five has been lower than for the population at large. Immediately after the ratification of the amendment, candidates courted the youth vote carefully, but it has since become less of a priority. This amendment was the latest in the evolution of national standards for voter eligibility, which is now almost completely in federal rather than state hands.

VOTER TURNOUT

With the additions to the electorate that the centuries have brought, one might expect that participation in elections would have risen sharply. During the elections of the late 1800s, at least 70 percent of the eligible voters went to the polls, the number at times getting as high as 80 percent. Voter turnout for the past several decades has remained about the same—between 50 and 60 percent of those eligible—and lags behind the large turnouts of the latter part of the nineteenth century.

The meaning of these figures is a source of debate. One view is that a popular decline in interest in elections and a weakening of the competitiveness of the two major parties have occurred. During the late nineteenth century, parties fought bitterly and had great influence over the electorate. They worked hard to get as many voters to the polls as possible, and caucuses and conventions provided other motivating opportunities to participate. Legal barriers to participation (such as complex registration procedures) were kept at a low level, and great general excitement surrounded elections. Interest waned in the early twentieth century as Republicans dominated national elections, and politics seemed to lose its relevance to the average voter.

Another view is that the perceived decline in turnout is misleading. Voting fraud during the late nineteenth century was more commonplace. The famous slogan "Vote early and often" was not meant as humor but as a fact. Parties controlled the counting of votes. As a result, the number of votes counted was often larger than the number cast, and the number cast was often larger than the number of individuals eligible to vote. As safeguards to the validity of voting developed in the early twentieth century, numbers of votes decreased. This may explain the decline in voter participation.

Strict voter-registration procedures were developed to fight the fraud of the late nineteenth century, but these have had unintended consequences. Voting declined because it was difficult for some groups of voters, such as those with little education, to register. Voter registration is one reason why Americans lag behind other democracies in voter turnout.

Most Americans believe low voter turnout reflects voter apathy. This is misleading. In this country, only two-thirds of the voting-age population is registered to vote. In most European nations, registration is done automatically, requiring no effort of the individual voter. Registering to vote in this country falls entirely on individual voters. They must learn how, when, and where to register; they must go to the time and trouble to process their registrations; they must register again if they relocate. The 1993 motor-voter law, which requires states to allow people to register to vote when applying for driver's licenses, was an attempt to simplify voter registration. There was an initial surge of new registrations, but results have been mixed since. (It has also been observed that states with election-day registration have significantly larger turnout rates without evidence of voter fraud.) The United States compares more favorably with other democracies when turnout of registered voters is the standard of comparison. The real problem, therefore, is the relative percentage of registered voters rather than apathy. Two careful studies found that almost all of the differences between voter turnout in the United States and other democracies could be explained by party strength, automatic registration, and compulsory voting laws.

PARTICIPATION

Voting is by far the most common form of political participation, but it is certainly not the only form. One model of participation assigns six levels of participation to Americans:

- **Inactive** About one-fifth of the population does not participate in any way. They do not vote, and probably do not even talk about politics very much. They would typically have little education and a low income and be young.
- **Voting specialists** These are people who vote but do not participate in any other substantial way. They tend to have little schooling and tend to be older than the average citizen.
- **Campaigners** These people not only vote but also enjoy getting involved in campaigns. They are generally better educated than the average citizen. They tend to engage in the conflicts, passions, and struggles of politics. They often have strong identification with a political party, and they have strong positions on issues.
- **Communalists** These have social backgrounds similar to campaigners' but are far more nonpartisan. They devote their time and energy to community activities and local problems, often contacting local officials about these problems.
- **Parochials** These stay away from elections but often contact local politicians about specific, often personal problems.
- **Activists** Constituting about one-ninth of the population, these are people who are often highly educated, have high incomes, and tend to be middle-aged. They participate in all forms of politics.

> ## AP Tip
>
> Profiles that suggest likelihood of voting and likelihood of not voting are generally found on the multiple-choice section of the AP exam.

Certain profiles are far more likely to produce voters and other forms of political participation. College graduates are more likely to participate than those with less education, and in fact the more education one has, the more likely he or she is to participate. Aside from the elderly who have difficulty getting to the polls, older people (especially those above the age of forty five) tend to vote and participate more than younger people do. Regular churchgoers tend to participate more than nonchurchgoers if all other factors are equal. Men and women vote at about the same rate. Minorities vote less than whites. However, this is most likely a socioeconomic phenomenon, as minorities with the same level of education and income as whites tend to vote more than whites. Political elites and those with high levels of external efficacy are the group most likely to vote. The charts below illustrate the correlations between age, schooling, and race and voter turnout.

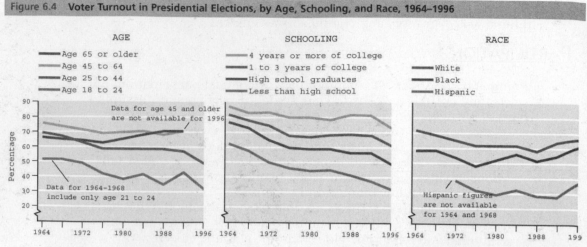

Figure 6.4   Voter Turnout in Presidential Elections, by Age, Schooling, and Race, 1964–1996

Sources: Updated from Gary R. Orren, "The Linkage of Policy to Participation," in *Presidential Selection,* ed. Alexander Heard and Michael Nelson (Durham, N.C.: Duke University Press, 1987). Data for 1996 are from *Statistical Abstract of the United States 1998,* 296, as supplied by Christopher Blunt.

Americans may be voting less, but there is evidence that they are participating more in campaigning, contacting government officials, and working on community issues. Other forms of participating seem to be growing as well. One helpful scheme groups participation into two camps:

- **Conventional** Widely accepted modes of influencing government such as voting, trying to persuade others, petitioning, giving money to campaigns and even running for office are considered conventional forms of participation. Aside from voting itself, these forms are all on the rise.
- **Unconventional** More dramatic activities such as protesting, civil disobedience, and even violence are considered unconventional. The media's frequent attention to protest can make it a successful kickoff of an effort to change a policy. Civil disobedience was very successful for the civil rights movement of the 1950s and 1960s. Although supported by very few people, violence has had a way of pressuring government to change its policies throughout the nation's history.

Although Americans vote at lower rates than do people abroad, the meaning of voting is different because of federalism. The United States has far more officials than any other country. One estimate of the number of elected offices in the United States is 521,000. It is likely that virtually every week of the year sees an election taking place somewhere in the country. A typical citizen can vote for a lengthy line of political offices: president, two senators, a member of the House of Representatives, a governor, a state senator, a state representative, a state attorney general, a state auditor, a state treasurer, and other state and local officials as well. Many Europeans, in contrast, vote for one member of a parliament once every four or five years.

Voter turnout rates in the United States, when compared with those in other democracies, should probably be considered less an embarrassment and more a matter of very different voting systems. While voter turnout is not a source of pride, it is the result of the nation's unique voting system and environment.

Multiple-Choice Questions

1. Which of the following is the best explanation for low voter turnout in the United States?
   (A) More than half of all Americans are apathetic towards politics.
   (B) The voting process is difficult to understand, and ballots are complicated.
   (C) Most potential voters do not identify with a political party.
   (D) The burden of registering falls on individual voters.
   (E) It is difficult for many voters to get enough information about the candidates to vote with confidence.

ANSWER: **D**. The most likely reason for low voter turnout is that the burden of registering falls upon individual voters. Although the motor-voter law has made the process easier, its results are mixed. In many countries, the government registers voters automatically (*American Government*, 8ᵗʰ ed., page 130 / 9ᵗʰ ed., page 132).

Table 6.1 Two Ways of Calculating Voter Turnout, 1996–2001 Elections, Selected Countries			
A Turnout as Percentage of Voting-Age Population		**B** Turnout as Percentage of Registered Voters	
Belgium	83.2%	Australia	95.2%
Denmark	83.1	Belgium	90.6
Australia	81.8	Denmark	86.0
Sweden	77.7	New Zealand	83.1
Finland	76.8	Germany	82.2
Germany	75.3	Sweden	81.4
New Zealand	74.6	Austria	80.4
Norway	73.0	France	79.7
Austria	72.6	Finland	76.8
France	72.3	Norway	75.0
Netherlands	70.1	Netherlands	73.2
Japan	59.0	UNITED STATES	63.4
United Kingdom	57.6	Japan	62.0
Canada	54.6	Canada	61.2
UNITED STATES	47.2	United Kingdom	59.4
Switzerland	34.9	Switzerland	43.2

Source: From the International Institute for Democracy and Electoral Assistance (IDEA), *Voter Turnout: A Global Survey* (Stockholm, Sweden, 2001). Reprinted with the permission of Cambridge University Press.

2. The table above supports which one of the following conclusions regarding voter turnout from 1996 to 2000?
   (A) Voter turnout in the United States, as a percentage of registered voters, was below 50 percent.
   (B) Mandatory voting, as required by law in Australia, has no impact on voter turnout.
   (C) Voters in the United States are more likely to vote if they have registered.
   (D) The main reason for not voting in the United States is apathy.
   (E) There is no more than a 5 percent difference between turnout as a whole than turnout among registered voters.

Answer: **C**. In the United States, turnout as a percentage of voting-age population was 47.2 percent. Turnout as a percentage of registered voters was 63.4 percent. This means that registered voters are more likely to vote (*American Government,* 8th ed., page 130 / 9th ed., page 132).

3. All of the following were used to keep blacks from voting EXCEPT
   (A) segregation
   (B) literacy tests
   (C) poll taxes
   (D) grandfather clauses
   (E) intimidation and threats

Answer: **A**. Literacy tests, poll taxes, grandfather clauses, the all-white primary, intimidation and threats were used to keep blacks from exercising their rights to vote. Jim Crow laws were used to segregate the races in public places (*American Government,* 8th ed., page 133 / 9th ed., pages 134-135).

4. The electorate has expanded as a result of all of the following EXCEPT
   (A) the voting age has been lowered to eighteen
   (B) states may not require residency of more than thirty days
   (C) areas with significant non-English-speaking populations must provide ballots written in other languages
   (D) residents of the District of Columbia may vote in presidential elections
   (E) state standards now govern almost every aspect of voter eligibility

Answer: **E**. While the states originally set most of the standards for voter eligibility, the national government now governs almost all aspects of this process (*American Government,* 8th ed., page 135 / 9th ed., page 136).

Table 6.3	Two Methods of Calculating Turnout in Presidential Elections, 1948–2000	
Year	Voting Age Population (VAP)	Voting Eligible Population (VEP)
1948	51.1%	52.2%
1952	61.6	62.3
1956	59.3	60.2
1960	62.8	63.8
1964	61.9	62.8
1968	60.9	61.5
1972	55.2	56.2
1976	53.5	54.8
1980	52.8	54.7
1984	53.3	57.2
1988	50.3	54.2
1992	55.0	60.6
1996	48.9	52.6
2000	51.2	55.6

Source: Adapted from Michael P. McDonald and Samuel L. Popkin, "The Myth of the Vanishing Voter," *American Political Science Review* 95 (December 2001): table 1, 966. Reprinted with permission of Cambridge University Press.

5. The table above supports which of the following conclusions?
   (A) National voter turnout as a percentage of the voting-eligible population has not fallen since the early 1970s.
   (B) Turnout as a percentage of the voting-age population has fallen every year since 1980.
   (C) There is never more than a 2 percent gap between turnout as a percentage of voting-age population and turnout as a percentage of voting-eligible population.
   (D) Turnout as a percentage of voting-eligible population has declined every year since 1988.
   (E) Voter turnout would increase if the voting age were raised to twenty-one.

ANSWER: **A.** Michael P. McDonald and Samuel L. Popkin adjusted measures of voter turnout to take into account eligible voters. They determined that, as a percentage of the eligible population, turnout has not decreased since the early 1970s (*American Government,* [not available in 8th ed.] / 9th ed., pages 139-140).

6. Which of the following citizens is most likely to vote?
   (A) a 65-year-old African American high school graduate
   (B) a 35-year-old white college-educated woman
   (C) a 70-year-old white college professor
   (D) a 40-year-old Hispanic with an associate's degree
   (E) an 18-year-old African American just starting college

ANSWER: **C.** Voter turnout increases with age and educational level. Turnout rates are highest for whites, followed by blacks and Hispanics. Some political scientists believe this may be related more to socioeconomic class than to race (*American Government,* 8th ed., page 138-141 / 9th ed., pages 141-144).

7. What is the best explanation for why Americans vote at lower
    rates than people abroad?
    (A) We have a truly democratic system, and most people are
        satisfied and see no reason to vote.
    (B) Unlike most countries, we have a federal system, which means
        we elect more officials at more levels of government.
    (C) Americans are less informed about politics compared with
        Europeans.
    (D) Less than 50 percent of Americans are involved in nonpolitical
        activities in their communities.
    (E) Americans are not required to vote, but most European
        countries levy fines on nonvoters.

ANSWER: **B**. Americans go to the polls frequently to elect officials at all
levels of government under our federal system. This may lead to "voter
fatigue" (*American Government*, 8th ed., pages 142-143 / 9th ed., page
144).

8. What is the impact of religion on political participation?
    (A) Religious people are less likely to vote, because they put their
        faith in a higher power.
    (B) Religious people are more likely to give money to charities, but
        less likely to vote.
    (C) Being active in a religious organization increases the likelihood
        of charitable volunteer work as well as voting.
    (D) Being active in a religious organization increases participation
        in nonpolitical activities but does not increase the likelihood of
        voting.
    (E) Religion has no measurable impact on the likelihood of voting.

ANSWER: **C**. The majority of religious people participate in several
forms of nonpolitical activities, including joining organizations,
attending church services, and making charitable and church
contributions. In addition, religious people are more likely to vote
(*American Government*, 8th ed., page 139 / 9th ed., page 141).

9. Which of the following make it difficult to compare voter turnout
    rates in the nineteenth century with voter turnout today?
    I.   In the nineteenth century parties printed ballots, and today we
         use the Australian ballot.
    II. Fraud in voting was more common in the nineteenth century.
    III. Voters are now required to register.
    IV. In the nineteenth century, political machines tried to control
         election outcomes.

    (A) I and II
    (B) I, II, and III
    (C) II and III
    (D) II, III, and IV
    (E) I, II, III, and IV

ANSWER: **E**. Because political machines tried to control elections in
order to put their own candidates into power, voter turnout rates for
the nineteenth century are probably inflated. This was because voting
was done in public, without a registration process. Although the

registration process has reduced fraud, it has also lowered voter turnout (*American Government,* 8th ed., page 136-137 / 9th ed., pages 138-139).

10. The drawing above best represents which time period?
    (A) the antebellum period
    (B) the Civil War
    (C) Reconstruction, while northern troops were still in control of the South
    (D) the period following Reconstruction, after northern troops were removed from the South
    (E) the colonial period, before African Americans were disenfranchised

ANSWER: **C.** This drawing depicts African Americans voting after the Civil War, while northern troops remained in the South. Once troops were removed, blacks were disenfranchised by literacy tests, poll taxes, grandfather clauses, terrorism, and white primaries (*American Government,* 8th ed., page 133 / 9th ed., page 135).

Free-Response Questions

1. Identify and explain two methods, other than voting, of participating in the political process.

RESPONSE: One method of participating in the political process is joining a civic association. By joining groups that provide services and do good works in the community, citizens can identify problems in their communities, lobby public officials, and even take steps to alleviate those problems themselves.

Another way to participate in the political process is by supporting social movements. People who have traditionally been the victims of discrimination may band together to work for change. One of the best examples of this is African American civil rights leaders, who worked to end segregation and lobbied for the passage of civil rights legislation.

Writing letters or sending e-mail to legislators is another form of political participation. Members of Congress have people on staff who read letters and respond to them. Such letters can be effective in getting the attention of Congress if individual letters are persuasive or enough letters are sent on a particular issue. One example is the 1981 Reagan tax cuts. Reagan asked for the public's support, and Congress was flooded with letters favoring the bill (*American Government,* 8th ed., page 141-144 / 9th ed., pages 144-146).

2. Over time, voting rights have been expanded to include groups previously excluded from the formal political process. For TWO of the groups below, explain how voting rights have been expanded and discuss the impact of these groups on the political process.

    Women
    African Americans
    Voters aged eighteen to twenty-one

RESPONSE: Women were given the right to vote nationwide by the Nineteenth Amendment, although several western states allowed women to vote prior to that time. The struggle for the franchise lasted for decades, and in one stroke the size of the eligible voting population doubled. Although women vote in slightly larger percentages than men, there has not been a dramatic change in the conduct of elections or the identity of the winners. However, there is a gender gap, with more women than men voting for the Democratic party.

African Americans were denied the right to vote nationwide until the passage of the Fifteenth Amendment. While northern troops occupied the South following the Civil War, African Americans voted in large numbers, ran for office, and were sometimes elected. However, following Reconstruction, several tactics were used to disenfranchise blacks. These included literacy tests, poll taxes, grandfather clauses, white primaries, and violence. With the passage of the Voting Rights Act of 1965, federal marshals ensured that African Americans were allowed to register and vote.

The Twenty-sixth Amendment gave eighteen-year-olds the right to vote. This amendment was a response to the Vietnam War—the United States was drafting soldiers as young as eighteen. However, turnout for voters aged eighteen to twenty-one is the lowest for all eligible age groups, and this group does not support any particular political party (*American Government,* 8th ed., page 132-135 / 9th ed., pages 134-136).

7

ELECTIONS AND CAMPAIGNS

American campaigns are unique. Running for national office requires an *individual* effort—in many other democracies, running for national office requires a party effort. The candidate decides to run, raises money, and appeals to voters on the basis of personality and definition of issues. Political parties are playing a decreased role in American elections.

KEY TERMS

caucus

Federal Election Commission

general election

gerrymandering

incumbency

independent expenditures

malapportionment

1974 Federal Campaign Reform Law

party coalitions

party realignment

political action
    committees

position issues

primary election

soft money

spots

valence issues

visuals

KEY CONCEPTS

- Presidential and congressional campaigns have significant differences.
- Campaigns are long and expensive, relying increasingly on media to communicate.
- Campaign finance is a continual source of reform in campaigns.

■ Elections can cause a realignment of coalitions that form political parties.

For a full discussion of elections and campaigns, see *American Government,* 8th ed., Chapter 8 / 9th ed., Chapter 8.

COMPARING PRESIDENTIAL AND CONGRESSIONAL CAMPAIGNS

Several striking differences exist between congressional and presidential elections. Presidential races are generally more competitive than congressional races, with the narrower margin of victory. While a president is limited to two terms of office, congressmen often serve for decades and hold a greater incumbency advantage. While congressmen can take credit in their home states or districts for grants, projects, and programs, constantly reminding constituents of these achievements via mail or visits home, presidents have significant national power but little local power. They must rely more and more on the media for communication. While a congressional candidate can detach his or her record from Washington and even campaign against the "insiders," presidents are held accountable for all that flows from the nation's capitol. With the reduced role of political parties in American politics, congressional candidates have stopped hanging on to presidential coattails and increasingly run campaigns independent of the president.

Running for president is a commitment of several years, of dizzying effort and energy, and of a staggering amount of money. When the media notices an individual and refers to him as having presidential "caliber," a candidacy has begun. Congressmen and senators running for president can stress their sponsorship of significant legislation. Governors, particularly from large and powerful states, often command attention quite naturally. Candidates set aside years to run for the presidency. Ronald Reagan, for instance, spent six years running a campaign. Huge sums of money must be raised. A large, paid staff must be established as well as hundreds of volunteers and advisors. Finally, a campaign strategy and campaign themes must be envisioned and coordinated, with incumbents defending their records and challengers attacking incumbents.

Running for Congress is a different sort of animal indeed. With no term limits in Congress, incumbents have an extraordinary advantage. Each state has two senators, who serve for six years, and House representatives (the number is determined by population), who serve for two years. House races can be affected by district boundaries, and these boundaries have traditionally been characterized by two problems:

■ **Malapportionment** Districts have at times been created with very different populations, giving votes in less populated districts more clout.
■ **Gerrymandering** District boundaries have been drawn to favor one party rather than another, which can lead to very odd-shaped districts. In addition, gerrymandering can be used

to make minorities the majority of a district, an issue that has received contradictory rulings from the Supreme Court.

National and state governments continue to wrestle with these problems.

With these as a backdrop, individuals start their quest for a seat in Congress by acquiring a state-mandated number of signatures. A primary election is often held to determine each major party's candidate, though parties have limited influence over who wins. In the general election, incumbents almost always win. Their independence from the party they represent creates a couple of important consequences. First, legislators are closely tuned in to local concerns and to those who elected them. Second, their lack of dependence on a party for election means that party leaders in Congress have little influence over them.

HOW CAMPAIGNS ARE CONDUCTED

Especially in presidential campaigns, strategies in primary and general elections are different. Primaries generally draw a party's activists, who are often more ideologically stringent than voters at large. Therefore, a Democratic candidate must appear more liberal than usual and a Republican more conservative. Without the help of party activists, candidates have little success mobilizing donors and volunteers. Political elites play a critical role during the presidential primaries.

The first test of the primary season for a presidential candidate is not a primary at all, but caucuses in the state of Iowa. Held in February of every presidential election year, caucuses are small, precinct-level meetings held simultaneously throughout the state to select party candidates. Candidates must do well in Iowa or face an immediate disadvantage in media attention and contributor interest. Winners tend to be the most liberal Democrats in the race and the most conservative Republicans, reflecting the characteristics of the party elites.

New Hampshire traditionally hosts the first primaries of a campaign year. The importance of the Iowa caucuses and the New Hampshire primaries presents a problem: those electorates hardly represent the American electorate in general. Southern states, sensing that northern states such as Iowa and New Hampshire have too much influence on the choice of the nominee, created Super Tuesday by moving all of their primaries to the same day in early March. As the primary season continues, candidates face the dilemma of being conservative or liberal enough to get nominated but mainstream enough so to hold on to moderate voters in the general election.

After the primary season has established the candidates from the two major parties, the general election campaign begins in order to determine who will be the final victor and officeholder. Two kinds of campaign issues emerge. *Position issues* are those on which the candidates have opposing views. Voters are also divided on these. For instance, in the 2000 election, candidates Bush and Gore disagreed on Social Security, defense, and public school voucher systems. Other issues are of a nature that does not divide the general public. These, called *valence issues*, focus on the extent to which a candidate emphasizes the issue, such as a strong economy or low crime rates.

Modern campaigns are increasingly waged through television, debates, and direct mail. Television time falls into two categories: paid advertising (known as "spots") and news broadcasts (known as "visuals"). Spots can have an important effect in some elections. Little-known candidates can increase visibility through frequent use of spots, a strategy employed successfully by Jimmy Carter in 1976. Spots tend to work better in primary elections than in general elections, as voters have far greater information from various sources available to them in general elections. Visuals are vital to any campaign because they cost little. Filmed by a news agency, a visual may have greater credibility for viewers than a spot does. Campaign staffs know that visuals depend on cameras and newsmen being around, so they work hard to have their candidate at a place and time that can be easily filmed and will be of interest to viewers. Ironically, visuals may be less informative than spots because visuals often display the "horse-race" aspect of a campaign while spots describe more substantial issues.

With the growing popularity of television over the past fifty years, debates have become an integral part of many campaigns. Even primaries often include televised debates. While some campaigns have profited from debates (notably John F. Kennedy's in 1960 and Ronald Reagan's in 1980), most debates do not profoundly affect campaigns. If anyone benefits, it is generally the challenger. In a debate, a candidate risks committing the dreaded slip of the tongue, which the media and opponents will then attempt to exploit. For this reason, candidates often resort to stock speeches with frequently repeated campaign themes and proven favorites among supporters.

The computer and the Internet are increasingly important factors in campaigns. The computer makes sophisticated direct-mail campaigning possible and enables candidates to address targeted voters with specific views. Howard Dean's extensive use of the Internet in establishing himself as a viable Democratic candidate in the 2004 Democratic primaries may well have a profound effect on the way money is raised in future elections.

Money and Campaigning

AP Tip

Campaign finance continues to be a hotly contested political issue. Knowledge of the 1974 law is critical to understanding recent reforms and will likely be part of the AP exam.

Campaigns acquire money from a variety of public and private sources. During the presidential primaries, candidates receive federal matching funds for all individuals' donations of $250 or less, creating incentives to raise money from small donors. During the general presidential election, all campaign money comes from the government unless the candidate decides not to accept federal money. Congressional elections are primarily funded by private donations, including those of individuals, political action committees (PACs), and political parties. Most individual donors give less than $200, with a maximum of $2,000. PACs are limited to contributions of $5,000, but most give significantly less than that. Incumbent candidates typically receive one-third of their campaign funds from PACs and rarely have to spend their own money on a campaign. Challengers often supply a greater percentage of their own campaign funds than incumbents do.

Coupled with other illegal donations, the Watergate scandal of the 1970s convinced Congress to pass the 1974 Federal Campaign Reform Law and, as part of it, create the Federal Election Commission (FEC). The law included several provisions:

- The limit on individual donations is $1,000 per candidate per election.
- The previous ban on corporate and union donations was reaffirmed, but PACs can be created to raise money instead.
- PACs have to consist of at least fifty volunteer members, give to at least five federal candidates, and limit their donations to $5,000 per election per candidate and $15,000 per year to any political party.
- Primary and general elections count separately for donations.
- Public funding for presidential campaigns includes matching funds for presidential primary candidates who meet funding stipulations; full funding for presidential general campaigns for major party candidates; and partial funding for minor party candidates that had at least 5 percent of the vote in the previous election.

Campaign spending increased dramatically as a result of the law. Loopholes in the law include independent expenditures, allowing PACs to spend as much as they want on advertising as long as it is not coordinated with a specific campaign; and soft money, by which unlimited funds can be donated to a political party as long as a candidate is not named. Soft money can then be passed on to candidates from the party.

Independent expenditures and soft money led to campaign finance reform in 2002. Reforms included a ban on soft money given to national parties, an increase in the limit of an individual donation (up to $2,000), and a restriction on advertisements referring to a candidate by name thirty days before a primary and sixty days before a general election. The full impact of these reforms remains to be seen.

Party affiliation, the state of the economy, and the character of the candidate probably influence voting more than money does. Congressional races are no doubt more affected by money. Challengers must spend a significant amount of money to be recognized, and big-spending incumbents also tend to do better. Even so, party, incumbency, and issues play a large role in congressional races. It is difficult for a challenger to overcome not only an incumbent's money but also his credit claiming, mailing privileges, and free publicity from sponsoring legislation.

ELECTIONS AND PARTY ALIGNMENTS

Several factors determine who wins elections. Party identification still matters, but Democrats are more likely to vote for a Republican than vice versa. Republicans also tend to get more of the independent vote. Issues, in particular that of the economy, help determine elections. A poor economy is difficult for an incumbent president to overcome; a strong economy generally means reelection. Campaigns do make a difference in an election, however, mainly by reawakening voters' loyalties and allowing voters to see the character and core values of a candidate. Retrospective voters, those who look at how things have gone in the recent past, often decide elections. They vote for the party in the White House if they like what has happened and vote against that party if they do not.

If a candidate is going to win, he or she must build a winning coalition, or combination of several distinct groups. Traditionally the Democratic coalition has been African Americans, Jews, Hispanics, Catholics, southerners, and union members. Republicans have long had a coalition of business and professional people as well as many farmers. Coalitions historically have been reorganized under certain conditions. Realignment describes this reorganization of a party's following. Realignment occurs when a new issue arises that cuts across existing party divisions—for example, slavery or a weak economy. Some political scientists feel that the nation is due for another realignment and that the 1980s might have started one. Yet neither the 1984 nor the 1988 election truly signaled a realigning shift among the voters. Perhaps parties are actually decaying far more than they are realigning as twenty-first-century politics begins to emerge— a process called dealignment by some.

Multiple-Choice Questions

1. Presidential and congressional races differ in all of the following ways EXCEPT
   A) presidential races are more competitive than races for the House of Representatives
   (B) a much smaller proportion of people vote in congressional races in nonpresidential election years
   (C) members of Congress can get credit for the constituent service they provide
   (D) candidates for Congress can disassociate themselves from what is going on in Washington, D.C.
   (E) congressional elections receive more national funding than presidential elections

ANSWER: E. All of the statements are true except the last one. Only qualifying presidential candidates receive federal funding (*American Government,* 8th ed., page 180 / 9th ed., page 186).

2. How does federal law restrict fund-raising for presidential campaigns?
   I. Individual contributions are limited to $2,000.
   II. PAC contributions are limited to $5,000.
   III. Federal matching funds are available to candidates who raise $5,000, in individual contributions of $250 or less, in twenty states.
   IV. Candidates are limited to $2,000 in spending their own personal funds.

   (A) I and II
   (B) I, II, and III
   (C) I, II, and IV
   (D) I, III, and IV
   (E) I and IV

ANSWER: **B**. There is a limit on spending by individuals of $2,000 and by PACs of $5,000. To qualify for matching funds, candidates must raise at least $5,000 in $250 contributions in twenty states. However, there is no limit on the amount a candidate may spend on his or her own campaign (*American Government*, 8th ed., page 182 / 9th ed., page 188).

3. Which of the following is the best example of gerrymandering?
   (A) drawing a congressional district boundary down a narrow strip of highway no wider than six blocks
   (B) drawing boundaries so that districts are of very unequal size
   (C) drawing boundaries to allow fair and equal representation of voters
   (D) creating a new district to reapportion seats following a census
   (E) eliminating an existing district to reapportion seats following a census

ANSWER: **A**. Gerrymandering means drawing a district boundary in some bizarre or unusual shape to make it easy for the candidate of one party to win an election (*American Government*, 8th ed., page 290 / 9th ed., page 189).

4. Which of the following factors explain the incumbency advantage and the "sophomore" surge?
   I. the ability to provide casework
   II. the ability to provide pork
   III. the use of franking privilege
   IV. the ability to take individual credit for major pieces of legislation

   (A) I and II
   (B) I, II, and IV
   (C) I, II, and III
   (D) I, III, and IV
   (E) I and IV

ANSWER: **C**. Incumbent congressmen have had the ability to provide constituent service and bring lucrative projects into their districts. They can use franking privileges to contact constituents. It would be unusual for a "sophomore" congressman to be able to take individual credit for a major piece of legislation (*American Government,* 8th ed., page 293 / 9th ed., pages 190-191).

5. Which of the following is a valid criticism of the caucus system?
   (A) Everyday citizens are not welcome to participate.
   (B) Caucuses are not held in convenient locations.
   (C) The first caucus is in Iowa, which is not representative of the population as a whole.
   (D) The first caucus is held in New Hampshire, which is not representative of the population as a whole.
   (E) Caucuses often last several days and become endurance contests.

ANSWER: **C.** Iowa receives a disproportionate share of attention from the media and candidates because it holds the first caucus. This state is not representative of the population as a whole (*American Government,* 8th ed., page 183 / 9th ed., page 193).

6. Which of the following groups would be most likely to receive direct mail from a conservative candidate?
   (A) college students and auto workers
   (B) fundamentalist Christians and business owners
   (C) teachers and small business owners
   (D) bankers and Native Americans
   (E) African Americans and Jews

ANSWER: **B.** Direct mail is usually sent to groups already sympathetic to the candidate. The groups most likely to sympathize with a conservative candidate are fundamentalist Christians and business owners, who tend to vote Republican (*American Government,* 8th ed., page 191 / 9th ed., page 200).

7. All of the following are part of the Bipartisan Campaign Finance Reform Act of 2002 EXCEPT
   (A) "soft money" contributions to national political parties from corporation were banned
   (B) money given to national parties must be in the form of individual donations and PACs
   (C) independent organizations cannot use their own money in ads that refer to a clearly identified federal candidate during the sixty days before an election
   (D) individuals can no longer spend unlimited amounts of their own money on their campaigns
   (E) "soft money" contributions to national political parties from unions were banned

ANSWER: **D.** The campaign finance reform law banned soft money contributions from unions and corporations. Independent organizations must stop advertising for a particular candidate in the sixty days before the election. Candidates are limited to accepting "hard money" from individuals and PACs (*American Government,* [not available in 8th ed.] / 9th ed., page 206).

8. Which of the following is most likely to help an incumbent
    president get reelected?
    (A) good economic times
    (B) a strong vice president
    (C) his stance on abortion
    (D) the addition of new groups of voters
    (E) favorable reporting by the press

ANSWER: **A.** In good economic times, the party holding the White
House normally does well. This is called the "pocketbook" vote
(*American Government,* 8th ed., pages 196-199 / 9th ed., page 207).

Table 8.3 The Incumbency Advantage in Congressional Campaign Spending (constant 1992 dollars)

Year	Average Incumbent Spending	Average Challenger Spending	Number of Races	Incumbent-to-Challenger Spending Ratio	Median Ratio
1978	$284,577	$202,863	235*	1.40	1.93
1980	$298,510	$174,031	338	1.72	3.82
1982	$400,630	$202,689	315	1.98	3.24
1984	$417,815	$192,433	338	2.17	4.47
1986	$488,447	$175,418	319	2.78	5.39
1988	$496,894	$148,723	328	3.34	7.08
1990	$479,969	$124,899	321	3.84	10.02
1992	$609,060	$172,802	307	3.52	5.35
1994	$573,374	$223,664	328	2.56	4.68
1996	$630,852	$254,964	357	2.47	5.11
Total	$473,421	$187,587	3,186	2.52	4.66

*Number of cases is small due to nonfilers.

Source: Stephen Ansolabehere and James Snyder, "The Sources of the Incumbency Advantage in Congressional Campaign Finance,"
Department of Political Science, Massachusetts Institute of Technology, June 1997, 29.

9. The table above supports which of the following conclusions?
    (A) Spending by incumbents has increased in every election since
        1978.
    (B) The candidate who spends the most money is the most likely
        winner.
    (C) Since 1984, incumbents have outspent challengers at a rate of
        more than 2 to 1.
    (D) Because of name recognition, incumbents do not have to spend
        as much money as challengers.
    (E) The average individual contribution received by incumbents is
        more than double the average individual contribution received
        by challengers.

ANSWER: **E.** Incumbents raised more than twice as much money as
challengers did, on average, since 1984. It is important to note that
success in fund-raising does not always translate into spending. Many
incumbents have large balances at the end of campaigns. The money
often goes to other candidates in later elections (*American
Government,* 8th ed., page 199 / 9th ed., page 208).

10. Which type of voters has the most impact on an election?
    (A) prospective voters, who cast their ballots for the person they think has the best ideas for handling matters in the future
    (B) ideological voters, who carefully match the candidates with their own views on the issues
    (C) split-ticket voters, who vote for one party for Congress and the other party for the presidency
    (D) retrospective voters, who look at how things have gone in the recent past
    (E) voters who are more interested in foreign affairs than in domestic policy

ANSWER: **D**. Elections are decided by retrospective voters, who look at how things have gone in the recent past. They vote for the party in the White House if they like what happened and vote against that party if they don't like what occurred (*American Government,* 8th ed., page 202 / 9th ed., page 210).

Free-Response Questions

1. Identify and explain three reasons for the incumbency advantage.

RESPONSE: Because of the incumbency advantage, people already holding office usually win reelection, regardless of party affiliation. One reason for this is casework. Incumbents have the ability to provide constituent service for citizens in their districts who need help. For example, a citizen may turn to his or her congressman when a Social Security check is late. The congressional staff may assist with the problem, and the satisfied constituent will vote to reelect that member of Congress.

Another reason for the incumbency advantage is the ability to bring financial resources into the district. Provisions in bills that provide funding within a state are known as "pork." For example, a member of Congress may take credit for funding a new community college. The professors hired, the students, and the community may reward the congressman with reelection.

Franking privileges also help incumbents. Members of Congress can mail letters to constituents using federal dollars. This enables congressmen to keep in touch with their districts, increasing name recognition. Although franking privileges cannot be used to campaign, they can be used to explain what the representative has been doing in Congress. This increases incumbents' chances of reelection because constituents know more about them (*American Government,* 8th ed., page 180-181 / 9th ed., pages 190-192).

2. Explain two differences between a primary or caucus and a general election.

RESPONSE: Primaries and caucuses are used to select a party's candidate for office. A primary involves individual voters going to the polls to make a selection of their party's candidate. A caucus is a meeting of voters to discuss and decide upon their party's candidate. A general election determines who will be the final winner and officeholder from among each party's candidates.

In general elections, candidates concentrate their efforts on big states with large numbers of electoral college votes. Before the national conventions, Iowa and New Hampshire receive a disproportionate amount of attention because they are the first states to hold caucuses and primaries, respectively. This focuses the candidates on states where the populations are not very representative of the population as a whole. In addition, the people who participate in the primaries and caucuses are more extreme ideologically than the rest of the population (*American Government,* 8th ed., page 183-185 / 9th ed., pages 193-194).

8

POLITICAL PARTIES

American political parties are among the oldest in the world. At one time parties could mobilize voters in a way that gave local machines enormous power. Today, parties are relatively weak because the laws and rules under which they operate have taken away much of their power. In addition, many Americans have lost their sense of commitment to any particular party.

KEY TERMS

divided government

economic-protest party

factional party

Federalists

ideological party

Jacksonian Democrats

minor party

nominating convention

one-issue party

plurality system

political machines

political party

realignment

Republicans

solidarity party

split ticket

sponsored party

superdelegates

third party

two-party system

Whigs

winner-take-all system

KEY CONCEPTS

- Political parties, once strong in the United States, are now increasingly weak.
- Political parties function differently at the national, state, and local levels.

- The United States has a strong two-party system that makes it difficult for minor parties to succeed.
- Political party delegates often differ ideologically from average voters.

For a full discussion of political parties, see *American Government*, 8th ed., Chapter 7 / 9th ed., Chapter 7.

THE RISE AND DECLINE OF POLITICAL PARTIES

A political party is a group that seeks to elect candidates to public office by giving those candidates an identification that is recognizable to the electorate. While European parties generally command great loyalty, parties in this country have become relatively weak.

Parties change over time. Critical periods produce sharp, lasting realignments of the parties. Such a shift might occur at the time of an election or just after. Good examples include the election of 1860, which made the Republicans a major party, and the election of 1932, which began the era of the New Deal. Electoral realignments seem to occur when a new issue of great importance cuts across existing party lines and replaces old issues that previously had held a party together. New coalitions combine to form a different composition within a party.

Although the Founders disliked parties and guarded against them, parties quickly emerged in the young republic. Thomas Jefferson and Alexander Hamilton had a number of policy disagreements even while serving in George Washington's administration. Their followers developed into loose caucuses that became the first political parties. Jefferson's followers were labeled the Republicans—*not* the precursors of today's Republican party—and Hamilton's followers were called the Federalists. Though the Republicans had early success in national elections that led to the demise of the Federalists, the parties were both relatively weak and little more than heterogeneous coalitions.

Andrew Jackson and his followers changed the party system by making it a fixture of the masses. By 1832, presidential electors were selected by popular vote in most states, giving the common man greater impact. Jackson's party, the Democrats—the original members of today's Democratic party—built from the bottom up. Presidential caucuses, at which party leaders nominated presidential candidates, were replaced by a national party convention. Another party, the Whigs, emerged to oppose the Jacksonian Democrats.

The two parties that came out of the Jacksonian period were the first truly national parties, but they were unable to survive the sectionalism created over the issue of slavery. The modern Republican party began as a third party and became a major party as a result of the Civil War. Republican dominance of the White House, and to a lesser extent of Congress, for the following seventy-five years was the result of two forces. Supporters of the Union during the Civil War became Republicans for several generations, while former Confederates consolidated as Democrats. Republicans later benefited from the presidential candidacy of Democrat William Jennings Bryan in 1896. Bryan's populist stances made him unpopular with Democrats in the Northeast, furthering the North-South split of the parties. Because of this sectionalism, most states came to be dominated by one party, with factions developing within each party.

Reform of the party system began with the progressives of the early 1900s and was amplified during the New Deal. Progressives pushed measures that were designed to curtail the power and influence of both local and national party activities. Primary elections were favored over nominating conventions. Nonpartisan elections at the local and sometimes state levels became commonplace. Party alliances with business were halted. Strict voter registration requirements became the norm, as did civil service reform to eliminate patronage. Initiative and referendum measures were started in many states to allow citizens to vote directly on proposed legislation. These reforms reduced the worst kinds of corruption. At the same time, they weakened the parties by allowing officeholders to be less accountable to them and by hindering coordination of parties across the branches of government.

In recent decades the Democrats and Republicans have seemed to be decaying and dealigning, not realigning as in earlier eras. The proportion of those identifying with a party declined between 1960 and 1980 while the proportion of those voting a split ticket (voting for one party for certain offices and another party for other offices) increased. Ticket splitting creates divided government, in which different parties control the White House and Congress. Divided government is strong evidence of the overall weakening of the parties.

AP Tip

The number of voters who practice ticket splitting continues to increase. Divided government is a direct result of ticket splitting. Both ticket splitting and divided government are likely to appear on the AP exam.

PARTIES AT THE NATIONAL, STATE, AND LOCAL LEVELS

At the national level, the two major parties appear to be quite similar. Both hold national conventions every four years to nominate the presidential candidates. Both have a national committee composed of delegates from the states, who manage affairs between conventions. Congressional campaign committees support congressional candidates with party money, and a national chair manages daily work.

The party structures of the Democrats and Republicans took different paths in the late 1960s and early 1970s. The Republicans became a well-financed, highly staffed organization devoted to funding and electing Republican candidates, especially to Congress. Democrats changed their rules for nominating presidential candidates, altering the distribution of power in the party. Consequently the Republicans became an efficient bureaucracy while the Democrats became quite factionalized. Republicans were also the first to take advantage of computerized mailings, building a huge file of names of people who had given or might give money to the party. Eventually the Democrats adopted the same techniques, and both parties began to focus on sending money to state parties, sidestepping federal spending restrictions, a loophole referred to as soft money.

The major event of the national parties is the national convention. The national committee sets the time and place for each convention, held every presidential election year. Different formulas are used to allocate delegates at the conventions. Democrats in recent decades have tended to shift delegates away from the South to the North and the West. Republicans have shifted delegates away from the East and towards the South and the Southwest. Ideologically this has caused the Democrats to move more to the left and the Republicans more to the right.

In addition, the Democrats have established different rules for their convention. In the 1970s, the McGovern-Fraser Commission was charged with making representation at conventions more diverse and democratic. As a result, the power of local party leaders was weakened and the proportion of women, African Americans, youth, and Native Americans attending the convention was increased. Later reforms reestablished some of the influence of elected officials by reserving 14 percent of the delegates for party leaders and elected officials, who would not have to commit themselves in advance to a presidential candidate. These became known as superdelegates.

Democrats have also changed the distribution of delegates drawn from state primaries and caucuses. A state's delegates are divided among candidates who receive at least 15 percent of the vote, rather than the traditional winner-reward system that gave primary and caucus winners extra delegates.

The conventions of both parties have changed fundamentally, and probably permanently. Primary elections and grassroots caucuses now choose delegates once selected by party leaders. As a result the national party conventions are no longer places where party leaders meet to bargain over the selection of their presidential candidates. They are instead places where delegates come together to ratify choices already made by party activists and primary voters.

National party structures have changed, but grassroots organizations have withered. As a result, state party systems have sought to redefine their role. Every state has a Democratic party and a Republican party, each of which typically consists of a state central committee, county committees, and sometimes various local committees. Distribution of power differs from state to state.

At one time, state and local parties held power through political machines. These recruited members through incentives such as money, jobs, and political favors. Party leaders held great control and power, and abuses were commonplace. Gradually the corruption of machines was controlled through voter registration, civil service, and the Hatch Act, which made it illegal for federal civil service employees to take an active part in a political campaign while on the job. Changes in the profiles of voters also doomed the machines. Voters grew in education, income, and sophistication, and they came to depend less on the advice, help, and leadership of local party officials.

Today state and local parties deal with several modern trends that seem to be taking parties in the opposite direction from the old political machines. Many voters are drawn to ideological groups for whom principle is more important than winning an election. These tend to be single-issue activists within one of the two parties. Other modern voters are motivated by the "game" of politics. Loyal voters, they nonetheless are often difficult to mobilize. Sometimes a strong party organization can be created from a preexisting organization. These are known as sponsored parties. For example, the local Democratic party in Detroit was developed out of the United Auto Workers union. The drawbacks of solidary groups (political party organizations based on a friendship network) and sponsored parties have led many candidates to seek personal followings at state and local levels. These require an appealing personality, an extensive network, name recognition, and money. The Kennedys in Massachusetts, the Talmadges in Georgia, the Longs in Louisiana, and the Byrds in Virginia, all have developed strong personal followings in their states. Dealing with these trends is difficult for local parties as they struggle to define their role in the twenty-first century.

THE TWO-PARTY SYSTEM AND MINOR PARTIES

The United States has a two-party system that dates back to the original parties—the Republicans and the Federalists. Several unique features are responsible for this system.

Elections at every level are based on the plurality, winner-take-all method. A plurality system means that the winner is the person who gets the most votes, even if he or she does not get a majority of all votes cast. Some countries require majorities through runoff elections or give legislative seats based on proportional representation. Either of these encourages a multiparty system. The most dramatic example of the winner-take-all principle is the electoral college. In all but two states, Nebraska and Maine, the presidential candidate who wins the most popular votes in a state wins all of that state's electoral votes. Minor parties cannot compete under this system because they are unable to get enough votes to defeat a major party candidate.

Another explanation for the endurance of the two-party system is found in the opinions of the voters. There has always been a rough parity between the two parties, and most voters have been satisfied to let their individual beliefs fall into one of the two broad coalitions that the parties represent. Bitter dissent within parties has been quite common, but only sparingly has such dissent driven voters to a third party.

Though rarely successful at getting candidates elected, minor parties, or third parties, have often come on the American political scene. These tend to fall into one of four categories:

- **Ideological parties** These tend to be at the edges of the political spectrum. Some examples are the Socialist party, the Communist party, the Green party, and the Libertarian party.
- **One-issue parties** Minor parties often address a single issue. Examples include the Prohibition party (to ban alcohol) and the Women's party (to obtain women's voting rights).
- **Economic protest parties** These parties, often regional, protest against depressed economic conditions. Examples include the Populist party, the Reform party (under Ross Perot), and the Greenback party.

■ **Factional parties** Splits in the major parties can create a factional party, usually over the identity and philosophy of the major party's presidential candidate. Examples include the "Bull Moose" Progressive party and the States' Rights party.

Through concessions, minor parties often have impact in getting the major parties to address their issues. The minor parties with probably the greatest influence on policy are factional parties. The threat of a factional split is significant to either party, and the major parties often go to great lengths to avoid such a split.

DELEGATES AND VOTERS

When a party nominates a presidential candidate, it must seek an appealing, moderate candidate but must also keep dissidents in the party satisfied by making compromises. Today's delegates are often issue-oriented activists. Democratic delegates are more liberal as a whole than the party's voters; Republican delegates, more conservative. Today's delegates are often issue-oriented activists. While they help create the broad coalition necessary to elect a president, they sometimes can nominate a candidate unacceptable to the party's rank-and-file voters.

This disparity between delegates and voters accounts to some extent for the low number of Democratic presidential candidates elected since 1968, with several liberal candidates lacking appeal to moderate voters. The 1964 candidacy of Barry Goldwater, a staunch conservative, illustrates the same phenomenon at work within the Republican party. On the campaign trail, candidates must limit themselves to issues that most of the party agrees on because of the wide range of beliefs within a party. However, by doing this, the candidate can risk losing the vote of the more ideologically extreme voters.

While the parties have far less impact than they did a century ago, they continue to play a significant role in the voting habits and political activities of Americans.

Multiple-Choice Questions

1. How do American political parties compare with political parties in Europe?
   (A) American parties are stronger and have more loyal members.
   (B) American parties are more centralized, with more control by the national party organizations.
   (C) Because of federalism, American political parties are decentralized, with significant power at the state and local levels.
   (D) For the past three decades, the party that controls Congress has usually controlled the presidency.
   (E) National law regulates European parties heavily.

ANSWER: **C.** Because of federalism, many important governmental decisions are made at the state and local levels. This gives state and local parties more authority, weakens the national party organizations, and decentralizes power (*American Government*, 8th ed., pages 150-152 / 9th ed., pages 152-154).

2. All of the following characterize a period of critical realignment EXCEPT
    (A) a sharp and lasting shift in the coalitions supporting the political parties
    (B) a series of crises, resulting in a reaction against the two major parties
    (C) the major defeat of a party, with another party taking its place
    (D) when a new issue of importance to voters cuts across existing party divisions
    (E) when voters become apathetic and turnout falls below 50 percent

ANSWER: **E.** Realignment occurs when there is a major shift in voting patterns. This can be caused by the formation of new coalitions, the major defeat of a party (such as the Federalists), a series of crises (such as economic depression), or an issue of importance (slavery) (*American Government*, 8th ed., pages 208-211 / 9th ed., pages 158-161).

3. The proportion of people identifying themselves with a political party declined between 1960 and 1980. One of the reasons for this is
    (A) decentralization of the party organizations
    (B) split-ticket voting
    (C) less media coverage of elections and campaigns
    (D) the realignment of coalitions
    (E) a decrease in the number of people identifying themselves as independents

ANSWER: **B.** Split-ticket voting, where people vote for one party in Congress and the other party for president, has characterized elections since 1960. This shows that the power of political parties is weakening (*American Government*, 8th ed., pages 211-212 / 9th ed., pages 161-162).

4. In the 1970s and 1980s, the Democratic party made reforms that unintentionally led to it becoming more fragmented. What was the original purpose of these reforms?
    (A) to include more union members as delegates to the Democratic convention
    (B) to improve the fund-raising efforts of the Democratic party
    (C) to make the delegations from both parties more reflective of the population as a whole
    (D) to make the Republican party delegations more reflective of the population as a whole
    (E) to make the Democratic party delegations more reflective of the population as a whole

ANSWER: **E.** The McGovern Commission reforms were intended to make the Democratic party more reflective of the population as a whole by including more women and minorities as delegates and changing the rules for delegate selection (*American Government,* 8th ed., pages 158-160 / 9th ed., pages 164-166).

5. Who are superdelegates?
   (A) powerful members of political parties and elected officials who become delegates without having to run in primaries or caucuses
   (B) delegates who have more than one vote
   (C) delegates who have veto power over the party's choice of candidates
   (D) delegates who write the party's platform and have a major influence over the issues emphasized
   (E) delegates, like movie stars, who have national recognition and, as a result, have great influence in choosing candidates

ANSWER: **A**. Superdelegates are powerful members of political parties and elected officials. They may attend the convention as a result of their status and are not required to run in primaries or caucuses. They are powerful within the party in selecting candidates (*American Government,* 8th ed., page 160 / 9th ed., page 166).

6. All of the following were problems with political machines EXCEPT
   (A) They traded votes for favors.
   (B) The federal bureaucracy grew with unnecessary jobs.
   (C) Unqualified people were given important government jobs.
   (D) They rarely delivered on their promises to help new immigrants.
   (E) They engaged in fraudulent practices in voting and government contracting.

ANSWER: **D**. Political machines exchanged votes for favors, particularly for new immigrants. As a result, they were able to help immigrants with social services and employment. However, their practices were fraudulent, unqualified people were put into the federal government, and the bureaucracy grew (*American Government,* 8th ed., pages 161-163 / 9th ed., pages 168-169).

7. Which of the following features have encouraged the development of a two-party system in the United States?
   I. the plurality system of voting, where a candidate need not win a majority of votes to win the election
   II. the winner-take-all feature of the electoral college
   III. the numerous state and local elections because of federalism
   IV. the fact that the House of Representatives is based upon a state's population

   (A) I and II
   (B) I and III
   (C) I, II, and III
   (D) II, III, and IV
   (E) I, II, and IV

ANSWER: A.   The "first past the post" plurality system allows a candidate to win an election without a majority of the votes. As a result, there are no runoff elections like the ones that make smaller parties more competitive in Europe. In addition, the winner-take-all feature of the electoral college makes it difficult for smaller parties to get any electoral college votes because, in order to do so, they must receive a majority of the votes in a state (*American Government*, 8th ed., pages 165-168 / 9th ed., pages 171-174).

8. Long-standing third parties, such as the Socialist, Libertarian, and Green parties, are examples of
    (A) ideological parties
    (B) one-issue parties
    (C) economic-protest parties
    (D) factional parties
    (E) candidate-centered parties

ANSWER: A.   Ideological parties profess a comprehensive view of American society and government that is radically different from that of the established parties. Ideological parties tend to last longer than the other types of third parties (*American Government*, 8th ed., page 170 / 9th ed., page 175).

Table 7.5	How Party Delegates and Party Voters Differ in Liberal Ideology			
Liberal Ideology	**1984**	**1988**	**1992**	**1996**
Democrats				
Delegates	66%	39%	47%	43%
Voters	31	25	28	27
Republicans				
Delegates	2	1	1	0
Voters	15	12	12	7

Sources: For 1984: *Los Angeles Times* (August 19, 1984); for 1988: *New York Times*/CBS News poll, in *New York Times* (August 14, 1988); for 1992: *New York Times* (July 13 and August 17, 1992) and unpublished CBS News poll, "The 1992 Republican Convention Delegates"; for 1996: *New York Times* (August 12 and 26, 1996).

9. According to the table above, how do party delegates and party voters differ?
    (A) Party delegates are more conservative than party voters.
    (B) Party delegates have become more conservative over time while party voters have become more liberal.
    (C) Republican delegates are more likely than Republican voters to support some liberal ideology.
    (D) Democratic delegates are more liberal than Democratic voters.
    (E) Delegates closely mirror the ideology of their party's delegates.

ANSWER: **D**. While the percentage of Democratic party delegates who describe themselves as liberal is decreasing, the delegates are more liberal than people who vote for the Democratic party (*American Government*, 8th ed., page 173 / 9th ed., page 178).

10. What is the major difference between a primary and a caucus?
    (A) Primaries choose delegates, while caucuses choose candidates.
    (B) Primaries are open only to voters who are registered with a party.
    (C) Caucuses are meetings of high-ranking party leaders.
    (D) Caucuses are meetings of party members, and primaries are elections.
    (E) Primaries have been replaced with caucuses in most states.

ANSWER: **D**. A caucus is a meeting of party followers at which party delegates are picked. A primary is an election prior to a general election in which voters select the candidates who will run on each party's ticket (*American Government*, 8th ed., page 173 / 9th ed., pages 178-179).

Free-Response Questions

1. Explain three ways political parties have changed over time, and discuss the results of these changes.

RESPONSE: Although the founding fathers did not envision the existence of political parties, beginning in the 1790s, two parties formed. The first party, the Federalists, favored a strong central government. The other party, the Democratic-Republicans, emphasized the rights of states and individuals. These parties were small groups of local notables. Their leaders did not see themselves as professional politicians. Neither party exists today, so there is no party that can trace its roots to the founding fathers.

The second two-party system emerged with the Jacksonian Democrats. An opposing party, called the Whigs, also emerged. The Jacksonian Democrats replaced the caucus with the nominating convention. This system was developed as a reform measure to give local officials some measure of control over the nominating process.

Following the Civil War, sectional divisions characterized the party system. Republicans were strong in the North and West; the South was a Democratic stronghold. This split had a profound effect on how parties were organized. Most states were one-party states. Parties used political machines to build loyalty and exchange votes for favors.

During the progressive era, reforms, such as the secret ballot and the direct election of senators, weakened political machines. Political parties were less able to hold officeholders accountable, and power became more fragmented. Party organizations were weakened.

Parties have been further weakened in recent years by a rise in split-ticket voting. This occurs when voters elect one party to Congress and another to the presidency. As a result, it is more difficult for either party to get things done. In addition, candidates are chosen before the national convention, robbing the conventions of their prior drama (*American Government*, 8th ed., pages 152-157, 208-212 / 9th ed., pages 154-162).

2. Identify and describe three kinds of third parties, and explain their role in a two-party system.

RESPONSE: Ideological parties value principles. Third parties such as the Socialists and Libertarians draw in people whose beliefs are not well represented by the major parties. Although they rarely win elections, these parties have staying power because they raise issues that the two major parties must address—for example, the issue of deficits raised by Ross Perot. They do serve as a means of political expression for those outside the mainstream.

One-issue parties seek a single policy, and tend to avoid other issues completely. Historical examples include the Free Soil and Prohibition parties. One-issue parties raise important issues and can often force the major parties to address these issues in their platforms.

Economic protest parties, such as the Greenback and Populist parties, form during times of economic distress, usually in a particular part of the country. Their concerns are often adopted by at least one of the major parties. Once the economy improves, these parties tend to disappear.

A split in a major party creates factional parties. For example, voters who split from the Democratic party and, more frequently, the Republican party created Ross Perot's Reform party. Ross Perot advocated campaign finance reform. His supporters probably took votes away from the Republican party, and may have cost it the election (*American Government,* 8th ed., pages 169-171 / 9th ed., pages 175-177).

9

INTEREST GROUPS

The United States is a country of diverse interests. The American constitutional system provides for many points where citizens and groups can access the government, including the president, the courts, and Congress. In addition, political parties have become relatively weak. These factors have made the United States ripe for the emergence of thousands of interest groups.

KEY TERMS

direct mail

environmental movement

feminist movement

grassroots lobbying

institutional interests

interest groups

lobbyist

membership interests

political action committees

social movement

unions

KEY CONCEPTS

- The growth of interest groups in recent decades is a significant change in American politics.
- Several types of interest groups exist in American politics.
- Interest groups engage in many different types of activities.

For a full discussion of interest groups, see *American Government,* 8th ed., Chapter 9 / 9th ed., Chapter 9.

THE GROWTH OF INTEREST GROUPS

Interest groups have existed since the country was founded— Independence-era groups such as the Sons of Liberty are early examples of interest groups. Federalists and Anti-federalists struggling over the ratification of the Constitution could be termed interest groups. The religious associations and antislavery movements of the 1830s and 1840s were also initial forms. By the 1860s, trade unions, farmers' groups, and fraternal organizations were developing. The late eighteenth and early nineteenth centuries brought business associations and charitable organizations. More modern organizations came in the 1960s in the form of environmental, consumer, and political reform organizations.

Several factors help explain the rise of interest groups:

- **Broad economic development** As the economy evolves, new interests are created and old interests need to be redefined. Farmers have had to change over the centuries from subsistence to commercial farming while adapting to unstable markets. The industrial revolution brought mass production that in turn created the need for labor unions. Stable economic times are less likely to produce interest groups.
- **Government policy** Public policy has often fostered new interest groups. Wars create veterans who demand pensions and benefits and are willing to organize in order to obtain them. New Deal policy nurtured the rise of strong labor unions. Because state governments determine who is qualified to become a doctor or a lawyer, professional associations have emerged.
- **Emergence of strong leaders** Magnetic leaders who are willing to make personal sacrifices draw an organized following that often develops into an interest group. These leaders are frequently young and energetic. The civil rights and antiwar movements of the 1960s are good examples of interest groups that developed because of strong leaders.
- **The expanding role of government** As the scope of government activities continues to swell, more organized groups are monitoring those activities. Interest group proliferation corresponds with the expansion of government activities over the past half century.

KINDS OF INTEREST GROUPS

Broadly defined, an interest group is any organization that seeks to influence public policy. Though they may target any level of government, they rarely run a candidate for office. Most groups fall into one of two categories: institutional interests and membership interests. Institutional interests are individuals or organizations that represent other organizations. Large corporations have representatives in the capital who work full time for the firm's interests. General Motors is a good example. Representatives of the car giant carefully watch for possible legislation affecting the industry and work hard to get the federal government to adopt favorable laws or halt potentially harmful ones. Institutional interests do not always represent business and corporate concerns. They also lobby for public interests such as state governments, foundations, and universities. The other category of interest groups is membership interests. These groups depend on Americans joining their cause through membership dues and other donations. Such groups span several categories, including social, business, professional, veterans, charitable, and religious.

General reasons individuals give for joining an interest group are political efficacy and civic duty, but there are often specific differences in what individuals hope to gain from their membership. Some people join to feel connected to their community. Interest groups such as the League of Women Voters, the NAACP, Rotary, and the American Legion have all had success by fostering strong local organizations. Other people join an interest group for the material incentives that accompany membership. Farm organizations offer discounted farm supplies to their members only. The American Association of Retired Persons (AARP) offers incentives from low-cost life insurance and discounted prescription drugs to tax advice and group travel plans. Still others join a group because they believe in the goal or purpose of the organization. Members of such groups—for example, the National Resources Defense Council or the Criminal Justice Legal Foundation— are attracted to the group's ideology or its commitment to benefit society at large. Groups in this category often use lawsuits and publicity to further their agenda.

Social movements—that is, widely shared demands for change in aspects of the social or political order—often give rise to interest groups. The environmental movement has produced several such groups. The Sierra Club, the Wilderness Society, and the National Wildlife Federation are earlier environmental groups, dating from the late nineteenth and early twentieth centuries, while the Environmental Defense Fund and Environmental Action came in the 1960s and 1970s. The environmental movement illustrates some important points about groups derived from social movements. First, one social movement may spawn several organizations. Second, the more extreme organizations within a movement will be smaller and more activist than the moderate organizations.

One broad social movement can draw members to a variety of interest groups within that movement. Some of these are more moderate than others, and some concentrate on specific aspects of the movement. The feminist movement has large, moderate solidarity groups such as the League of Women Voters. The movement also has groups drawn by material incentives such as the National Federation of Republican Women, which is openly supportive of the Republican party. Yet perhaps the best-known feminist group, the National Organization of Women (NOW), exists for ideological incentives.

Organized labor, in the form of unions, once was a social movement, but now few unions exist for the purpose of altering society. Unions have lost a lot of their clout over the decades. Economic changes have not helped in member recruitment, and the public's approval of unions has declined. Yet the benefits of collective bargaining sustain many unions and preserve them as significant national interest groups.

INTEREST GROUPS IN ACTION

> ### AP Tip
> Because interest groups are growing in influence and political parties are weakening, the activities of interest groups are likely to be part of several questions on the AP exam.

Interest groups need money to operate effectively. Those groups that are membership-based rely heavily on membership dues. Foundation grants are responsible for financing many groups, particularly public-interest lobbies. Federal grants are provided to interest groups that are engaged in a project of public interest. Direct mail is used increasingly by most interest groups to raise money. Through the use of computers, a specialized audience can be selected for mailings. Direct mailings are expensive, so sophisticated techniques have been developed to attract the public's attention, such as teasers on the envelope, famous-name endorsements, and personalization of the letter.

Interest groups engage in a wide range of activities that include the following:

- **Supplying credible information** Legislators are policy generalists who must vote on a staggering number of complicated issues. Providing information is perhaps the most important tactic available to interest groups. A lobbyist can build a strong relationship and increase access as well as influence by providing detailed and current information. The value of the information is often greatest on a narrow or technical issue that legislators are unable to gather for themselves. Officials also look to lobbyists for an assessment of the values at stake and how those values fit with their own political beliefs.

- **Raising public support** Traditionally interest groups have favored face-to-face contact between lobbyist and politician. A recent trend is grassroots mobilization. Grassroots lobbying is designed to generate public pressure directly on government officials. This strategy works well when an issue affects a large number of people. Radio, fax machines, and the Internet can now get news out almost immediately. Satellite television can link voters in various locations across the country. Toll-free phone numbers and e-mail enable voters to contact the offices of members of Congress without a charge (these are particularly important now that all mail goes through decontamination for possible chemical tampering and may take weeks to reach a member of Congress). These modern communications have allowed interest groups to bring far more attention to their issues and exert far more direct pressure on legislators. These technologies have also allowed the creation of so-called Astroturf lobbying—a series of phone calls from widely dispersed places that look like grassroots reactions but are really carefully organized lobbying efforts by professionals.

- **Creating PACs and making campaign contributions** Although giving money is perhaps the least effective way to influence politicians, it is a very common activity among interest groups. The campaign finance reform law of 1973 had two important provisions. It restricted the amounts that could legally be given to candidates, and it made it legal for corporations and unions to create political action committees (PACs)—organizations that finance candidates and may lobby as well—for the purpose of campaign contributions. These contributions are made regularly, but they probably do not lead to vote buying. More money is now available on all sides of the issues. Members of Congress commonly take the money but still decide for themselves how to vote. Incumbents get most of the PAC money, and PACs tend to give money to candidates who already support their position. Labor PACs give almost exclusively to Democrats. Business PACs split their money between Democrats and Republicans. If PAC money influences politics at all, it is most likely in the realm of providing access to members of Congress or influencing committee actions.
- **Employing former government officials** Hundreds of people have left government jobs to work as lobbyists. This is termed the "revolving door." Many fear that this potentially leads to corruption. If the promise of a future job influences an official to vote or act in a certain way, then a real conflict of interest exists. Studies have been inconclusive in finding if there is indeed a pattern of impropriety in government officials taking jobs as lobbyists.
- **Seizing opportunities through protest and disruption** Although protest, picketing, and violence have always been a part of American politics, they have generally been considered more acceptable since the 1960s. Interest groups on both ends of the political spectrum have used public displays and disruption to publicize their causes. On the left, feminists, antinuclear power groups, and the American Indian Movement represent interest groups who have engaged in disruptive practices. On the right, the neo-Nazis, parents opposed to forced busing, and right-to-life groups have used the same techniques. The goals of these groups are generally to disrupt an institution and force negotiations, to enlist the support of others, or to create martyrs to draw public concern and support.
- **Leading litigation** Interest groups have financed and provided legal representation in many landmark Supreme Court cases, such as *Brown v. Board of Education*.

Interest group activity is a form of political speech and is protected by the First Amendment. Nevertheless, there have been attempts to control interest groups. One, a 1946 law, required groups and individuals seeking to influence legislators to register with Congress and file quarterly financial reports. This accomplished little because grassroots activity was not restricted and no staff was provided to enforce the law through review of the registrations or reports. A 1995 act provided a broader definition of lobbying and tightened reporting requirements. This more recent act also authorized the Justice Department to undertake investigations into possible violations.

With the trend towards weaker political parties and increased diversity of public interest, interest groups will likely provide an expanded role in linking the American voter and the government.

Multiple-Choice Questions

1. All of the following explain the proliferation of interest groups EXCEPT
    (A) America is diverse, with countless immigrants, races, and religions
    (B) because of its federal system, there are multiple points of access to government
    (C) political authority is shared by several branches of government, each of which might be targeted by interest groups
    (D) interest groups often run candidates for office to give their supporters a voice in government
    (E) political parties are relatively weak, which helps explain the strength and number of interest groups

ANSWER: **D**. Interest groups occur because of diversity. They target all levels of government. American political parties are weaker than in many other countries, but interest groups may be stronger. However, interest groups do not usually run candidates for office (*American Government*, 8th ed., pages 217-218 / 9th ed., pages 223-224).

2. Throughout American history, which of the following conditions has led to an increase in interest groups' activity?
    I.   a strong economy with low inflation
    II. the rise of professional societies, such as the American Medical Association (AMA)
    III. government policies that create new groups, such as veterans
    IV. leaders who are willing to make personal sacrifices

    (A) I and II
    (B) I, II, and III
    (C) II, III, and IV
    (D) I, II, and IV
    (E) III and IV

ANSWER: **C**. Interest groups have been created by professional organizations, such as the AMA, and new government policies, such as wars that create veterans. Interest groups often have a strong leader—historically, the NAACP has had many—who is willing to make personal sacrifices. Interest groups are less likely to arise in good economic times (*American Government*, 8th ed., pages 219-221 / 9th ed., pages 225-226).

3. "Free riders" occur when interest groups fight for benefits to the public as a whole, such as consumer protection. How can interest groups prevent the free- rider problem?
    (A) by ensuring that the benefits they seek will help only their members
    (B) by providing people an incentive to join the interest group, such as a subscription to a magazine
    (C) by limiting membership to a few carefully screened members
    (D) by lobbying members of Congress only in the district where the interest group operates
    (E) there is no practical way for interest groups to prevent the "free-rider" problem

ANSWER: **B**. Interest groups, such as AARP, often provide incentives to their members, such as magazines and travel discounts. This encourages people to pay a fee to become members of the group (*American Government,* 8th ed., pages 223-224 / 9th ed., pages 228-229).

4. Environmentalists, women, and union members have worked over the years to advance their interests. What is the best description of these causes?
    (A) They are social movements that have spawned several related interest groups.
    (B) They are PACs, which give money to political campaigns.
    (C) They are social movements because all of them have liberal goals.
    (D) They are interest groups because they lobby Congress for favorable legislation.
    (E) They are social movements because they do not take strong positions and tend to support moderate policies.

ANSWER: **A**. A social movement is a widely shared demand for change in some aspect of the social or political order. These movements, such as those led by environmentalists, women, and unions, often result in the creation of several related interest groups (*American Government,* 8th ed., pages 225-229 / 9th ed., pages 231-235).

5. Why are lobbyists useful to members of Congress in considering legislation?
    (A) because most lobbyists are lawyers and can draft bills using technical legal language
    (B) because lobbyists have bigger research staffs than members of Congress
    (C) because lobbyists are policy generalists who have knowledge about a broad range of topics
    (D) because members of Congress must listen to lobbyists in order to get electoral support
    (E) because members of Congress are policy generalists and lobbyists are policy specialists with expert knowledge in their area

ANSWER: **E**. Members of Congress are policy generalists who must decide about a broad range of issues. Lobbyists have expertise in specific fields. Members of Congress need credible information and often rely on lobbyists to provide it (*American Government*, 8th ed., page 232 / 9th ed., page 237).

6. An interest group would use grassroots lobbying on all of the following issues EXCEPT
   (A) abortion
   (B) Medicare
   (C) Social Security
   (D) complex tax legislation affecting a few people
   (E) affirmative action

ANSWER: **D**. Not every issue lends itself to grassroots lobbying, which encourages individual interest group members to contact members of Congress. The more people are directly affected by a policy, the more likely an interest group will use grassroots lobbying (*American Government*, 8th ed., page 234 / 9th ed., page 239).

7. A group representing a corporation, labor union, or special interest that raises and spends campaign contributions on behalf of candidates or causes is a
   (A) special interest group
   (B) grassroots lobbying committee
   (C) political action committee
   (D) social movement
   (E) tax-exempt entity

ANSWER: **C**. Political action committees raise and spend money on behalf of candidates and causes. The Federal Election Commission regulates them (*American Government*, 8th ed., pages 236-238 / 9th ed., pages 241-242).

Table 9.4 **How PACs Spent Their Money in 2000 (in millions of dollars)**

PAC Sponsor	House					Senate				
	Dem.	Rep.	Incumbent	Challenger	Open	Dem.	Rep.	Incumbent	Challenger	Open
Corporate	$22.0	$39.9	$54.3	$2.2	$5.3	$5.1	$16.9	$19.3	$1.5	$4.5
Trade/professional	22.3	32.6	45.6	3.5	5.7	3.8	9.4	9.3	1.2	2.8
Labor	39.9	3.5	30.1	7.9	5.2	6.2	0.4	2.3	2.8	1.4
Nonconnected	11.4	15.6	15.1	5.7	6.3	3.0	5.5	4.9	1.4	2.2

Source: Federal Election Commission.

8. The table above supports which of the following conclusions?
   (A) Most PAC money goes to open seats.
   (B) More PAC money is spent on Senate races than on races in the House of Representatives.
   (C) Corporate PACs give twice as much money to Republicans in the House than to Democrats.
   (D) Labor PACs spend more money on challengers than on incumbents in the Senate.
   (E) Independent candidates rarely receive PAC money.

ANSWER: **D**. On races in the Senate, labor PACs spend more money on challengers than incumbents (*American Government*, 8th ed., page 238 / 9th ed., page 242).

9. Which of the following are sources of funding for interest groups?
   I. foundation grants
   II. federal grants
   III. federal contracts
   IV. direct-mail solicitations

   (A) I, II, and III
   (B) I and II
   (C) II, III, and IV
   (D) I and III
   (E) I, II, II, and IV

ANSWER: E. Interest groups receive funding from foundation grants given by private groups, along with federal grants and contracts. In addition, they may use direct mail to solicit funds from their members (*American Government,* 8th ed., pages 229-230 / 9th ed., pages 235-236).

10. Which of the following is a concern about the influence of lobbyists on government?
   (A) Many lobbyists are former federal officials who gave up their positions in government to work for interest groups.
   (B) Many lobbyists are attorneys who have undue influence because of their legal expertise.
   (C) Many lobbyists also work as congressional staff members.
   (D) Many members of Congress are former lobbyists who still have strong connections with interest groups.
   (E) Because lobbyists do not have to register with the government, it is difficult to control their activities.

ANSWER: A. Many people worry about the "revolving door," the practice of officials leaving their government positions to accept more lucrative jobs as lobbyists. This may give them undue influence over policy-making (*American Government,* 8th ed., pages 238-239 / 9th ed., pages 243-244).

Free-Response Questions

1. Interest groups attempt to influence the policy-making process in a number of ways and through multiple access points. For TWO of the following, explain how interest groups advance their causes, and give a specific example for each:

      litigation
      donating money through PACs
      grassroots lobbying

RESPONSE: Litigation means the bringing of a lawsuit. Interest groups go to the courts to advance their causes. This may happen when Congress is not responsive to the interest group's demands. For example, during the 1950s, civil rights groups supported legislation to bring equal rights to African Americans. However, these efforts were frequently blocked in Congress, sometimes through filibusters in the Senate. So, the NAACP turned to the courts to end segregation. In

Brown v. Board of Education, the Supreme Court ruled that school segregation violated the Constitution.

Interest groups may contribute money to candidates and causes through political action committees (PACs). Some people worry that the sea of all this political money has resulted in our having "the finest Congress that money can buy." This concern was raised during the savings and loan scandal when it was found that the same congressmen who delayed the investigation of the savings and loan industry had received substantial campaign contributions from these very institutions. However, so much PAC money is available on so many issues that members of Congress may be able to vote freely.

Grassroots lobbying is designed to generate public support directly on government officials. Interest groups contact their members, asking that they contact the members of Congress representing their district or state. Modern technology has made this even easier with e-mail. No one enjoys dealing with people who are upset, and members of Congress want to satisfy their constituents. An example of this is the American Association of Retired Persons and its use of grassroots lobbying in support of a prescription drug benefit (*American Government,* 8th ed., pages 230-238 / 9th ed., pages 237-243).

2. Although lobbying by interest groups is no longer considered synonymous with vote buying, it still has its critics.

    a. Explain the viewpoint expressed by the above cartoon.

    b. Describe one negative influence of interest groups and PACs on the policy-making process.

    c. Describe one benefit of interest groups and PACs on the policy-making process.

RESPONSE: Part (a): This political cartoon shows a congresswoman besieged by lobbyists, each one carrying a document that represents a policy agenda. The viewpoint expressed is that lobbyists pester members of Congress, making it difficult for them to consider thoughtfully the best interests of the constituents.

Part (b): One negative influence of interest groups and PACs is the potential for exchanging votes for favorable legislation. Although PACs have a right to participate in the political process, they represent groups instead of large numbers of people, and PACs can make contributions to political parties. The result is that interest groups have more influence than individual voters. There is a concern that this hinders the policy-making process because legislation favorable to PACs is passed, to the detriment of individual constituents.

Part (c):   Interest groups are an important institution linking individual citizens to the policy-making process. After all, most interest groups are simply made up of like-minded individuals in support of a cause. By pooling their resources, they can utilize experts and become more influential in the policy-making process (*American Government,* 8th ed., pages 217-221 / 9th ed., pages 223-226).

10

MASS MEDIA

The media in the United States enjoy a degree of freedom greater than that in virtually any other nation. Nowadays, government officials have a love-hate relationship with the media. Politicians need the media to advance their careers, but they fear the media's power to criticize, expose, and destroy.

KEY TERMS

adversarial press	national media
attack journalism	party press
C-SPAN	press secretary
feature stories	popular press
Federal Communications Commission	routine stories
insider stories	sensationalism
Internet	sound bite
investigative journalism	trial balloon
muckrakers	yellow journalism

KEY CONCEPTS

- The media have evolved as more sophisticated forms of communication have become available, changing the role of media in American politics.
- Government has some control over the media, but the recent trend of deregulation is changing what media are allowed to do.
- The media are the major source of information about the government for the American public, and they have a major impact on how politics are conducted.

- The media are often accused of bias in their reporting of government officials and activities.

For a full discussion of mass media, see *American Government*, 8th ed., Chapter 10 / 9th ed., Chapter 10.

THE BACKGROUND AND STRUCTURE OF THE MEDIA

Changes in the organization and technology of the media have had great impact on American politics. In general, four periods of journalistic history can be identified:

- **The party press** In the early decades of the new nation, parties created, subsidized, and controlled various newspapers that had relatively small circulation and high subscription rates. These partisan newspapers were typically circulated only among the political and business elites.
- **The popular press** High-speed presses later made self-supporting, mass readership, daily newspapers possible. Telegraphs gave local papers greater access to the news. By 1848, the Associated Press, a wire service, fostered objective reporting and systematic distribution of information. The urbanization of the late nineteenth century provided concentrated populations to support newspapers and their advertisers. These papers were typically partisan, often engaging in yellow journalism (or sensationalism) to increase subscriptions. Their success made a press independent of the government feasible, and they demonstrated that criticizing government policies could create profits.
- **Magazines of opinion** As yellow journalism increased, the middle class sought alternative news and supported progressive periodicals. Individual writers from publications such as *McClure's* and the *Atlantic Monthly* gained a national following initially through investigative journalism. Later, the term "muckraker" would be applied to journalists seeking to expose conduct contrary to the public interest. The readership of these national magazines was indicative of the growing level of education and sophistication among Americans.
- **Broadcast journalism** With the arrival of radio in the 1920s and television in the late 1940s, politicians could address voters directly. The rise of entertainment choices through these two media also meant that people could easily ignore politicians. Fewer politicians could be covered by radio and television than by newspapers. Presidents were routinely covered, but other officials had to be controversial or have a national reputation to receive attention. Nightly news broadcasts started the sound bite, a short video clip of an official boiling down an entire speech into a few catchy phrases. The brevity of sound bites created problems for officials and candidates in clearly conveying their messages. The development of cable and satellite television has brought about narrowcasting—the targeting of a segmented audience by radio and TV stations.

■ **The Internet** The recent growth of the Internet may create an entirely new era in media and politics. Methods of campaign finance and facilitation between voters and political activists are two areas already being revolutionized by the Internet.

Competition between two—and sometimes more—major newspapers once characterized the press in most major cities. Now fewer than 4 percent of major American cities have more than one. Radio and television, intensely competitive, are becoming more so. Much of the nation's press has been locally owned and managed, orienting it to local markets, though this is increasingly less common. Concentration of media ownership is one of the major issues in the evolution of the media.

A national media has evolved, one which draws great attention from Washington. The national press includes the following:

■ the wire services (AP, UPI)
■ national magazines such as *Time, Newsweek,* and *U.S. News and World Report*
■ televised evening news broadcasts (ABC, CBS, NBC, PBS)
■ cable News Network
■ Fox News Network
■ newspapers with national readerships such as the *Wall Street Journal,* the *Christian Science Monitor, USA Today,* the *New York Times*, and the *Washington Post*

The national press is significant not only for the attention it gets from politicians but also because national reporters and editors are better paid, tend to come from prestigious universities, have a more liberal outlook (with the exception of Fox News, known for its appeal to conservatives and Republicans), and often do investigative or interpretive stories. The national press traditionally takes on the following roles:

AP Tip

The traditional roles of gatekeeper, scorekeeper, and watchdog are often the subject of questions on the AP exam.

■ **Gatekeeper** The national press influences what subjects become national political issues and for how long.

■ **Scorekeeper** The national press tracks political reputations and candidacies. It covers elections as though they are horse races rather than choices among policy alternatives. Media momentum during the presidential primary season is crucial.

■ **Watchdog** The national press investigates personalities and exposes scandals.

GOVERNMENT INFLUENCE ON THE MEDIA

Newspapers are almost entirely free from government regulation. Upon publication, newspapers can be sued only for libel, obscenity, or incitement to an illegal act. Each of these conditions has been narrowly defined by the courts to enhance the freedom of the press. The Supreme Court has ruled repeatedly that there can be no prior restraint on published materials.

Sometimes the government is eager to coerce reporters to reveal their sources. Reporters are steadfast in maintaining the confidentiality of sources, sometimes to the point of willingness to accept jail time. The Supreme Court allows the government to compel reporters to divulge information in court if it bears on a crime.

Radio and television are licensed and regulated. The Federal Communications Commission (FCC) issues licenses that must be renewed periodically. In addition, stations must serve "community needs." Recently, strong movements have arisen to deregulate radio and TV, which could prove to revolutionize the media in the United States. Radio has experienced the most deregulation. The 1996 Telecommunications Act allowed one company to own as many as eight radio stations in large markets (five in smaller ones) and as many as it wished nationally. This trend has had two results: first, a few large companies now own most of the big-market radio stations; second, the looser editorial restrictions that accompanied deregulation mean that a greater variety of opinions and shows can be found on radio, resulting in more radio talk shows.

Several rules still exist for radio and television in regard to campaigns:

- Equal access must be provided for all candidates.
- Rates must be no higher than the cheapest commercial rate.
- Debates at one time had to include all candidates, but recent debates have been sponsored by the Commission on Presidential Debates and can be among only the major candidates. Fairness regarding debates remains a hotly contested topic, particularly inflaming third-party candidates and negotiators for candidates from the two major parties.

EFFECTS OF THE MEDIA ON POLITICS

Although studies of the impact of the media on elections have been inconclusive, there is no doubt that the media have a major effect on how politics is conducted, how candidates are perceived, and how policy is formulated. National conventions have been changed to fit the needs of television broadcasts. Some candidates have won their party's nomination for senator or governor with media advertising campaigns that bypass parties. Interest groups (particularly environmental and consumer groups) have used the media effectively to get a variety of issues on the national agenda. Studies indicate that television news stories affect the popularity of presidents and that political commentary has a large effect. Politicians also use the media to float "trial balloons"—statements intentionally leaked by unnamed sources to test the public's reaction to a controversial issue.

Today's media focus far more on the president than any other public official. Theodore Roosevelt was the first to court the press heavily. He favored reporters who wrote friendly stories over those who did not, and he was the first to give reporters space in the White House that was near the oval office. Franklin Roosevelt made the press secretary a major job, one that would carefully cultivate and manage the press. Modern press secretaries head large staffs, meet regularly with reporters, brief the president on questions he is likely to be asked, and attempt to control the flow of news coming from the White House.

Congress receives less coverage than the president. The House of Representatives has a history of being quite restrictive; it allowed no cameras on the floor until 1978. With the introduction of cable TV's C-SPAN in 1979, gavel-to-gavel coverage of House proceedings became available. The Senate has a history of being more open; Senate hearings have been broadcast on television since 1950. Senate sessions have been available on C-SPAN since 1986.

INTERPRETING POLITICAL NEWS

Though the percentage of people who think the media are biased is increasing, most people still believe that the press is objective. This is especially true of television, because it allows us to judge not only words but also images. Members of the press generally think of themselves as unbiased, but polls indicate that journalists are much more liberal than the public at large, and those in the national media are the most liberal of all. Having liberal views does not mean that stories will inevitably be biased, however. Conservative talk radio and the increasingly popular Fox News Network offer views that some use to counter claims of a liberal bias in the media. Many factors influence how a story is written, among them urgent deadlines, a desire to attract an audience, a professional obligation to be fair, and the need to develop sources. The type of story also affects whether a reporter or editor will tend towards bias. Stories can be classified as:

- **Routine stories** Regularly covered stories such as public events are typically simple and easily described. All media tend to report these similarly, and the opinions of journalists have little effect. For example, a presidential trip, a bill passing in Congress, or a Supreme Court ruling would typically be reported without much bias.
- **Feature stories** Stories not routinely covered are called feature stories, and these require reporter initiative. Selection of topics for these stories involves a reporter's or editor's perception of what is important. Liberal and conservative papers often do different feature stories.
- **Insider stories** Stories that involve investigative reporting or political leaks are called insider stories. These stories require a reporter to select which facts to use, so the ideology of the reporter or editor may surface. The motive of the person who leaks the story might also be a source for bias.

Leaks to the press are becoming more frequent. One reason is that the separation of powers creates competition among government officials who give secrets to the press as a weapon. It is not illegal to print most secrets in the United States. Another reason is that, since Vietnam, Watergate, and the Iran-contra affair, the press has often had an adversarial relationship with the government. The press and politicians tend to mistrust each other. The cynicism of the past few decades has created an era of attack journalism. Journalists hounding politicians have had a negative impact on the press, however, because people often do not like this kind of news. Attack journalism is partially responsible for the growing cynicism among the public towards the media.

Intense competition among the media means that each has a smaller share of the audience. The press relies increasingly on sensational news stories that often include sex, violence, and intrigue among politicians. Sensationalism draws an audience and is cheaper than investigative reporting, but it is often drawn from unreliable sources. The result is less substantive news and often even greater cynicism towards the press. Fewer and bigger players in this intense competition mean that the stakes are even higher and the pressures to win audience are greater.

Politicians fight bias and sensationalism in a number of ways. The number of press secretaries in both executive and legislative branches has increased dramatically. They work full time to control and manipulate unwanted stories. Press releases, which are often uncontroversial and sterile, are another way to fight bias. Presidents are often known to reward and punish reporters based on their stories.

As communication technology evolves, the role of the press in politics will continue to increase. Mass media will maintain a central role in linking average citizens to the government.

Multiple-Choice Questions

1. How does the American media differ from the media in most other countries?
   (A) Almost all American radio and television stations are privately owned.
   (B) The United States government has little power to regulate broadcasters.
   (C) The United States has very strict libel laws, and untruths about public officials usually result in fines.
   (D) Most other countries have a Freedom of Information Act that permits the media to request information about the government.
   (E) Because of federal grants and special funding, the media in the United States do not have to worry much about profit.

ANSWER: **A.** Almost all American radio and television stations are privately owned. Because they need to make a profit, they must satisfy a variety of interests (*American Government*, 8th ed., page 246 / 9th ed., page 252).

2. Broadcast journalism changed the media's coverage of politics in all of the following ways EXCEPT
   (A) a broadcast allows public officials to speak directly to audiences without their remarks being filtered through editors
   (B) politicians can reach voters on a national scale without the support of political parties
   (C) people could easily ignore a speech by changing the channel
   (D) citizens get more detailed and specific information about programs and policies than they could get from the print media
   (E) public officials must do something bold or sufficiently colorful to gain free access to the broadcast media

ANSWER: **D**. Although the broadcast media reach a large audience, their coverage of the issues is generally less detailed than coverage in the print media (*American Government,* 8th ed., page 250 / 9th ed., pages 255-256).

3. When Gary Hart ran for the Democratic nomination in 1987, he told the press to go ahead and follow him, because "they would be bored." The resulting sexual scandal that arose is an example of the media's role as
   (A) a gatekeeper who influences what subjects become national political issues and for how long
   (B) a scorekeeper who keeps track of and helps make political reputations
   (C) a reporter who covers important facts in an unbiased manner
   (D) a referee who carefully balances coverage of all the candidates
   (E) a watchdog who closely scrutinizes candidates' backgrounds and activities

ANSWER: **E**. During the Gary Hart scandal, the media acted as a watchdog by staking out his apartment. As a watchdog, the media delve into the backgrounds and personal lives of candidates (*American Government,* 8th ed., pages 254-255 / 9th ed., pages 259-260).

4. Which of the following have to be proved in order for a public official to recover damages for libel?
   I. the statements were made with malice
   II. the statements are untrue
   III. the statements were made with a reckless disregard for the truth
   IV. the statement caused harm to the public official

   (A) I and II
   (B) I, II, and II
   (C) II, and III
   (D) III and IV
   (E) I, II, III, and IV

ANSWER: **E**. The United States has a stringent standard a public official must meet in order to recover damages for libel. He or she must prove not only that the statement was false and damaging but also that it was made with malice—that is, a reckless disregard for the truth (*American Government,* 8th ed., pages 255-256 / 9th ed., pages 260-261).

5. The government can use all of the following tools to encourage positive stories and constrain negative stories written by journalists EXCEPT
    (A) "spinning" a story by attacking a politician's critics
    (B) closing the "leaks" given to particular reporters
    (C) revoking the licenses of stations that give unfavorable coverage
    (D) using the press corps to release favorable stories
    (E) refusing to give important background information

ANSWER: C. The FCC cannot revoke a station's license simply for giving a government official unfavorable press coverage. However, government officials can spin a story to their advantage, close information leaks, and refuse to give background information. In addition, the press corps can release favorable stories about White House officials (*American Government*, 8ᵗʰ ed., page 269 / 9ᵗʰ ed., pages 273-274).

6. Which of the following is the best example of a trial balloon?
    A) A candidate for office runs ads in one state on a single issue to see how the public will react.
    (B) An anonymous White House source makes a statement that is then reported on the news.
    (C) A newspaper covers the flooding in a neighboring state and chooses to delete stories of local interest.
    (D) A TV special report covers drug dealers in a community but does not cover efforts to end drug abuse.
    (E) The president holds a news conference to announce a new program to stop the spread of AIDS.

ANSWER: B. A "trial balloon" is a statement issued by an unnamed source to test the public's reaction (*American Government*, 8ᵗʰ ed., page 257 / 9ᵗʰ ed., page 263).

7. Why is there more news coverage of the president than of Congress or the courts?
    A) because the president is one person and is viewed by the public as the center of government
    (B) because the president has the ability to call news conferences, whereas members of Congress must act through their leaders
    (C) because the courts issue opinions that are difficult to understand, and it is difficult for the press to explain court decisions clearly
    (D) because congressional committee hearings are usually closed to the press and the public
    (E) the statement is inaccurate; Congress actually gets as much press coverage as the president does

ANSWER: A. It is easier to cover the president because he is one person and is seen as the center of government. There are 535 members of Congress, which makes it difficult to cover. Although there are only nine justices on the Supreme Court, it is difficult for the press to cover them because they are not allowed to discuss current cases (*American Government*, 8ᵗʰ ed., pages 261-263/ 9ᵗʰ ed., pages 266-267).

Table 10.2	Journalist Opinion Versus Public Opinion	
	Journalists	The Public
Self-described ideology:		
Liberal	55%	23%
Conservative	17	29
Favor government regulation of business	49	22
U.S. should withdraw investments from South Africa	62	31
Allow women to have abortions	82	49
Allow prayer in public schools	25	74
Favor "affirmative action"	81	56
Favor death penalty for murder	47	75
Want stricter controls on handguns	78	50
Increase defense budget	15	38
Favor hiring homosexuals	89	55

Sources: Los Angeles Times poll of about 3,000 citizens and 2,700 journalists nationwide, as reported in William Schneider and I. A. Lewis, "Views on the News," *Public Opinion* (August/September 1985): 7. Reprinted with permission of American Enterprise Institute for Public Policy Research.

8. Which of the following statements does the table above best support?
    (A) The content of news stories has a liberal bias.
    (B) Fewer than 20 percent of journalists describe themselves as conservatives.
    (C) Newspaper owners are more conservative than the reporters who work for them.
    (D) Reporters are most liberal on the issue of affirmative action.
    (E) While the majority of the public is conservative, the majority of journalists are liberal.

ANSWER: A. Fifty-five percent of journalists describe themselves as liberal, 17 percent as conservative. However, this does not necessarily mean that the content of news stories is biased. It may be, but this is not measured on the table (*American Government,* 8th ed., page 263 / 9th ed., page 268).

9. Since the early 1970s, how has the relationship between the president and the press changed?
    (A) It has become friendlier because presidents are now more willing to answer questions.
    (B) It has become more adversarial, partly as a result of the Vietnam War and Watergate.
    (C) It has become more adversarial because embarrassing stories sell more newspapers.
    (D) It has not changed, because we have always had a free press.
    (E) It has become less critical of the president because surveys show that people do not like the cynicism of the media.

ANSWER: **B**. After the Vietnam War, Watergate, and the Iran-contra affair, the press became more adversarial with presidents. Although the public does not like this negative coverage, the relationship between the president and the press remains more adversarial than it was in the past (*American Government,* 8th ed., pages 266-267 / 9th ed., page 271).

10. Which of the following stories would most likely receive media coverage?
    (A) a discussion of the detailed party platforms of each presidential candidate
    (B) a story about a missing woman and her romantic relationship with a member of Congress
    (C) a report about the safety recommendations made for all new SUVs
    (D) a discussion of the leading economic indicators
    (E) a study comparing birth defects in the United States with birth defects in Canada

ANSWER: **B**. The media often cover health, safety, and economics issues, but newspapers and TV outlets know that sensational stories sell. As a result, the media have a strong incentive to rely on these stories to get readers and viewers (*American Government,* 8th ed., page 269 / 9th ed., page 273).

Free-Response Questions

1. According to Wilson and DiIulio, "Important changes in the nature of American politics have gone hand in hand with major changes in the organization and technology of the press." Identify TWO changes that have occurred as a result of technology, and describe the impact of those changes on the media's coverage of politics.

RESPONSE: By the mid-nineteenth century, the high-speed press made it possible to print large quantities of newspapers quickly and cheaply. Wire services, such as the Associated Press, allowed national news to reach most Americans the same day it happened. Mass readership of newspapers developed. As political parties no longer controlled the press, press bias came to be a reflection of the views of editors, not political parties.

Broadcast journalism—radio and television—precipitated a major change in the way news was gathered. Public officials could speak directly to audiences, but people could just as easily turn off the broadcasts. This led the media to feature exciting stories to catch and keep the viewers' attention. The news again became sensationalized, and complex stories were reduced to sound bites that oversimplified coverage of the political process (*American Government,* 8th ed., pages 246-251 / 9th ed., pages 252-257).

2. Although the United States has one of the freest presses in the world, the media are still subject to some constraints. Identify and explain one formal and one informal constraint on the media.

RESPONSE: One formal constraint on the media is the prohibition against libelous or obscene material. However, the laws against libel of a public official make the charge difficult to prove. In order to recover for libel, a public official must prove publication of an untrue and damaging statement. In addition, the statement must have been made with malice and a reckless disregard for the truth.

Another formal constraint on the media is FCC regulations. The FCC licenses broadcasters. If a formal request for the review of a station's license is received, a hearing must be held prior to license renewal. In addition, the FCC requires stations to provide public service programming. On political issues, stations must provide equal time and a right of reply to the major candidates.

One informal constraint on the media is the need to make a profit. Unlike the press in many European countries, the American press is usually privately owned. Because of the profit motive, stations literally cannot afford to offend viewers or advertisers. As a result, stations must avoid appearing too biased or risk losing viewers and, eventually, advertising dollars.

Another informal constraint on the media is that politicians and press officers want favorable coverage. When a paper runs a negative story that reflects badly on a government official, that official and his staff may stop providing valuable leads to that reporter, newspaper, or television station. As a result, the media may be hesitant to report negative stories for fear of losing important sources of information (*American Government,* 8th ed., page 255-258, 264-266, 269-270 / 9th ed., pages 260-262, 269-270, 274).

11

CONGRESS

Congress was given significant constitutional powers, making it the "first branch" in the minds of the Founders. It has the power over the federal budget, can pass a law even if the president vetoes it, and can alter the way laws are administered.

KEY TERMS

bicameral

caucus

closed rule

cloture

cloture rule

committee system

conference committees

Congressional Budget Office

Congressional Research Service

discharge petitions

division vote

double-tracking

filibuster

franking privileges

General Accounting Office

House Rules Committee

incumbency

joint committees

majority leader

minority leader

multiple referrals

open rule

pork

presidential veto

president pro tempore

quorum

restrictive rule

roll-call vote

Rule 22

safe district

select committees

seniority system

Seventeenth Amendment

Speaker of the House

standing committees

subcommittees

teller vote

term limits

voice vote

whip

KEY CONCEPTS

■ The United States Congress is a bicameral legislature that has evolved into two very distinct chambers.

■ Three theories (representational, organizational, attitudinal) attempt to explain how members of Congress behave in their voting patterns.

■ Congress is organized in various ways, including party, committee, and staff organizations.

■ The process of a bill becoming a law is complex and laden with a multitude of rules.

■ The ethics of legislators continue to be a concern for the public.

For a full discussion of Congress, see *American Government,* 8th ed., Chapter 11 / 9th ed., Chapter 11.

THE EVOLUTION AND COMPOSITION OF CONGRESS

The Framers of the Constitution created Congress as a bicameral (two-chamber) legislature. They wanted to avoid a concentration of power in a single institution, and they wanted a balance between large and small states. They fully expected Congress to be the dominant institution of the federal government. Congress was generally dominant over the presidency until the twentieth century. Most of the nation's early political struggles—including those over slavery, admission of new states to the Union, internal improvements, tariffs, and business regulation—were played out in Congress.

The dynamics of power in the House of Representatives has varied over the years. The late nineteenth century witnessed powerful Speakers who seized new authority by personally selecting the chairmen and members of all committees, deciding what business would come up for a vote, and placing limitations on who could speak and what the limitations of debate would be. Early twentieth-century Houses revolted against the power of the Speaker and distributed power to party caucuses (associations of members of Congress created to advocate on behalf of a political ideology or constituency), the Rules Committee (the committee that decides which bills come up for a vote and in what order), and chairmen of standing—or permanent—committees. In the 1960s and 1970s, Democratic-controlled Houses changed the rules so that powerful southern committee chairs could not block civil rights legislation. Subcommittees were strengthened, and the House became more democratic. Because of inefficiencies, the House moved back to strong Speakers in the 1990s.

The Senate escaped many of the tensions encountered by the House because it is a smaller chamber. The smaller size of the Senate precludes the need for a Rules Committee. Prior to 1913, senators were elected by the state legislatures, so senators focused on pleasing party leaders and funneling jobs and contracts back to their states. The

Seventeenth Amendment changed the way senators were elected in 1913. As a result, senators were elected directly by the people and, as a consequence, became more interested in pleasing the general electorate.

Senators are allowed to filibuster (give a prolonged speech or series of speeches made to delay legislative action). By the end of the nineteenth century, it had become a common and unpopular practice. In 1917 Rule 22 was enacted, which allowed debate to be cut off if two-thirds of the senators present and voting agreed to a cloture motion to end debate. It has since been revised to allow sixty senators to cut off debate.

Though the typical representative or senator is a middle-aged, white, Protestant, male lawyer, the characteristics of legislators have changed:

- **Sex and race** The House has become less male and less white since 1950. The Senate has been slower to change. Members of color may gain influence more quickly in the future because the former tend to come from safe districts (districts where the winner carries more than 55 percent of the vote). Republican control of both houses in the last decade has reduced minority influence.

AP Tip

The advantages of being an incumbent are important in understanding the dynamics of Congress. Incumbency will certainly appear on the AP exam in some form.

- **Incumbency** Prior to the 1950s, many legislators served only one term. In recent decades, membership in Congress has become a career, causing very low turnover. Although the Republican Revolution of the early 1990s brought many new members to the House, incumbents still hold a great electoral advantage. Most House districts are safe, with one party holding a significant numerical advantage over the other party. Senators are less secure as incumbents. Voters tend to support incumbents for several reasons. Media coverage is higher for incumbents. Further, incumbents have greater name recognition because of franking (mailing privileges), travel to the district, credit claimed for projects brought to a state or district (called pork-barrel projects), and individual case help.
- **Party** Democrats were the beneficiaries of incumbency from the 1930s to 1992. During that time, the Democrats controlled both houses in twenty-five Congresses and at least one house in twenty-eight Congresses. In 1994 voters opposed incumbents because of budget deficits, scandals, and legislative-executive bickering. A conservative coalition of southern Democrats (who often vote conservatively on legislation) and Republicans today controls Congress.

TYPES OF REPRESENTATION

There are at least three theories about how members of Congress behave in terms of voting and formulating policy:

- ▪ **Representational view** One view is that legislators vote to please their constituents in order to get reelected. This is most likely true when constituents have a clear view on an issue and the legislator's vote is likely to attract attention. Studies show that legislators are more likely to vote in accord with constituent desires in the areas of civil rights and social welfare but less so on foreign policy issues.
- ▪ **Organizational view** When constituency interests are not vitally at stake, legislators may respond to their party leaders or respected colleagues.
- ▪ **Attitudinal view** Another view is that a legislator's ideology determines his or her vote.

Members of Congress are increasingly divided by political ideology. This has made the ideological view of voting more important. Taking cues from the party is of decreasing importance. Polarization among members has led to many more partisan attacks and to less constructive negotiations on bills and policies.

THE ORGANIZATION OF CONGRESS

Congress is not a single organization but, rather, a vast and complex collection of organizations by which the business of the legislative branch is carried out and through which its members form alliances. At least three levels of organization exist in Congress: party, committee, and staff.

PARTY ORGANIZATION IN CONGRESS

The president pro tempore formally leads the Senate. Largely a ceremonial office, the president pro tempore is the member of the Senate with the most seniority in the majority party. The true leaders of the Senate are the majority and minority leaders, elected by their respective party members. The majority leader schedules Senate business, usually in consultation with the minority leader. Party whips keep leaders informed and pressure party members to vote in accord with the party line. Each party has a policy committee that schedules Senate business and prioritizes bills. Committee assignments are handled by groups of senators from each party. Committee assignments emphasize ideological and regional balance.

The greater size of the House gives its leadership more power. The Speaker of the House is the leader of the majority party and presides over the House. The Speaker's powers are formidable and include deciding who will be recognized on the House floor; interpreting rules on motions; assigning bills to committees; influencing which bills are brought up for a vote; and appointing members of special and select committees. The majority party in the House also elects a floor leader, called the majority leader. The minority party elects a minority leader.

Each party has a whip, who is in charge of rounding up votes. Each party has a committee for making committee assignments.

Congressional rules have changed since the Republican takeover in the mid- 1990s. No committee chairman serves for more than six years. Seniority is less of a standard for selecting committee chairmen. The Senate is now less party-centered and less leader-oriented.

Though party unity in voting is still evident, there is less cohesion among the parties than during the 1990s. Ideological splits between parties and party leaders are more common. Caucuses—associations of members of Congress created to advocate on behalf of an ideology, constituency, or regional and economic interest—within and between the two major parties have become rivals to the parties in policy formulation. Three types of caucuses have emerged:

- **Intraparty** Members share the same ideology (for example, the Conservative Opportunity Society).
- **Personal interest** Members share an interest in an issue (for example, the human rights caucuses).
- **Constituency concerns** Members have similar constituencies (for example, the Congressional Black Caucus).

COMMITTEE ORGANIZATION IN CONGRESS

Committees do most of the work in Congress. Committees consider bills, maintain oversight of executive agencies, and conduct investigations. There are three types of committees:

- **Standing Committees** These are permanent bodies with specified legislative responsibilities. Examples include the Armed Services Committee and the Judiciary Committee.
- **Select Committees** These are groups appointed for a limited purpose and limited time. Examples include various intelligence committees.
- **Joint Committees** Both representatives and senators serve on joint committees. Conference committees are a type of joint committee appointed to resolve differences in Senate and House versions of the same piece of legislation.

Both Senate and House committees have similar practices. The majority party has the majority of seats on the committees and elects the chair. Usually the ratio of Democrats to Republicans on a committee corresponds roughly to their ratio in that house of Congress, but on occasion the majority party will try to take extra seats on key panels, such as the House Appropriations or Ways and Means committees. Chairs are usually the most senior members of the committee, despite the fact that the seniority system has been under attack in both parties in recent decades.

Two House committees are noteworthy for their prominence in the dynamics of the House. The House Rules Committee is unique to the House because it reviews all bills except revenue, budget, and appropriations bills coming from a House committee before the bills go to the full House. The House Ways and Means Committee is powerful because it drafts tax legislation.

STAFF ORGANIZATION IN CONGRESS

Congressional staffs grew rapidly during the twentieth century. Staffs have several important tasks, but perhaps the most important is taking care of constituency service. Approximately one-third of a congressman's staff works in the home district, and almost all have at least one full-time district office. Staff members also have legislative functions that include devising proposals, negotiating agreements, organizing hearings, and meeting with lobbyists and administrators. Congressional committees also have their own staffs, usually one for the majority side and one for the minority side. Members of Congress can no longer keep up with increased legislative work, so they must rely heavily on their staffs.

In addition to increasing the number of staff members, Congress has also created staff agencies that work for Congress as a whole. These have largely been created to give Congress specialized knowledge equivalent to what the president has:

- **Congressional Research Service (CRS)** The CRS is part of the Library of Congress and responds to congressional requests for information. It does not recommend policy but looks up facts and indicates the arguments for and against proposed policy. It also tracks the status of every major bill before Congress.
- **General Accountability Office (GAO)** Formerly known as the General Accounting Office, the GAO continues in its traditional role of auditing the money spent by executive departments. In addition, the GAO now investigates agencies and policies and makes recommendations on almost every aspect of government.
- **Congressional Budget Office (CBO)** The CBO advises Congress on the likely economic effects of different spending programs and provides information on the costs of proposed policies.

HOW A BILL BECOMES A LAW

In viewing the following chart of how a bill becomes a law, it must be kept in mind that the complexity of these procedures ordinarily gives a powerful advantage to the opposition of a bill. There are many points at which action can be blocked. If a bill is not passed by both houses and signed by the president within the life of one Congress, it is dead and must be reintroduced during the next Congress.

The process of a bill becoming a law is as follows:

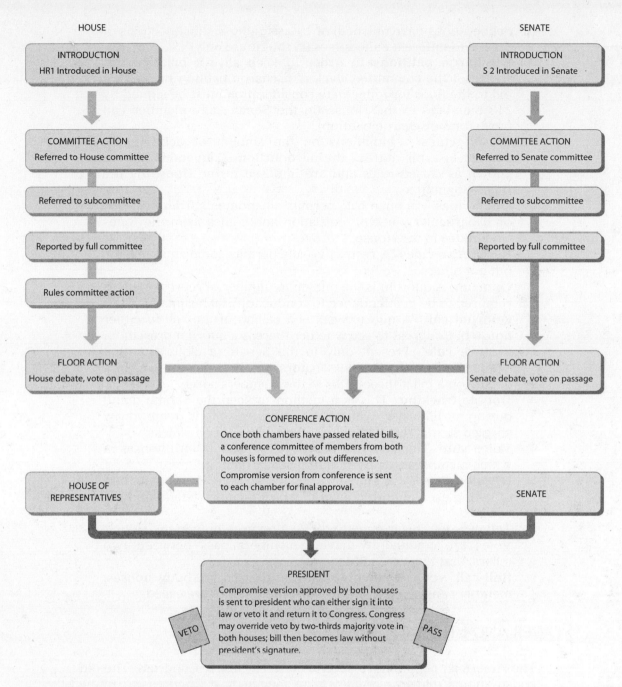

In addition to the actions illustrated in the chart above, the following procedures and rules can influence the passage of a bill:

■ **Multiple referrals** Although sending bills to committees is necessary and valuable, committees fragment the process of considering bills dealing with complex matters. To deal with this problem Congress has established a process whereby a bill may now be referred to several committees that simultaneously consider it in whole or in part. This process is called a multiple referral. Following the 1995 reforms, these can be done only sequentially (one committee acting after another's deliberations have finished) or by assigning distinct portions of the bill to different committees (in the House only).

- **Discharge petitions** In order to keep alive a bill that has stalled at the committee level, a discharge petition bringing a bill to the floor for immediate consideration must be signed by 218 members in the House (in the Senate, any member can move for a discharge petition).
- **Closed rules** Limitations on the amount of debate time allotted to a bill and on the introduction of amendments are known as closed rules and are imposed in the House by the Rules Committee.
- **Open rules** An open rule permits amendments from the floor on a particular piece of legislation and comes from the Rules Committee in the House.
- **Restrictive rules** A restrictive rule permits some amendments but not others.
- **Quorum** A quorum is the minimum number of representatives required to be in attendance to conduct official business.
- **Quorum call** A quorum call is a calling of the roll in either house of Congress to see whether there is a quorum present.
- **Cloture rule** Present only in the Senate, a cloture motion (signed by at least sixteen senators) provides for the end of a debate on a bill if three-fifths of the members agree.
- **Double-tracking** This is a method to keep the Senate going during a filibuster whereby a disputed bill is temporarily shelved so that the Senate can go on with other business.
- **Voice vote** This is a method of voting used in both houses in which members vote by shouting yea or nay.
- **Division vote** Also known as a standing vote, this is a method of voting used in both houses in which members stand and are counted.
- **Teller vote** This is a method of voting used only in the House. Votes are counted by having members pass between two tellers, first the yeas and then the nays.
- **Roll-call vote** A method of voting used in both houses, members answer yea or nay when their names are called.

POWER AND ETHICS IN CONGRESS

The American people have several concerns about Congress. The old constitutional dilemma remains: Are members of Congress to refine public opinion or mirror it? James Madison believed that national laws should transcend local interest, that legislators should make reasonable compromises among competing societal interests, and that legislators should not be captured by special interests. Yet now many interest groups represent a significant proportion of the public interest. Another problem is the perception of policy gridlock. The Framers designed Congress to act deliberatively, yet many Americans view this as not acting at all.

Many Americans favor term limits because of the high reelection rate of incumbents and the perception that career politicians act more out of self-interest than out of public interest. The Supreme Court has ruled term-limit proposals unconstitutional. Those opposing term limits argue that they would likely produce amateur legislators who would be less prone to compromise and more influenced by lobbyists. Other reforms aim at reducing the power and perks of congressmen, claiming, for instance, that franking (or mailing) privileges need to be regulated and that pork—projects aimed at benefiting a congressman's home district or state—needs to be trimmed to avoid wasteful projects.

Americans continue to question the ethics of legislators. Scandals do occur in Congress, and most cries for reform are aimed at rules about the influence of money. Ethics codes and related reforms enacted in 1978, 1989, and 1995 have placed members of Congress under tight rules governing financial disclosure. The problem with these codes is that they assume that money is the only source of corruption. This is certainly not the case. For example, corruption can also come in the form of bargaining, involving the exchange of favors and votes, among members of Congress (known as logrolling) or between members of Congress and the president. In addition, jobs offered to former legislators create an ethics issue. While there are limits on how soon former legislators can lobby their former colleagues on certain issues, the rules are vague and their intentions are often circumvented.

Twenty-first century Congresses are complex and powerful organizations. Although reforms are often suggested, traditional patterns continue to dominate much congressional practice.

Multiple-Choice Questions

1. All of the following make it difficult for Congress to make policy EXCEPT
   (A) Congress must worry about voters' preferences, so it engages in arguments on important issues
   (B) Congress does not choose the president, so there is no guarantee a bill will become law
   (C) Congress operates through coalitions of several political parties, each of which represents different interests
   (D) Congress is bicameral, and a bill must pass both houses
   (E) each member of Congress faces reelection, and the interests of the members of his or her district must be considered

ANSWER: **C**. Each member of Congress must consider the preferences of the voters in his or her district. This can lead to arguments over policy. In addition, a bill must pass both houses of Congress and be signed by the president (or have a veto overridden) to become law. Unlike many countries, the United States has a two-party system that does not require party coalitions (*American Government*, 8th ed., pages 278-279 / 9th ed., pages 284-285).

2. How did the composition of Congress change between 1950 and 2002?
   (A) There was no change in the number of ethnic minorities, but the number of women increased.
   (B) There was no change in the number of women, but the number of African Americans increased.
   (C) The percentage of African Americans in Congress is similar to the percentage of African Americans in the country as a whole.
   (D) There are fewer Hispanics but more African Americans and women.
   (E) Although representation does not mirror the population as a whole, there are more minorities and women.

ANSWER: **E**. Congress has gradually become less white and less male (*American Government*, 8th ed., pages 284-285 / 9th ed., page 289).

3. What role does incumbency play in congressional elections?
   (A) Incumbents are more likely to be reelected in the House of Representatives than in the Senate.
   (B) More than 90 percent of all incumbent members of Congress are reelected.
   (C) Incumbents are more likely to be reelected in the Senate than in the House of Representatives.
   (D) Incumbency is helpful only when the economy is strong; more than half of all incumbents lose their reelection bids in a weak economy.
   (E) There is no correlation between incumbency and reelection.

ANSWER: **A**. There is an incumbency advantage for all members of Congress. However, incumbents in the House of Representative are more likely to be reelected than incumbents in the Senate (*American Government*, 8th ed., pages 284-286 / 9th ed., pages 290-291).

4. During the 1960s and 1970s a conservative coalition was an important factor in Congress. Why is that coalition less important today?
   (A) because African American southern Democrats have become more moderate in their ideology
   (B) because white southern Republicans have become less conservative
   (C) because many southern Democrats in Congress have been replaced by Republicans
   (D) because the regional issues that brought the coalition together, like race relations, have been resolved through civil rights legislation
   (E) because the southern states have changed and are less conservative than they were in the past

ANSWER: **C**. The conservative coalition of the 1960s and 1970s was made up of Republicans and southern Democrats. Republicans have replaced many southern Democrats in Congress (*American Government*, 8th ed., page 289 / 9th ed., page 294).

5. The representational view of Congress is based on the assumption that members want to get reelected and therefore vote to please their constituents. Under what circumstances is a member of Congress most likely to vote according to this view?
(A) when a bill will bring "pork" to the congressman's district
(B) when constituents have a clear view on some issue and the issue has attracted attention
(C) when constituents have a clear view on an issue and the member of Congress agrees with constituents' views
(D) when there is a close race for reelection and a member of Congress is eager to please constituents
(E) when a small group of constituents goes to great lengths to make its views known to their senator or representative

ANSWER: B. Congressmen act according to the representational view when constituents have a clear view on an issue that has attracted attention (*American Government*, 8th ed., pages 295-296 / 9th ed., pages 294-295).

6. Of the following members of Congress, who will most likely be chosen to head the House Appropriations Committee when the majority is Republican?

Rep.	Party	Years in Congress	Years on Appropriations Committee
Smith	R	18	2
Jones	R	5	5
Gonzales	D	22	8
Wilson	D	26	4
Jefferson	I	12	12

(A) Smith
(B) Jones
(C) Gonzales
(D) Wilson
(E) Jefferson

ANSWER: B. Although this rule is not always followed, the chairman of the committee is usually the member who has served the longest on that committee from the majority party (*American Government*, 8th ed., pages 307-308 / 9th ed., page 306).

7. A congressional committee was created to investigate any intelligence failures that might have occurred prior to the terrorist attacks of September 11, 2001. What kind of committee does this represent?
(A) standing
(B) joint
(C) select
(D) conference
(E) oversight

ANSWER: **C**. A select committee is a group appointed for a limited purpose and lasting for only a few Congresses (*American Government*, 8th ed., page 306 / 9th ed., page 305).

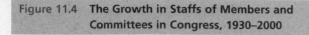
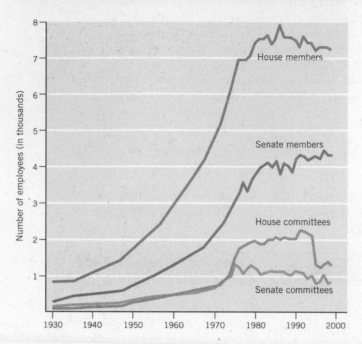

Figure 11.4 **The Growth in Staffs of Members and Committees in Congress, 1930–2000**

Source: From Harold Stanley and Richard Niemi, *Vital Statistics on American Politics 2001–2002* (Washington, D.C.: Congressional Quarterly Press, 2001). Reprinted with permission.

8. The chart above best supports which of the following conclusions?
   (A) From 1980 until 2000, both House and Senate committees saw a growth in staffs.
   (B) Senators have larger staffs than members of the House of Representatives.
   (C) Most congressional staffers work on committees.
   (D) In 1999 there was a decline in the number of staff members in both houses of Congress, as well as on committees.
   (E) There are more committees in the House than in the Senate; as a result, there has been more growth in House committee staffs.

ANSWER: **D**. From 1999 to 2000, there was a decline in the number of staff members in both houses of Congress, as well as on committees (*American Government*, 8th ed., page 310 / 9th ed., page 309).

9. The House Rules Committee does all of the following EXCEPT
   (A) adopts procedures under which the House will consider a bill
   (B) sets time limits on debate
   (C) permits or forbids certain amendments on the floor
   (D) reviews bills and places them on a calendar
   (E) establishes the number of votes needed for a bill to pass in the House

ANSWER: **E.** The House rules committee reviews bills and puts them on the agenda. It sets time limits and can limit the kinds of amendments allowed. Bills must pass the House of Representatives by majority vote (*American Government*, 8th ed., page 315 / 9th ed., page 315).

10. A filibuster in the Senate can be used to talk a bill to death. A cloture vote can end a filibuster. Taken together, what is the impact of these practices?
    (A) Neither political party can control the Senate unless it has at least sixty votes.
    (B) A party with fifty-one votes can get most of its legislative agenda passed.
    (C) The Senate rarely passes legislation on controversial issues.
    (D) Most important decisions are made in committees because it is difficult to pass a bill in the Senate as a whole.
    (E) The president's party has a significant advantage because the vice president of the United States can vote to break a tie in the Senate.

ANSWER: **A.** It takes sixty votes to end a filibuster. This means that neither party can control the Senate unless it has sixty votes. Otherwise, the minority party can use the filibuster to block legislation sponsored by the majority party (*American Government*, 8th ed., pages 317-318 / 9th ed., page 317).

Free-Response Questions

1. a. Identify and explain two ways party leadership (Speaker of the House, president pro tem of the Senate, majority leaders, minority leaders, and whips) influences members of their party in Congress.
   b. Identify and explain one factor that makes it difficult for party leadership to influence members of their party in Congress.

RESPONSE: Part (a): The Speaker is the most important person in the House. He is elected by the majority party and presides over all House meetings. The Speaker decides which bills will be assigned to which committees. This is one way he or she can use party leadership to influence members of their party in Congress. If a wayward member is sponsoring a bill, the Speaker may assign that bill to a committee where the bill is likely to get an unfavorable reception and be killed. Conversely, the Speaker can assign the bill to a safe committee where the bill will receive a favorable reception in exchange for the sponsor's party loyalty.

In addition, party leadership assigns members to committees. These assignments are especially important for newly elected members in Congress. Their political careers, opportunities for favorable press coverage, and chances for helping their states with important issues and "pork" all depend upon being assigned to the right committees.

Part (b): Despite the importance of party leadership, members of Congress represent their states or districts, and they want to be reelected by their constituents. This means that they do not always act in accordance with their party's platform. Sometimes they run for office as outsiders who will "clean up the mess in Washington." As a result, they are independent actors, and it is difficult for their political parties to control their votes on particular issues (*American Government*, 8th ed., pages 278, 299 / 9th ed., pages 284, 298).

2. In addition to having personal staff members, members of Congress have staff agencies to assist them. For TWO of the following, identify the role of the agency and explain how the agency assists Congress in policy-making:
> Congressional Research Service (CRS)
> General Accountability Office (GAO)
> Congressional Budget Office (CBO)

RESPONSE: The CRS is part of the Library of Congress and answers requests for information made by members of Congress and their staffs. It is nonpartisan, but it will look up facts, as well as the arguments for and against a particular position. It keeps track of every major bill pending before Congress. The CRS assists Congress in policy-making by providing detailed and specific information about the positive and negative aspects of proposed policies. Members of Congress are policy generalists, and although they often receive specialized information from interest groups, those groups are self-interested. By relying on information supplied by the CRS, Congress can act in a more informed manner, and the result is better policy-making.

The GAO investigates agencies and policies and makes recommendations involving a broad range of governmental activities. Although the president appoints the comptroller general (the head of the GAO) for a fixed term, the GAO serves Congress, not the president. Congress provides funding for everything from the FBI to Medicare. The GAO holds each of these programs accountable for their financial practices. This enables Congress to make better policies, because it can determine how the money it appropriates is spent.

The CBO advises Congress about the economic impact of budgetary decisions. It analyzes the potential impact of the budget proposed by the president. One of its most important tasks is economic forecasting: the CBO determines economic trends and considers the impact of federal spending on particular economic sectors of the economy as well as on the country as a whole. Often, the CBO's economic forecast differs from that of the president. This has an impact on policy-making because it enables Congress to question specific aspects of the president's budget proposals and recommend changes that will benefit the economy (*American Government*, 8th ed., page 311 / 9th ed., page 310).

12

THE PRESIDENCY

The American presidency is a unique office. Presidents can send the most formidable military forces of the world into combat but can also have Congress reject their most treasured programs. The key to understanding this paradox is found in the system of separation of powers.

KEY TERMS

ad hoc structure

cabinet

circular structure

divided government

electoral college

executive privilege

impeachment

impoundment of funds

independent agencies

pocket veto

presidential coattails

presidential succession

pyramid structure

Twenty-fifth Amendment

Twenty-second Amendment

unified government

veto

White House office

KEY CONCEPTS

- The powers of the presidency are constrained by the separation of powers in the Constitution.
- The executive branch includes the president's personal staff, the cabinet, and many other agencies that report to him.
- Presidential power often rests on the president's ability to persuade, as well as the checks and balances he has on other branches of government.
- Presidents bring to office a program they hope to enact during their terms.
- Succession to presidents who leave office because of death, impeachment, or incapacitation has been clarified over the span of American history.

For a full discussion of the presidency, see *American Government,* 8th ed., Chapter 12 / 9th ed., Chapter 12.

DIVIDED GOVERNMENT AND THE POWERS OF THE PRESIDENCY

Unlike parliamentary systems that often assure that one party will be in power, American elections often produce divided government (a government in which one party controls the White House and a different party controls one or both houses of Congress). Even in periods of unified government (when the same party controls the White House and both houses of Congress), presidents and congresses can often work at cross-purposes. Conflicts between the president and Congress are the result of separation of powers.

The Framers of the Constitution had several fears that shaped the powers of the presidency: they feared the military power of the president; they feared presidential bribery in ensuring reelection; they feared lack of balance between the legislative and executive branches.

The electoral college was the answer to some of these fears. The original system included the following:

- Each state would choose its own method of selecting electors, whose number would match the state's number of representatives in Congress.
- Electors would meet in each state capital and vote for president and vice president.
- If no candidate won a majority, the House would decide the election, with each state delegation casting one vote.

Large states would have their say, but small states would have a minimum of three votes. Ultimately, because of our two-party system, the electoral college has worked differently than expected. Today there is a winner-take-all system in forty-eight states. Only in very rare cases does an elector vote for a presidential candidate other than the one who carried his or her state.

The Framers settled on a four-year term, and George Washington set the precedent of serving no more than two terms. Later, the Twenty-second Amendment limited the presidency to two terms. The Framers gave the president the following constitutional powers:

- serve as commander in chief of the military
- commission officers of the military
- grant reprieves and pardons for federal offences
- convene special sessions of Congress
- receive ambassadors (by implication giving the president the power to make foreign policy because he decides which ambassadors to recognize and which to ignore, as well as which countries receive U.S. ambassadors)
- faithfully execute the laws
- wield the "executive power"
- appoint officials to lesser offices

The Framers also gave the president the power to make treaties and to appoint ambassadors, judges, and high officials, but because the Senate must give its consent, these powers are shared. In addition, the Framers gave the president the power to approve legislation.

Perhaps even greater than these explicit presidential powers have been those informal powers that lie in manipulating politics and public opinion. Americans increasingly look to the president for leadership and hold him responsible for a large and growing portion of our national affairs.

THE EXECUTIVE BRANCH

The executive branch includes four areas:

- **The White House Office** The president's closest assistants have offices in the White House, usually in its West Wing. Titles vary from administration to administration, but in general the men and women who hold these offices oversee the political and policy interests of the president. They are not confirmed by the Senate and can be hired and fired at the president's will. There are three ways that presidents can organize their personal staffs:

> ### AP Tip
>
> A president's leadership style, which says much about the way an administration will evolve, is often a topic on the AP exam.

- **Pyramid structure** Most assistants report through a hierarchy to a chief of staff, who then deals directly with the president. The Eisenhower, Nixon, and Reagan administrations are examples of this.
- **Circular structure** The assistants in the West Wing report directly to the president, with no screening by the chief of staff. Carter's administration is a good example. This is also known as a wheel-and-spokes structure.
- **Ad hoc structure** Task forces, committees, and informal groups of friends and advisers deal directly with the president. For example, Clinton's health care policy was headed not by a cabinet member but by First Lady Hillary Clinton.

- **The Executive Office of the President** Agencies in the Executive Office report directly to the president and perform staff services for him. Unlike the White House staff, Executive Office appointments must receive Senate confirmation. The principal agencies are the Office of Management and Budget (which assembles the budget), the Central Intelligence Agency, the Council of Economic Advisers, the Office of Personnel Management, and the Office of the U.S. Trade Representative.

- **The cabinet** The cabinet is composed of the secretaries of the executive branch departments and the attorney general. There are fifteen major departments. Some of the oldest include State, Treasury, Defense, and Justice. Although not explicitly mentioned in the Constitution, every president has had a cabinet. The secretaries become advocates for their departments, but they also serve at the president's will. Heads of other agencies, such as the chief of the Environmental Protection Agency, have been elevated to cabinet-level status. Some cabinet departments and secretaries are inevitably closer to the president than others.
- **Independent agencies and commissions** The president appoints members of agencies that have quasi-independent status. The difference between an executive agency and an independent agency is not precise. In general, heads of independent agencies serve for a fixed term and can be removed only for cause; executive agencies have heads that can be removed at any time. Examples of independent agencies include the Federal Reserve Board and the Consumer Product Safety Commission. Executive agencies include the Postal Service and all cabinet departments.

PRESIDENTIAL POWER IN ACTION

Presidents rely heavily on persuasion. The president has the only true *national* constituency of any elected office, and this can be used to enlarge his powers. Presidents have three audiences to persuade: fellow politicians and leaders in the nation's capital; party activists and officials outside of Washington; the general public.

Presidents try to transform popularity into congressional support for their programs, though this is more difficult than it used to be. Presidential coattails (by which members of Congress are elected based on the president's popularity) seem to be a thing of the past. Congressional elections are relatively insulated from presidential elections because of weakened party loyalty and the direct relationships congressional members have with constituents. Nevertheless, Congress tends to avoid the political risks of opposing a popular president by passing more of that president's legislative agenda.

Presidential popularity and its impact on getting legislative proposals passed are difficult to measure. Getting a high number of proposals passed can be misleading if the president's major bills are never passed. Presidents can get a high number of favorable bills passed by avoiding controversial measures. The timing of proposing bills is also critical. A president is generally most popular immediately after he is elected—the "honeymoon period." Most will decline in popularity as the term continues. A sluggish economy, scandal, and an unpopular war, all can hurt a president's popularity. National emergencies, such as the attacks on September 11, 2001, can give the president at least a temporary spike in popularity.

Another form of presidential power is the ability to prevent other branches of government from pushing their agendas. Presidents can use their powers by saying "no" in a number of ways:

- **The budget** The president's staff and the Office of Management and Budget put together budget proposals to present to Congress. An administration's priorities and policies show up there, and the president can say "no" by excluding agency proposals from the final budget.
- **Veto** The president can send a veto message to Congress within ten days of the bill's passage. In it he sets forth his reasons for not signing the bill. A bill that has been returned to Congress with a veto message can be passed if two-thirds of each house votes to override the veto. Congress rarely overrides vetoes. Attempts at line-item vetoes (approving some provisions of a bill but rejecting others) were made in 1996, but the Supreme Court has ruled them unconstitutional. A bill that is not signed or vetoed within ten days while Congress is still in session becomes law automatically, without the president's approval. A pocket veto occurs when the president does not sign the bill within ten days and Congress has already adjourned. The bill does not become law.
- **Executive privilege** Confidential communications between the president and his advisers do not have to be disclosed. The justification for this practice has been the separation of powers and the need a president has for candid advice. During the Watergate scandal, President Nixon refused to turn over tape recordings of White House conversations. The Supreme Court, ruling on executive privilege for the first time, held that there was a sound basis for the practice, particularly in military and diplomatic matters, but there was no immunity from judicial process under all circumstances.
- **Impoundment of funds** From time to time presidents have refused to spend money appropriated by Congress. In response to President Nixon's impoundments in 1972, the Budget Reform Act of 1974 was passed. The act requires presidents to notify Congress of funds they do not intend to spend. Congress must agree within forty-five days to delete the item. If Congress doesn't agree with the impoundment of funds, the president is required to spend the money. The act also requires presidents to notify Congress of delays in spending.

THE PRESIDENT'S PROGRAM

Modern presidents are expected to have a program when they take office—for example, Reagan's commitment to tax cuts and larger military expenditures, Franklin Roosevelt's New Deal. There are two ways for a president to develop a program. One, exemplified by Presidents Carter and Clinton, is to have a policy on almost everything. Another way, illustrated by President Reagan, is to concentrate on three or four major initiatives or themes and leave everything else to subordinates. In either case, a president's resources in developing a program include interest groups, aides, campaign advisers, federal departments and agencies, and various specialists.

A president's program will often meet many constraints. Public and congressional reactions can encourage or discourage a president's plan. The limited amount of time and attention a president can give to one program can also constrain its development. At other times, programs can be put aside when an unexpected crisis occurs. Presidents are also hampered by the fact that federal programs and the federal budget can be changed only marginally.

Virtually all modern presidents have attempted some type of reorganization of the executive branch. President George W. Bush's establishment of the Homeland Security Department is an example of a long-standing practice: presidents often reorganize because the large number of agencies that report to them can be overwhelming. It is also tempting to reorganize because it is much easier to change policy through reorganizing than through abolishing an old program or agency.

VICE PRESIDENTS AND PRESIDENTIAL SUCCESSION

The vice president's role is unclear. The extent to which vice presidents participate in the White House is left up to individual presidents. Vice presidents do have the constitutional role of presiding over the Senate and voting in the case of a tie. In practical terms, however, the vice president's leadership powers in the Senate are weak, especially in times of divided government.

A vice president becomes president when a president dies or is convicted of a bill of impeachment. The issue of succession also arises when a president becomes seriously ill and is unable to perform his duties. In eight historical cases, no *elected* official was available to succeed the new president should he subsequently die in office because there was no clear provision for a new vice president when a former one moves up to become president.

The first attempt to clarify succession was the Succession Act of 1886, which was amended in 1947. At first this designated the secretary of state as next in line for the presidency should the vice president die, followed by the other cabinet officers in order of seniority. But this meant that the president could pick his own successor by choosing the secretary of state. A 1947 amendment to the law made the Speaker of the House and the president pro tempore of the Senate next in line for the presidency. This also seemed like a poor solution because those positions are often filled based on seniority and not on executive skill.

Both problems were addressed in 1967 by the Twenty-fifth Amendment, which allows the vice president to serve as "acting president" whenever the president declares that he is unable to discharge the powers and duties of his office or whenever the vice president and a majority of the cabinet declare that the president is incapacitated. The amendment deals with the succession problem by requiring a vice president who assumes the presidency to nominate a new vice president. This person takes office if the nomination is confirmed by a majority vote of both houses of Congress.

Presidents can be removed upon impeachment and conviction. The House votes to indict the president. The impeached president must be convicted by a two-thirds vote of the Senate (which sits as a court, hears the evidence, and makes its decision) to be removed. Only two presidents—Andrew Johnson and Bill Clinton—have ever been impeached. Richard Nixon surely would have been if he had not resigned before a vote was taken in the House. Neither Johnson nor Clinton was convicted.

Multiple-Choice Questions

1. Why is it more difficult for an American president to get his program enacted in comparison with a prime minister in a parliamentary system?
   (A) because of divided government, when one or both houses of Congress differ from the president's political party
   (B) because the president has fewer constitutional powers than a prime minister
   (C) because the president has less control over the cabinet than a prime minister
   (D) because prime ministers can enact their programs without the approval of parliament
   (E) because the Supreme Court in the United States frequently uses judicial review to overturn presidential programs

ANSWER: **A.** Divided government occurs when at least one house of Congress differs from the political party of the president. This makes it difficult for a president to get his programs passed. In parliamentary systems, the prime minister is a member of the biggest party in parliament, and divided government does not occur (*American Government*, 8th ed., page 335 / 9th ed., page 331).

2. All of the following are features of the electoral college system EXCEPT
   (A) there is a winner-take-all system in forty-eight states
   (B) if no one wins a majority of electoral college votes, the election is decided by the House of Representatives
   (C) when the House of Representatives decides an election, each member has one vote
   (D) state electoral ballots are opened and counted before a joint session of Congress
   (E) occasionally an elector will vote for a presidential candidate other than the one who carried his or her state

ANSWER: **C.** Each state's vote is allotted to the candidate preferred by a majority of the state's House delegation. Each state has one vote in the event the House of Representatives decides a presidential election (*American Government*, 8th ed., pages 340-341 / 9th ed., pages 336-337).

3. President Cleveland used federal troops to break up a labor strike, and President Eisenhower sent federal troops to desegregate Central High School in Little Rock, Arkansas. Which clause of the Constitution gave them this power?
   (A) serve as commander in chief of the armed forces
   (B) convene Congress in special sessions
   (C) commission officers in the armed forces
   (D) take care that the laws be faithfully executed
   (E) wield the "executive power"

ANSWER: **D**. The president's duty to "take care that the laws be faithfully executed" has become one of the most elastic phrases in the Constitution. Both Cleveland and Eisenhower interpreted this broadly in deploying federal troops (*American Government*, 8ᵗʰ ed., pages 344-345 / 9ᵗʰ ed., pages 340-341).

4. One of the criticisms of President Carter was that he was so involved with the minor details of policies that he couldn't see the forest for the trees. How did President Carter structure his White House staff?
   (A) ad hoc
   (B) circular
   (C) bureaucratic
   (D) pyramid
   (E) business model

ANSWER: **B**. Carter used a circular, or wheel-and-spokes, model. While this model guarantees openness to many sources of advice, it makes it difficult to manage the complexities of the government (*American Government*, 8ᵗʰ ed., pages 346-347 / 9ᵗʰ ed., pages 342-343).

5. How are cabinet secretaries and the attorney general selected?
   (A) The president appoints cabinet secretaries and the attorney general, subject to Senate confirmation, and they serve at his will.
   (B) The president usually retains his predecessor's cabinet secretaries and attorney general.
   (C) The president appoints cabinet secretaries and the attorney general for fixed fourteen-year terms of office.
   (D) Cabinet secretaries and the attorney general are appointed by the president and can be removed by Congress at will.
   (E) The president appoints cabinet secretaries and the attorney general, and they must resign at end of the presidential term.

ANSWER: **A**. Cabinet officers are the heads of the fifteen major executive departments. The attorney general runs the Justice Department. Upon taking office, presidents can appoint all new cabinet heads and a new attorney general. Sometimes they retain some of the existing cabinet secretaries. They serve at the will of the president (*American Government*, 8ᵗʰ ed., pages 349-350 / 9ᵗʰ ed., pages 345-346).

6. Which of the following statements most accurately describes the president's power to get his programs enacted?
   (A) Presidents often rule by decree and executive order; as a result, much of their program becomes law.
   (B) Presidents often have a majority of both houses of Congress; as a result, many of their proposals are adopted.
   (C) The president must rely heavily on persuasion to get things done.
   (D) Because the president can always call a press conference, he often uses the media to his advantage to get his program passed.
   (E) The president has more power to get things done in the second half of his term because by then he has established himself in office.

ANSWER: **C.** Because the constitutional powers of the president are sketchy, he must rely predominantly on persuasion, rather than power, to get things done (*American Government*, 8th ed., pages 354-355 / 9th ed., pages 351-352).

Table 12.3	Partisan Gains or Losses in Congress in Presidential Election Years			
			Gains or Losses of President's Party In:	
Year	President	Party	House	Senate
1932	Roosevelt	Dem.	+90	+9
1936	Roosevelt	Dem.	+12	+7
1940	Roosevelt	Dem.	+7	-3
1944	Roosevelt	Dem.	+24	-2
1948	Truman	Dem.	+75	+9
1952	Eisenhower	Rep.	+22	+1
1956	Eisenhower	Rep.	-3	-1
1960	Kennedy	Dem.	-20	+1
1964	Johnson	Dem.	+37	+1
1968	Nixon	Rep.	+5	+7
1972	Nixon	Rep.	+12	-2
1976	Carter	Dem.	+1	+1
1980	Reagan	Rep.	+33	+12
1984	Reagan	Rep.	+16	-2
1988	Bush	Rep.	-3	-1
1992	Clinton	Dem.	-9	+1
1996	Clinton	Dem.	+9	2
2000	Bush	Rep.	-3	-4

Sources: Updated from Congressional Quarterly, *Guide to U.S. Elections,* 928; and *Congress and the Nation,* vol. 4 (1973–1976), 28.

7. The table above supports which of the following conclusions?
   (A) Democratic presidents have partisan gains in the House, while Republican presidents have partisan gains in the Senate.
   (B) When a president's party gains seats in Congress, it always gains more seats in the House than in the Senate.
   (C) President Truman received the most partisan gains in Congress of all the presidents on the chart.
   (D) The president's party always loses seats in Congress in a second-term election.
   (E) Since 1980, presidential coattails are getting shorter.

ANSWER: **E.** The effect of presidential coattails (when voters vote for members of Congress because they belong to the same party as a popular president) has declined in recent years (*American Government*, 8th ed., page 356 / 9th ed., page 353).

8. Which of the following had a negative impact on presidential approval ratings?
   I.   the poor economy during George H. W. Bush's administration
   II. the impeachment proceedings against Clinton
   III. the Vietnam War during the Johnson administration
   IV. the Watergate investigation during the Nixon administration

   (A) I and II
   (B) I, II, and III
   (C) II, III, and IV
   (D) I, III, and IV
   (E) I and IV

ANSWER: **D**. The poor economy, the Vietnam War, and Watergate caused presidential approvals ratings to drop. On the other hand, Clinton's approval ratings actually went up during his impeachment (*American Government*, 8th ed., pages 357-359 / 9th ed., pages 354-356).

9. What happens to a bill that is not signed or vetoed within ten days while Congress is still in session?
   (A) It becomes law automatically, without the president's approval.
   (B) It is "pocket vetoed" and does not become law.
   (C) It becomes law as soon as Congress adjourns; until then, the president may veto it.
   (D) It is held over until the next session of Congress.
   (E) It becomes law if 60 percent of both houses of Congress approve it.

ANSWER: **A**. A bill that is not signed by the president within ten days while Congress is in session automatically becomes law. If Congress adjourns within ten days, the bill is "pocket vetoed" (*American Government*, 8th ed., page 358 / 9th ed., page 356).

"15% LIKE YOU AS A CONSERVATIVE, 15% LIKE YOU LIBERAL, AND 70% DON'T CARE ... SO MY ADVICE IS TO REINVENT YOURSELF AS THE 'I DON'T CARE' CANDIDATE."

10. What is the viewpoint represented in the cartoon above?
   (A) Most voters do not know whether the president is a liberal or a conservative.
   (B) Most voters are apathetic.
   (C) Polling does not provide useful information to presidents.
   (D) Presidents should rely on polls in determining their stance on the issues.
   (E) Polling influences the government because some presidents use it to decide how to address the issues.

ANSWER: E. Presidents use polling to determine the public's stance on the issues. Some presidents have been criticized for relying on polls rather than making up their own minds. On the other hand, presidents represent the people, and polling helps determine the views of the people (*American Government*, 8th ed., page 365 / 9th ed., page 362).

Free-Response Questions

1. There are several constraints that make it difficult for a president to develop a program. For TWO of the constraints below, identify a specific example and explain why it made it difficult for a president to pursue his program:

   crisis
   the federal budget
   adverse popular reaction

RESPONSE: One constraint that makes it difficult for a president to pursue his programs is crisis. For example, President Johnson proposed a number of social programs as part of the Great Society. He even declared war on poverty. However, the growing crisis in Vietnam and the war's increasing unpopularity took much of his attention. Although much of Johnson's social welfare program was enacted, it soon took a back seat to the war in Vietnam.

Another constraint that stands in the way of a president's programs is the federal budget. The budget contains certain uncontrollable expenditures. These are programs, like Social Security, that have been promised to a large sector of the population. Eliminating these programs would be political suicide, and they must be accounted for in the federal budget. Although President George H. W. Bush promised not to raise taxes, he was forced to break that promise in light of a slow economy and budgetary concerns.

Adverse popular reaction also may prevent a president from enacting his program. For example, President Reagan proposed tax cuts, larger military expenditures, adjustments to Social Security, and certain budget cuts. When these proposals became public, the first two were popular, but the last two met with resistance. As a result of this adverse reaction, the unpopular proposals were scaled back

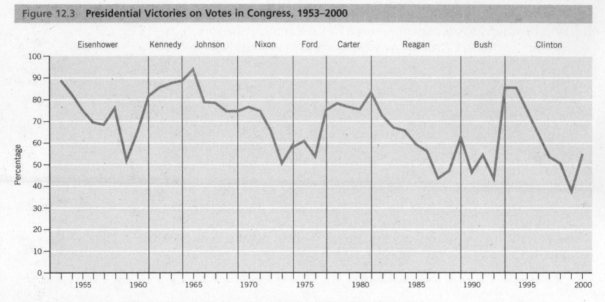

Figure 12.3 Presidential Victories on Votes in Congress, 1953–2000

Note: Percentages indicate number of congressional votes supporting the president divided by the total number of votes on which the president has taken a position.
Source: From Harold Stanley and Richard Niemi, *Vital Statistics on American Politics,* 2001–2002 (Washington, D.C.: Congressional Quarterly Press, 2001); and Gallup News Service, February 6, 2001. Reprinted with permission.

(*American Government,* 8th ed., pages 362-364 / 9th ed., pages 359-361).

2. Using the information in the figure above and your knowledge of United States politics, complete the following tasks:
    a. Describe what the figure demonstrates about presidential victories on votes in Congress from 1953 until 2000.
    b. Identify and explain one politically relevant factor that has caused presidential victories in Congress to rise above 80 percent.
    c. Identify and explain one politically relevant factor that has caused presidential victories in Congress to decline.

RESPONSE: Part (a): Although the percentage of presidential victories in Congress has varied over time, there is a slight overall decline in those victories from 1950 until 2000.

Part (b): One factor that has caused presidential victories in Congress to rise above 80 percent is the honeymoon period that follows a presidential election. At this time the president may claim to have a mandate from the people to enact his proposed program. For example, president Reagan promised tax cuts. He presented his tax-cut program during the first year of his presidency, and Congress enacted it.

Part (c): One factor that has caused presidential victories in Congress to decline is the loss of public support because of an unpopular war. In the beginning of his presidency, Lyndon Johnson was able to get much of his proposed civil rights and social welfare programs enacted. However, as the Vietnam War continued and public support dropped, so did the president's credibility. As a result, his percentage of victories in Congress declined (*American Government*, 8th ed., pages 357-359 / 9th ed., pages 354-356).

13

THE BUREAUCRACY

The federal bureaucracy is a complex web of federal agencies with overlapping jurisdictions. Most people think of the bureaucracy as wasteful, confusing, and rigid. Because the bureaucracy has such a large and complex organization, it is easy to find examples supporting this view. A closer look at the bureaucracy reveals that there is satisfaction with many aspects of government services and that many of the bureaucracy's problems are the result of actions taken by Congress, the courts, and the president.

KEY TERMS

civil service

competitive service

congressional oversight

discretionary authority

excepted service

iron triangle

issue networks

laissez-faire

merit system

National Performance Review

Office of Personnel Management

patronage

Pendleton Act

red tape

KEY CONCEPTS

- The federal bureaucracy grew dramatically as a result of the Great Depression and World War II.
- Federal agencies have substantial power in setting policy.
- The characteristics of bureaucrats generally reflect those of the American public.
- Congressional oversight is an important check on the powers of the bureaucracy.
- Several impressions of the federal bureaucracy are constant subjects of reform.

For a full discussion of the bureaucracy, see *American Government*, 8th ed., Chapter 13 / 9th ed., Chapter 13.

GROWTH OF THE BUREAUCRACY

The Constitution made scarcely any provision for a bureaucracy. The president appoints the heads of executive agencies and nominates cabinet secretaries, subject to Senate confirmation. Congress has the right to appropriate money, to investigate the agencies, and to shape the laws they administer. As a result, both Congress and the president have control over the bureaucracy.

The appointment of public officials has changed over time. These appointments are significant because officials affect how laws are interpreted and the tone and effectiveness of their administration. Patronage—appointments based on political considerations—dominated appointments in the nineteenth and early twentieth centuries. Patronage rewarded supporters, created congressional support, and built party organizations. The Pendleton Act of 1883 began a slow but steady transfer of federal jobs from the patronage system to the merit system (hiring on the basis of an individual's qualifications for the job).

After the Civil War, industrialization and the emergence of a national economy necessitated federal regulation of interstate commerce, foreshadowing the growth of government agencies. The numbers of agencies and bureaucrats grew. The new agencies provided services like administering military pensions. They did not create a huge body of regulations because:

- there was still a belief in limited government
- states' rights continued to be important
- there was a fear of concentrated discretionary power
- there was a commitment to laissez-faire (a freely competitive economy)

The Great Depression and World War II led to increased government activism. As a consequence, agencies took on a heightened regulatory role. The Supreme Court upheld laws that granted discretion to administrative agencies. The introduction of income taxes supported a larger bureaucracy. Most of all, the public became convinced that continuing military preparedness and ongoing social programs were in the best interests of the nation. These attitudes still prevail.

ACTIVITIES OF AGENCIES

Although there has been only a modest increase in the number of federal government employees since 1960, there has been significant growth in the number of privately contracted employees as well as state and local government employees. Far more important than any of these trends, however, is the growth of discretionary authority—the ability of agencies to choose courses of action and to make policies not set out in the statutory law.

Congress has delegated substantial authority to administrative agencies in three areas:

- paying subsidies to particular groups and organizations in society (for example, farmers, veterans, scientists, schools, universities, hospitals)
- transferring money from the federal government to state and local governments through grants
- devising and enforcing regulations for various sectors of society, particularly the economy, schools, health care, roads, and telecommunications

BUREAUCRATS

Bureaucrats—employees of agencies or bureaus—are distinct from elected officials. While in practice bureaucrats have some discretionary authority (for example, police do not arrest every lawbreaker they see), only elected officials are supposed to have discretionary authority. This explains why bureaucrats are insulated from being fired for political purposes and why bureaucrats must engage in seemingly redundant procedures and rules. These assure that policies made at the top are carried out throughout the organization and that every citizen is treated the same way.

The activities and powers of various agencies have tremendous impact on public policy. An understanding of who runs and works in those agencies is important:

- **Recruitment and retention** The federal civil service system was designed to recruit qualified people on the basis of merit and to retain and promote employees on the basis of performance. Many federal officials belong to the *competitive service*, in which they are appointed only after they have passed a written examination. Employees hired outside the competitive service are part of the *excepted service*—they are not hired based on an exam but, typically, are hired in a nonpartisan fashion. Most bureaucrats cannot be easily fired, although there are informal methods of discipline. When bureaucrats do get fired, the process of dismissal often takes more than a year.
- **Personal and professional attributes** The bureaucracy is a cross section of American society in terms of the education, sex, race, and social origins of its members. As is the case in the general workforce, African Americans and other minorities are most likely to be heavily represented in the lowest grade levels and tend to be underrepresented at the executive level. Because of the civil service system, bureaucracies were, for a long time, less discriminatory in hiring minorities and women than private businesses were. At higher levels, the typical civil servant is a middle-aged male with a college degree whose father was somewhat more advantaged than the average citizen. While career civil servants are more progovernment

than the public at large, on most policy questions they do not have extreme positions.

- **The nature of their jobs** Career bureaucrats often differ politically from their supervisors and the political appointees who head their agencies. Nevertheless, most bureaucrats try to carry out policy, even policy with which they disagree. "Whistle-blower" legislation protects them from punitive action by supervisors for reporting waste, fraud, or abuse in their agencies. Moreover, most civil servants have highly structured jobs that make their personal attitudes irrelevant. For example, the Environmental Protection Agency attracts bureaucrats who want to protect the environment and public health as well as free marketers who want to insulate companies from unnecessary regulation. Both end up performing their jobs in similar ways. Within each agency there is a culture and informal understanding among employees about how they are supposed to act. This culture can motivate employees, but it also can make agencies resistant to change.

- **Involvement in iron triangles and issue networks** Agencies have often used their positions to form useful power relationships with a congressional committee or an interest group. At one time scholars described the relationship between an agency, a committee, and an interest group as an iron triangle (for example, the Department of Veterans Affairs, the House and Senate committees on veterans' affairs, and veterans' organizations such as the American Legion). Through iron triangles, the self-interest of all three groups is served. Iron triangles are far less common today because politics has become too complicated. Issues involve more powerful actors than they once did because of the interchange among agencies, Congress, lobbyists, think tanks, academia, and corporations. This interchange has created issue networks—composed of members of interest groups, professors, think tanks, and media who regularly debate government policy on a certain subject. Issue networks have largely replaced iron triangles.

CONGRESSIONAL OVERSIGHT

AP Tip

The power of Congress to oversee the bureaucracy is fundamental to the system of checks and balances and is likely to appear on the AP exam.

Congressional supervision of the bureaucracy takes several forms. First, no agency can exist without congressional approval, and Congress influences agency behavior by the statutes it enacts. Second, no money can be spent unless Congress has first authorized it. Authorization legislation starts in a congressional committee and states the maximum amount of money that an agency can spend on a given program. This may be permanent, or it may be renewed each year. Third, even funds that have been authorized cannot be spent unless they are also appropriated. The House Appropriations Committee and its various subcommittees make appropriations annually.

The House Appropriations Committee has special power over agencies. The committee can recommend an amount lower than what an agency has requested and can revise or amend an agency's budget request. Both practices have the effect of strong congressional influence on agency policy. Although the Appropriations Committee does not have the power it once did, it still is the single most powerful influence on agency spending and policy.

Congress can also investigate agencies by holding hearings. Although the power to investigate is only implied in the Constitution, the Supreme Court has consistently upheld Congress's right to investigate. Investigations are generally used as a means for checking agency discretion and also for authorizing agency actions independent of presidential preferences.

REFORMING THE BUREAUCRACY

There are five frequently mentioned problems with the bureaucracy:

- **Red tape** Too many complex rules and procedures must be followed to get something done.
- **Conflict** Some agencies seem to be working at cross-purposes with other agencies.
- **Duplication** Two government agencies seem to be doing the same thing.
- **Imperialism** Agencies tend to grow without regard to the benefits that their programs confer or the costs that they entail.
- **Waste** Agencies spend more than is necessary to buy some products and services.

These problems do exist, but they are overstated and have logical origins in the Constitution and the policy-making process. For example, conflict and duplication occur because Congress, in setting up agencies and programs, often wants to achieve a number of different, partially inconsistent goals or cannot decide which goal it values most. Red tape and waste result from the obligation of bureaucrats to execute policy in accord with the rules set by elected officials and political appointees. It is noteworthy in regard to bureaucratic problems that while people are likely to say that they have a poor opinion of "the bureaucracy," they also often say that they have had good experiences with the bureaucrats with whom they have dealt personally.

Bureaucratic reform is always difficult to accomplish. Most rules and red tape grow out of struggles between the president and Congress. Periods of divided government make matters worse. This does not mean that reform is impossible, only that it is very difficult. There have been many attempts to make the bureaucracy work better for less money. Several reforms have stressed presidential control over the bureaucracy for the sake of efficiency, accountability, and consistency. The latest attempt, laid out in a report called the National Performance Review (NPR), in 1993, suggested a new kind of organizational structure that would encourage less centralized management, more employee initiatives, and fewer detailed rules, all leading to more customer satisfaction.

Despite attempts to decrease the size of the federal bureaucracy, it remains a huge, complex, and powerful part of the federal government. As with any large organization, it has both strengths and weaknesses, but its critical role in implementing and defining public policy is unquestioned.

Multiple-Choice Questions

1. Who exercises control over the bureaucracy?
   (A) There is very little control over the bureaucracy because agencies make regulations that have the force of law.
   (B) The executive branch controls the bureaucracy by appointing all federal employees.
   (C) Congress controls the bureaucracy because it has the power to fire agency heads after oversight hearings and for cause.
   (D) The judicial branch controls the bureaucracy by reviewing regulations to make sure they are constitutional before they go into effect.
   (E) Both Congress and the executive branch have controls over the bureaucracy.

ANSWER: **E.** Both Congress and the executive branch have control over the bureaucracy. The executive appoints agency heads and proposes agency budgets. Congress must approve budget proposals and can hold oversight hearings (*American Government*, 8th ed., page 376 / 9th ed., page 374).

2. How has the appointment of federal officials changed over time?
   (A) It has become more political because more government jobs have been created and are filled through patronage.
   (B) It is now based solely on merit; all federal government employees must take a civil service exam.
   (C) It is a combination of merit and political appointment with most jobs in the bureaucracy based on an exam or specific job qualifications.
   (D) Prospective employees take a civil service exam, and the person with the best score who is also a member of the president's political party is awarded the position.
   (E) There is no set procedure for filling jobs in the bureaucracy; each agency has its own rules.

ANSWER: **C.** Top-level jobs in the bureaucracy are filled by political appointment. However, most federal jobs are based upon a competitive exam or the applicant's ability to meet specific criteria (*American Government*, 8th ed., pages 377-384 / 9th ed., pages 375-382)

3. A postal clerk asks a customer if her package contains anything flammable. The customer responds that she is mailing a bottle of nail polish to her elderly aunt, who lives across town. The postal service employee allows the package to be mailed. The clerk's decision is an example of
   (A) discretionary authority
   (B) standard operating procedures
   (C) standard deviation
   (D) abuse of power
   (E) complexity and red tape

ANSWER: **A.** Street-level bureaucrats have discretionary authority when rules are not spelled out clearly (*American Government*, 8ᵗʰ ed., page 380 / 9ᵗʰ ed., page 378)

4. Which of the following has been a criticism of the process for firing a bureaucrat?
   (A) It is too political, and bureaucrats are often terminated for expressing their political beliefs.
   (B) Although bureaucrats must be given written warnings before they are terminated, there is not enough time given for them to improve their performance.
   (C) It is too difficult to fire bureaucrats because the process is elaborate and time-consuming.
   (D) Many good people do not enter the bureaucracy because most federal bureaucrats are fired when a new president takes office.
   (E) The process for terminating an employee differs from agency to agency, making the firing process too inconsistent.

ANSWER: **C.** The process for firing a bureaucrat is elaborate and time consuming, often taking more than a year (*American Government*, 8ᵗʰ ed., pages 384-385 / 9ᵗʰ ed., page 383).

5. How does the bureaucracy compare with the rest of the government in employing women and minorities?
   (A) Women and minorities mirror the population as a whole at all levels of the bureaucracy.
   (B) There are more women and minorities in Congress (including congressional staffs) than in the bureaucracy.
   (C) There are more women in the bureaucracy than in the rest of the government, but there are fewer minorities than in the population as a whole.
   (D) There are more women and minorities in the bureaucracy, but they are clustered in lower level jobs.
   (E) The bureaucracy is overwhelmingly white and male.

ANSWER: **D.** There are more women and minorities in the bureaucracy than in the other branches of government. However, they are clustered in lower paying, lower level jobs (*American Government*, 8ᵗʰ ed., page 386 / 9ᵗʰ ed., page 384).

6. From the standpoint of a federal agency, what is the advantage of an iron triangle?
    (A) It gives the agency allies in Congress, as well as in the private sector.
    (B) It allows federal agencies to receive funding directly from interest groups.
    (C) It provides agency heads with access to the media, so they can publicize their programs.
    (D) It gives the federal agency a direct link to the White House staff.
    (E) It prevents Congress from using oversight hearings as a means of cutting agency budgets.

ANSWER: **A**. Iron triangles consist of a federal agency, interest groups, and a congressional committee or subcommittee involved in a specific policy area. Iron triangles are important links between the agency, Congress, and the private sector (*American Government,* 8th ed., page 392 / 9th ed., page 390).

7. How can Congress check the activities of the bureaucracy?
    I.   through appropriations
    II. by appointing new agency heads
    III. through oversight hearings
    IV. through annual authorization legislation

    (A) I and II
    (B) I, II, and III
    (C) I, III, and IV
    (D) II, III, and IV
    (E) I and III

ANSWER: **C**. Congress can check the bureaucracy by appropriating funds and holding oversight hearings. An authorization bill is required to establish an agency. Some authorizations are subject to annual review (*American Government,* 8th ed., page 393 / 9th ed., pages 391-393).

8. The Pentagon paid $91 for screws that cost 3 cents at a hardware store. This is an example of which problem inherent in bureaucracies?
    (A) red tape
    (B) imperialism
    (C) duplication
    (D) waste
    (E) conflict among agencies

ANSWER: **D**. Although the problem is often exaggerated, waste is one criticism of the bureaucracy (*American Government,* 8th ed., page 396 / 9th ed., page 396).

9. The Department of Homeland Security was established to coordinate policies among the Federal Bureau of Investigation, the Transportation Security Administration, and the Central Intelligence Agency, as well as other federal agencies. What is the most serious problem that the creation of this department attempted to resolve?
   (A) red tape
   (B) imperialism
   (C) duplication
   (D) waste
   (E) conflict and lack of coordination among agencies

ANSWER: **E**. Although the Department of Homeland Security was established to reduce a number of problems, the most serious was conflict and lack of coordination among agencies (*American Government*, [not available in 8th ed.] / 9th ed., pages 392-393).

10. In general, what is the opinion of the American public regarding the bureaucracy?
    (A) When people have personal dealings with bureaucrats, they generally have positive experiences, although they have a less favorable attitude about the federal government as a whole.
    (B) When people have personal dealings with bureaucrats, they generally have negative experiences, although they have a favorable attitude about the federal government as a whole.
    (C) People have negative experiences with individual bureaucrats and feel negatively about the government as a whole.
    (D) People have positive experiences with individual bureaucrats and feel positively about the government as a whole.
    (E) People believe that bureaucrats try to be helpful, but they believe that the bureaucracy is too small to provide services effectively.

ANSWER: **A**. In general, people have good experiences with street-level bureaucrats, but they have a less favorable attitude about the bureaucracy as a whole (*American Government*, 8th ed., page 397 / 9th ed., page 397).

Free-Response Questions

1. Identify and explain one factor that has increased the role of the bureaucracy over time. Identify and explain one factor that restrains the growth of the bureaucracy.

RESPONSE: The bureaucracy has grown from three cabinet departments into the "fourth branch" of government. One factor that caused this is a change in public attitude. As a result of the New Deal, people expect the government to play an active role in dealing with economic and social problems. For example, President Nixon established agencies that implemented wage and price controls. The regulations created by these agencies expanded the role of the federal government in controlling the economy.

One factor that restrains the growth of the bureaucracy is legislative oversight. Although tales of wasteful spending may be exaggerated, Congress is sensitive to the public's perception that the bureaucracy does not spend money wisely and is mired in red tape. Oversight hearings are held to determine whether the bureaucracy is operating efficiently and effectively. If Congress believes that an agency's budget is bloated, it can cut funding to that agency when it passes appropriations bills in the next session (*American Government*, 8th ed., pages 379-380, 393 / 9th ed., pages 377-378, 391-393).

2. Iron triangles are examples of client politics, in which every member of the group benefits, and iron triangles have benefited bureaucratic agencies. With respect to this issue, complete the following tasks:
   a. Identify the members of a specific iron triangle.
   b. Explain the exchange of benefits among the members of an iron triangle.
   c. Identify issue networks and explain their impact on iron triangles.

RESPONSE: Part (a): An iron triangle is a network consisting of an agency, an interest group, and a congressional committee or subcommittee. One example is the Department of Agriculture, a congressional subcommittee on tobacco, and an interest group made up of tobacco growers.

Part (b): Each member of an iron triangle has something to offer that benefits the other members. For example, the Department of Agriculture can provide grants for tobacco farmers who are experimenting with new farming techniques; an interest group made up of tobacco farmers can assist members of Congress in writing technical bills that provide for tobacco subsidies; and members of the subcommittee can recommend appropriations for the Department of Agriculture's budget. As a result, all three groups work to insure their existence and increase their power.

Part (c): Issue networks include a variety of organizations, such as congressional committees, public interest groups, the media, scientists, and academics, who debate certain issues. An antismoking interest group, for example, and a medical association might form an alliance and work together to further their interests. In this case, a media campaign might cause the public to put pressure on members of Congress to support antitobacco policies. This would weaken the tobacco triangle (*American Government*, 8th ed., pages 392-393 / 9th ed., pages 390-391).

14

THE FEDERAL COURTS

The judicial branch plays a large role in making public policy. The major power that the federal courts have is judicial review, the right to declare laws of Congress and acts of the president unconstitutional.

KEY TERMS

amicus curiae	judicial review
briefs	"litmus test"
class action suits	*Marbury v. Madison*
concurring opinion	*McCulloch v. Maryland*
courts of appeals	opinion of the Court
dissenting opinion	senatorial courtesy
district courts	solicitor general
Dred Scott v. Sandford	stare decisis
in forma pauperis	strict construction
judicial activism	writ of certiorari

KEY CONCEPTS

- The federal courts have evolved into an institution that has significant impact on public policy.
- The selection of federal judges is a very political process.
- A limited number of cases are heard in federal courts, and an even more limited number reach the Supreme Court.
- Judicial activism is a philosophy in which judges make bold policy decisions.
- The other branches of government and the public have checks on the powers of the federal courts.

For a full discussion of the federal courts, see *American Government*, 8th ed., Chapter 14 / 9th ed., Chapter 14.

THE DEVELOPMENT OF THE FEDERAL COURTS

Most of the Founders probably expected judicial review to be an important judicial power, but it is unlikely that they thought the federal courts would play a large role in policy-making. The original view of the Founders was known as strict construction: judges would be bound by the wording of the Constitution and precedent, which was drawn mainly from the British legal system. Within a few decades, however, an activist approach emerged, and judges looked at the underlying *principles* of the Constitution.

The federal courts have evolved toward judicial activism, shaped by political, economic, and ideological forces of three historical eras:

- **National supremacy and slavery (1789-1861)** Two early court cases, *Marbury v. Madison* (1803) and *McCulloch v. Maryland* (1819), helped establish the supremacy of the national government. *Marbury* gave the Supreme Court the power to declare a congressional act unconstitutional. *McCulloch* established that federal law is supreme over state law. Both suggested that powers granted to the federal government should be construed broadly. The power of the federal government to regulate commerce among the states was also established, and state law that conflicted with federal law was declared void. A major case, *Dred Scott v. Sandford* (1857), made the Supreme Court a major player in setting the stage for the Civil War. The Supreme Court ruled that blacks were not citizens of the United States and that federal law prohibiting slavery in northern territories was unconstitutional.
- **Government and the economy (1865-1936)** The dominant issue during this period was deciding when the economy would be regulated by the states and when by the national government. Most court decisions protected private property. The Court upheld the use of injunctions to prevent labor strikes, struck down the federal income tax, sharply limited the reach of the antitrust laws, restricted the powers of the Interstate Commerce Commission, refused to eliminate child labor, and prevented states from setting maximum hours of work. These restricted the federal government's ability to regulate the economy. Yet the Court also authorized various kinds of regulation, such as requiring railroads to improve their safety, approving mine safety laws, and regulating fire-insurance rates. While the Court was supportive of private property, it could not develop a principle distinguishing between reasonable and unreasonable regulation.
- **Government and political liberty (1936-present)** During this period the Court has deferred to the legislature in regulating the economy. It has shifted its attention to personal liberties and is active in defining rights. The Warren Court, which began in 1953, redefined the relationship of citizens to the government and protected the rights and liberties of citizens.

During the past fifteen years, the Supreme Court has begun to rule that the states have the right to resist some federal action. It is possible that this is the beginning of a new era in which the Court will return certain powers to the states, a process known as devolution.

THE SELECTION OF JUDGES

All federal judges are nominated by the president and confirmed by the Senate. Presidents almost always nominate a member of their own political party, and party background does have some effect on how judges behave. However, rulings are also shaped by other factors, such as the facts of the case, precedent, and lawyers' arguments.

Confirmations are often contentious. Senate delays on confirmations often leave many seats open on the appellate courts. One tradition regarding nominations is senatorial courtesy: senators from the president's party review an appointee for a federal district court in their state; senators can "blue-slip"—that is, veto—a nominee, a practice that has been criticized because it gives senators virtual power in nominating judges.

Another concern is the use of the "litmus test," a test of ideological purity used by recent presidents, in nominating, and senators, in confirming, judges for federal courts. Presidents seek judicial appointees who share their political ideologies. Because various presidents appoint judges, different circuits issue different rulings over similar cases. While candidates cannot be asked how they would rule in a specific case, they can be asked about judicial philosophy. Litmus tests are most apparent in Supreme Court confirmations, for which there is no tradition of senatorial courtesy.

THE JURISDICTION OF THE FEDERAL COURTS

The United States has two court systems—one state, one federal—which can complicate the questions of which cases the federal courts may hear, and how cases beginning in the state courts may end up before the Supreme Court.

The Constitution lists the kinds of cases over which federal courts have jurisdiction; all others are left to state courts. Federal courts can hear all cases involving the U.S. Constitution, federal law, and treaties; these are known as federal-question cases. Federal courts may also hear cases involving different states or involving citizens of different states; these are known as diversity cases. Some cases, such as those where both state and federal laws have been broken, can be tried in either state or federal courts.

The Constitution specifies a very limited original jurisdiction for the Supreme Court. Nearly every case the Supreme Court hears is on appeal and chosen by the court. It does this by issuing a writ of certiorari. If four justices agree to hear a case, a "writ of cert" is issued, and the case is scheduled for a hearing. The Court tends to take cases that pose a significant federal or constitutional question, involve conflicting decisions by circuit courts, or contain a constitutional interpretation by one of the highest state courts regarding state or federal law. Only about one hundred appeals are granted certiorari in a given year.

Some Americans criticize the courts as undemocratic. The Supreme Court rejects all but a few of the applications for certiorari. In addition, the costs of appeals are high. Nevertheless, costs can sometimes be lowered or even covered in full in the case of indigents (called in forma pauperis), for which the government pays the costs. Those who are unable to afford counsel are provided a lawyer at no charge. Interest groups are also sources of funding for litigation. Court costs are also affected by the practice of fee shifting, which enables plaintiffs to collect their costs from a defendant if the defendant loses.

Getting to court requires legal standing. To have standing there must be a real controversy between adversaries, and the litigants must demonstrate personal harm. Under certain circumstances, a citizen can benefit from a court decision without ever going to court. In these cases, courts recognize class-action suits, in which an identifiable group of people has standing. If the case is won, all who have circumstances similar to the active plaintiffs receive a share of the judgment. Since 1974, the Supreme Court will not hear class-action suits unless every ascertainable member of the group is notified individually. This is often prohibitively expensive.

THE POWERS OF THE SUPREME COURT

Once a case gets to the Supreme Court, lawyers for each side submit briefs. A brief is a document that sets forth the facts of the case, summarizes the lower-court decision, gives the arguments for the side represented, and discusses precedents on the issue.

Oral arguments are presented later. Each side has one half-hour, but justices can interrupt with questions. Because the federal government is either the plaintiff or defendant in about half the cases that the Supreme Court hears, the solicitor general of the United States appears frequently before the Court. The solicitor general, the third ranking officer in the Justice Department, decides which cases the government will appeal from the lower courts and personally approves every case presented to the Supreme Court.

Written briefs and even oral arguments may be offered by a "friend of the court," or amicus curiae. An amicus brief is from an interested party not directly involved in the suit. The reasoning and research found in academic law journals are also sources of ideas used by the justices in reaching decisions and writing their opinions.

After briefs are submitted and oral arguments are heard, justices develop their opinions and decisions. Much of this work is performed by clerks, who are often recent graduates of the top law schools in the country. These drafted opinions are circulated among the justices and their clerks. Next, the justices meet in conference to allow for the exchange of ideas and arguments and to vote. The chief justice counts the votes, writes the decision of the court (or assigns someone to write the official decision if he is among the minority), and manages the process.

In deciding a case, a majority of justices must be in agreement. Sometimes the opinion is brief and unsigned; this is known as a per curiam opinion. There are three kinds of opinions:

▣ An opinion of the Court is the majority opinion.

▣ A concurring opinion is an opinion that agrees with the decision but uses different reasoning to reach that conclusion.

▣ A dissenting opinion is a minority opinion. Disagreeing with the decision, it has no value as precedent but may form the basis for later appeals or reversals of precedent.

The federal courts have the power to make public policy in three ways:

▣ by interpretation of the Constitution or law
▣ by extending the reach of existing law
▣ by designing remedies that involve judges acting in administrative or legal ways

These powers can be measured in several ways. Over 130 laws have been declared unconstitutional. Over 260 cases have been overturned—to let a prior decision stand is called stare decisis. Judges now handle cases once left to the legislature. Further, judges now often go beyond what is narrowly required by imposing remedies for issues and problems.

AP Tip

Judicial activism versus judicial restraint is a major issue when considering the federal courts. The issue will certainly appear on the AP exam in some form.

Judicial activism, the philosophy by which judges make bold policy decisions, has both supporters and critics. Supporters believe courts should correct injustices when other branches or state governments refuse to do so and when change creates new circumstances not foreseen by the Founders. They also argue that the courts are the last resort for those without the power or influence to provoke new laws. Promoting the philosophy known as judicial restraint, critics argue that judges cannot put themselves above the law and that they lack expertise in designing and managing complex institutions. These critics also note that the courts are not accountable because judges are not elected.

Judicial activism increased during the twentieth century because government has tended to do more and courts have interpreted a greater number of laws. Also, activist judges have become far more widely accepted in American political culture as our values, society, and technology have changed.

CHECKS ON JUDICIAL POWER

Like the other branches of the federal government, the judicial branch does not have unrestrained powers. There are several checks on the powers of the federal courts:

- Courts rely on others to implement their decisions. Congress can check the courts in several ways:
  - Confirmation proceedings gradually alter the composition of the courts.
  - Impeachment proceedings, though rare, can also change the composition of the courts.
  - Congress can change the number of judges, giving the president more or fewer appointment opportunities.
  - Revising legislation can undo Supreme Court decisions.
  - Amending the Constitution can alter the jurisdiction of the Court.
  - Defying public opinion may be dangerous for the legitimacy of the Supreme Court. Public confidence in the Supreme Court since the 1960s has varied as the Court has issued controversial rulings. Today there is often more popular support for the executive and legislative branches.

The courts have substantial power, and judicial review in particular makes the courts an important part of the complex process of establishing and revising American public policy.

Multiple-Choice Questions

1. Using the power of judicial review, the Supreme Court can do all of the following EXCEPT
   (A) declare a law passed by Congress unconstitutional
   (B) declare a law passed by a state unconstitutional
   (C) declare acts of the executive branch unconstitutional
   (D) determine the meaning and application of the Constitution
   (E) overturn a Constitutional amendment as a violation of civil rights

ANSWER: E. Judicial review allows the Supreme Court to determine the meaning and application of the Constitution and overturn a law or regulation that violates the Constitution. Because amendments are part of the Constitution, they are, by definition, constitutional, and the Supreme Court may not overturn them (*American Government*, 8th ed., pages 403-404 / 9th ed., pages 403-404).

2. Justice Clarence Thomas believes that the Constitution should be interpreted according to its clearly implied language. This judicial philosophy can best be described as
   (A) strict construction
   (B) judicial activism
   (C) conservatism
   (D) liberalism
   (E) constitutionalism

ANSWER: A. Justice Thomas is a strict constructionist who believes the Constitution should be interpreted directly by the language of the Constitution (*American Government*, 8th ed., page 404 / 9th ed., page 404).

3. Which chief justice of the Supreme Court is considered to have been the most activist in expanding civil liberties?
    (A) John Marshall
    (B) Earl Warren
    (C) William Rehnquist
    (D) Warren Burger
    (E) Roger Taney

ANSWER: **B**. Beginning in 1953, the Warren Court began interpreting the Constitution using judicial activism. The result was an expansion of civil rights, civil liberties, and defendants' rights (*American Government*, 8th ed., page 410 / 9th ed., page 410).

4. The federal courts have jurisdiction over the following cases EXCEPT
    (A) civil suits between citizens of different states in which the amount exceeds $50,000
    (B) criminal cases involving violations of laws passed by Congress
    (C) bankruptcy cases
    (D) state appeals cases in which the defendant alleges his or her constitutional rights were violated
    (E) prosecutions under state criminal law.

ANSWER: **E**. The federal courts do not have jurisdiction to hear criminal cases involving violations of state law unless there is an alleged violation of the defendant's constitutional rights (*American Government*, 8th ed., page 415 / 9th ed., page 415).

5. The Supreme Court will often grant certiorari when
    I.   there is a circuit conflict over the same issue
    II. the highest court in a state has held a federal law to be in violation of the Constitution
    III. the highest court in a state has held a state law to be in violation of the Constitution.
    IV. the case is between citizens of different states and the amount at issue exceeds $50,000.

    (A) I and II
    (B) I, II, and III
    (C) I and III
    (D) I, III, and IV
    (E) I, II, III, and IV

ANSWER: **B**. The Supreme Court often grants certiorari when circuits rule differently on the same issue or when either a state or federal law has been ruled unconstitutional by a state's highest court (*American Government*, 8th ed., page 416 / 9th ed., page 416).

6. National supremacy over the states was expanded by the Supreme Court in cases involving all of the following issues EXCEPT
    (A) railroad regulations issued by the Interstate Commerce Commission
    (B) the creation of a national bank
    (C) the use of injunctions to prevent labor strikes
    (D) laws regulating wages and hours
    (E) state laws regarding marriage and divorce

ANSWER: **E.** Over time, the Supreme Court has expanded the power of the federal government by allowing the creation of a national bank, upholding railroad regulations, permitting the use of federal injunctions in labor disputes, and validating wage and hour regulations (*American Government*, 8th ed., pages 406-409 / 9th ed., pages 406-409).

7. Why has the practice of senatorial courtesy been criticized?
    (A) because it puts too much of the judicial nomination process in the hands of the president
    (B) because it keeps the senate from confirming judicial appointments
    (C) because it is the equivalent of reversing constitutional powers—a senator basically nominates the candidate and the president consents
    (D) because it prevents qualified people from obtaining positions in the circuit courts of appeals
    (E) because the president is able to bypass Senate confirmation if one senator approves of the appointment

ANSWER: **C.** A senator can "blue slip" a nominee from his state, killing a nomination. The can be an undemocratic way of blocking the will of the majority (*American Government*, 8th ed., page 412 / 9th ed., pages 412-413).

8. All of the following make it difficult to get a case to the Supreme Court EXCEPT
    (A) the Supreme Court does not take all cases
    (B) appeals cost money for lawyers and copies
    (C) by the time a case gets to the Supreme Court, the case has already gone through an expensive trial and appeals process
    (D) it can take a long time to settle a matter in federal court
    (E) the government does not supply lawyers for the appeals court process

ANSWER: **E.** The Supreme Court chooses the cases it accepts by issuing a writ of certiorari. Although it is expensive and time consuming to take a case to the Supreme Court, the government provides lawyers for people who are in forma pauperis (*American Government*, 8th ed., page 417 / 9th ed., page 417).

9. Long after the Supreme Court ruled prayer in the public schools unconstitutional, schools all over the country were still allowing prayer and Bible readings. What explains this?
    (A) The Supreme Court's decision was vague, and schools were not sure how to implement it.
    (B) The courts have no police force or army; hence, they have no enforcement powers.
    (C) School districts could still legally engage in school prayer because they continued to file appeals.
    (D) Both President George H. W. Bush and President Clinton supported school prayer, so they ordered the executive branch not to enforce the Court's decision.
    (E) The areas where school prayer was still being held were all Christian, so no one challenged the practice.

ANSWER: **B**. The courts have no enforcement power. Unless the failure to comply is easily detected and brought to the Court's attention, it is difficult to ensure compliance with decisions (*American Government*, 8th ed., pages 426-427 / 9th ed., page 427).

10. Congress has all of the following checks on the judicial branch EXCEPT
    (A) it can alter the number of judges and courts
    (B) it can impeach justices
    (C) it can propose a constitutional amendment
    (D) it can change the courts' jurisdiction
    (E) it can change the length of judges' terms

ANSWER: **E**. Congress can change the number of judges and courts, alter the courts' jurisdiction, impeach judges for cause, and begin the constitutional amendment process when the court reaches an unpopular decision (*American Government*, 8th ed., pages 426-427 / 9th ed., pages 426).

Free-Response Questions

1. The federal courts are part of the system of checks and balances created by the Constitution. With respect to this issue, complete the following tasks:
    a. Identify and explain one check on judicial power held by Congress.
    b. Identify and explain one check on judicial power held by the executive.
    c. Identify and explain one check on the other branches held by the judiciary.

RESPONSE: Part (a): Congress has several methods of checking the power of the judicial branch. One method is by proposing an amendment to the Constitution. An example of this is the income tax. The Supreme Court ruled that a congressional law establishing an income tax was unconstitutional. After the ruling, several members of Congress proposed a constitutional amendment to provide for a federal income tax. This proposal was ratified by the states. The Sixteenth Amendment, in effect, overturned the Supreme Court's decision.

Part (b): The president also has a check on the judiciary. The president must nominate all candidates for the federal bench. While it is improper to ask candidates how they would rule in specific cases, the executive branch can inquire about their ideology. Of course, most judicial nominees are affiliated with the president's political party. In addition, the president can use executive agencies, such as the FBI, to investigate their backgrounds. This gives the president significant power over who sits on the federal bench.

Part (c): The Supreme Court's most important power is judicial review. This is the power to determine the meaning of the Constitution and invalidate state and federal laws accordingly. For example, the

Supreme Court determined that the Gun-Free School Zone Act exceeded Congress's power under the commerce clause. This was a check on Congress's power because it kept Congress from using powers that, in the Supreme Court's view, should be reserved to the states (*American Government*, 8th ed., pages 411-413, 426-429 / 9th ed., pages 411-413, 427-429).

2. The federal courts have played a larger role in our government over time. With respect to TWO of the following issues, explain how the court enlarged the role of the federal government:

> slavery
> the economy
> civil liberties

RESPONSE: By dealing with the issue of slavery, the Supreme Court played a large role in setting the stage for the Civil War. In the *Dred Scott* case, the court tackled the issue of whether a slave must be given his freedom once he was taken into a free state. The Court ruled that, under the Constitution, African Americans could never be citizens. This meant that there would be no dividing line between slave states and free states. Because slaves were considered property, they could be taken north, thus expanding slavery and preventing its prohibition. In rendering this decision, the court played a major role in exacerbating the tensions between North and South that would lead to the Civil War.

The federal courts have expanded the government's role in the economy. They have upheld railroad regulations, anti-child-labor laws, and regulations setting minimum wages and maximum hours. In addition, they have upheld wage and price controls. Until the late nineteenth century, this level of government regulation of the economy was unheard of, but because of court decisions, the government now regulates (but does not control) the economy.

Judicial activism, particularly by the Warren Court, has enlarged the scope of government in protecting civil rights and civil liberties. For example, in *Brown v. Board of Education*, the Supreme Court held that school segregation is unconstitutional. Later, when Central High School, in Little Rock, Arkansas, refused to desegregate, President Eisenhower called in federal troops. This expanded the scope of government—all as a result of the *Brown* decision. When the Court held that indigent defendants must be provided with counsel, this also expanded the scope of government through the creation of public defenders offices (*American Government*, 8th ed., pages 404-409 / 9th ed., pages 404-409).

15

POLICY-MAKING IN THE FEDERAL SYSTEM

Policy-making at the federal level is rarely accomplished consistently and routinely. An issue must first find its way to the political agenda, and then decisions must be made about how to address the issue. Coalitions are formed that struggle over the issue, and the policy that results depends on who gains, who loses, and the perceptions, beliefs, and values of key political actors.

KEY TERMS

client politics

costs and benefits

entrepreneurial politics

interest group politics

majoritarian politics

policy entrepreneurs

political agenda

KEY CONCEPTS

- The political agenda determines which issues will receive consideration in formulating new policy.
- Costs and benefits determine who supports a policy, who opposes it, and the coalitions that form to compete over a policy.
- Business regulation is an excellent case study of the different types of policies and policy-making.
- Perceptions, beliefs, interests, and values all play a critical role in the policy-making process.

For a full discussion of policy-making in the federal system, see *American Government,* 8th ed., Chapter 15 / 9th ed., Chapter 15.

SETTING THE POLITICAL AGENDA

> ### AP Tip
>
> The political agenda involves virtually all of the participants in the policy-making process and is a term likely to appear on the AP exam.

The most important decision affecting policy-making is determining what belongs on the political agenda—the issues about which public policy will be made. At any given time, certain shared beliefs determine what is legitimate for the government to do. This legitimacy is affected by shared political values, the weight of custom and tradition, the impact of events, and changes in the way that political elites think and talk about politics.

The legitimate scope of government action is constantly growing larger. Government activity is rarely scaled back because people have certain expectations of government that are difficult for politicians to change. Changes in the attitudes of the public and new events generally increase government activities. It is unfair to attribute government growth to one political party.

Three forces enlarge government activity, sometimes without public demand or even when conditions are improving:

- **Groups** Many policies are the result of small groups of people enlarging the scope of government by their demands. These may be organized interests—for example, corporations, unions—or unorganized yet intense groups—for example, urban minorities. Such groups may be reacting to a sense of relative deprivation.
- **Institutions** Major institutions such as the courts, bureaucracy, and Congress may add new issues to the political agenda. The courts make decisions that force action by other branches—for instance, school desegregation. They can facilitate change even when there is no popular majority for change. The bureaucracy has become a source of policy proposals. Congress, especially the Senate, produces potential presidential candidates who focus on activism as a means of gathering recognition.
- **Media** By publicizing issues the media help shape the political agenda. The public often becomes aware of issues through the media.

The political agenda can change because of shifts in popular attitudes, elite interest, critical events, or government actions. Popular attitudes tend to change slowly, often in response to critical events. Elite attitudes and government actions are far more volatile.

COSTS, BENEFITS, AND POLICY

The costs and benefits of a proposed policy provide a way to understand how an issue affects political power. A cost is any burden (monetary or nonmonetary) that people must bear from the policy. It might be a fee or higher taxes, but costs are often nonmonetary items, such as:

- requiring formal reports (for example, the number of team sports for boys and for girls in a school district)
- restricting activities (for example, farming on land that is a protected wetland or discriminating in hiring on the basis of gender)
- performing functions for the government (for example, collecting income and FICA taxes)

A benefit is any satisfaction (monetary or nonmonetary) that people expect to receive from the policy. It might be a tangible reward, but benefits are often intangible items, such as:

- restricting competition (for example, ownership restrictions on television stations or monopolies allowed in professional sports)
- accessing resources owned by the public (for example, mining rights on public land or use of patents developed by government-sponsored research)
- coordinating actions by government agencies (for example, amber alert procedures)

The perception of costs and benefits is also vital in the policy-making process as people consider whether the group to benefit and the costs incurred are legitimate. Political coalitions form over the distribution of costs and benefits.

The politics of policy-making can be illustrated by four kinds of policies:

- **Majoritarian politics** Some policies promise benefits to large numbers of people at a cost that large numbers of people will have to bear (for example, Social Security or military defense). The debate over such policies is generally conducted in ideological or cost terms, not as a rivalry among interest groups. Majoritarian issues are usually resolved in public debate and public votes on bills.
- **Interest group politics** In interest group politics, a proposed policy will confer benefits on some relatively small, identifiable group and impose costs on another small, equally identifiable group (for example, bills requiring business firms to give benefits to labor unions). Interest groups generally carry on the debate over these policies with minimal involvement by the wider public.
- **Client politics** With client politics, some identifiable, often small, group will benefit, but a large part of society will pay the costs (for example, regulated milk prices benefit dairy farmers but increase the cost of milk to consumers). Because the benefits are concentrated, the group that will receive those

benefits has an incentive to organize and work to get them. The costs are widely distributed, affecting many people only slightly, and those who pay the costs may be either unaware of any costs or indifferent to them.

■ **Entrepreneurial politics** In entrepreneurial politics a large part of society benefits from a policy that imposes substantial costs on some small, identifiable segment of society (for example, antipollution and safety requirements for automobiles, proposed as ways of improving the health and well-being of all people but at the expense of automobile manufacturers). A key element in the adoption of such policies is often the work of a policy entrepreneur, who acts on behalf of the unorganized or indifferent majority. Entrepreneurial politics can also occur if voters or legislators in large numbers suddenly become disgruntled by the high cost of some benefit that a group is receiving or become convinced of the urgent need for a new policy to impose such costs (for example, cleaning up toxic waste sites).

BUSINESS REGULATION: A CASE STUDY

Efforts by government to regulate business illustrate not only the four kinds of policy-making processes but also the relationship between wealth and power. Some observers believe that economic power dominates political power. In this view wealthy Americans have great access to political power. Politicians and business people with similar backgrounds and ideologies often form mutually beneficial relationships. At times, economic power allows individuals or groups to buy political power. Politicians must defer to business in order to keep the economy healthy. Other observers view political power as a threat to a market economy. Neither extreme is correct. Business and government relations depend on many variables.

Not all efforts to regulate business pit one group against another. Some laws have reflected majoritarian politics, in which the majority of voters were in favor of some form of regulation. For instance, antitrust legislation in the 1890s (for example, the Sherman Act and the Federal Trade Commission Act) was sparked by public support. By the early twentieth century, presidents were taking the initiative in encouraging the enforcement of antitrust laws. Support for antitrust laws came mainly from the ideological convictions of the public and were not the result of interest group activism.

Labor-management conflict in the twentieth century is a good example of interest group politics. Labor unions sought government protection for their rights to strike and engage in other forms of collective action. Business firms opposed labor vigorously. Labor won a victory with the creation of the National Labor Relations Board in the mid-1930s. Management won victories in the 1940s and 1950s (for example, the Taft-Hartley Act and the Landrum-Griffin Act). In those decades winners and losers were determined by economic conditions and the partisan composition of Congress. Costs and benefits involved specific groups, not the general public.

Client politics is also evident in business regulation. State licensing of occupations such as law and medicine are justified as ways of preventing fraud, malpractice, and safety hazards, and they no doubt serve these purposes. But they also have the effect of restricting entry into the regulated occupation, thereby enabling its members to charge higher prices than they otherwise might. Citizens generally do not object to this because they believe that the regulations protect them and that the higher prices are spread over so many customers as to be unnoticed.

Entrepreneurial politics have often been evident in regulating businesses. The 1906 Pure Food and Drug Act, an early example, forced meatpacking plants to sanitize their conditions following revelations of frightful practices in the widely read novel *The Jungle*. The 1960s and 1970s brought a large number of consumer and environmental protection statutes aimed at specific industries and businesses (for example, the Clean Air Act and the Toxic Substance Control Act). Ralph Nader is an excellent example of a policy entrepreneur, associating himself with many consumer and environmental interests.

PERCEPTIONS, BELIEFS, INTERESTS, AND VALUES

The perception of costs and benefits affects politics. For instance, if people think that laws fighting pollution will be expensive for companies but not for consumers, they will generally favor such measures. However, if they believe that they will pay for the laws in the form of fewer jobs or higher prices, they will not be as supportive.

Individuals and groups attempt to frame and define issues in ways that work to their advantage. Interest groups try to give the impression that their issue is vital to the welfare of the entire country and should be thought of in majoritarian terms. Likewise, opponents will try to frame an issue in client-politics terms so that the self-interest of the original group is emphasized. Political conflicts are a struggle to make one definition of the costs and benefits of a proposal prevail over others.

Values also play a vital role in policy-making. Concepts of what is good for the community or the country vary widely. What happens now or in the near future is more important to most people than what happens in the distant future—economists label this the short-term/long-term disconnect. Most people seem to react more sharply to what they will lose if a policy is adopted than to what they may gain.

The way people think makes a difference, even in the case of policies where money interests are at stake. Deregulation during the 1980s of industries such as the airlines, long-distance telephone companies, and trucking is a good example. The idea emerged among academic economists that governmental regulations were inefficient in industries that could be competitive. Politicians from both major parties embraced the idea of deregulation because they had the support of regulatory agencies and consumers, even though the industries themselves opposed deregulation. The affected industries feared more competition, lower prices, and fewer profits. The enactment of deregulation signaled the weakening of client politics and the power of ideas in policy-making.

Policy-making at the federal level is a complex and often confusing process that requires an understanding of the policy agenda, the costs and benefits of various issues, and the perceptions of groups involved.

Multiple-Choice Questions

1. The political agenda is affected by all of the following EXCEPT
   (A) a crisis, such as the terrorist attacks of September 11, 2001
   (B) pressures by interest groups, such as organized labor, to address certain issues, such as working conditions
   (C) pressures by institutions, such as the Supreme Court, to change practices, such as segregation
   (D) pressures by unfriendly foreign nations to change U.S. foreign policy
   (E) the use of the media to publicize matters, such as automobile safety

ANSWER: **D**. Interest groups, institutions, and the media all impact the policy agenda. In addition, the agenda changes when there is a crisis (*American Government*, 8th ed., pages 436-439 / 9th ed., pages 436-439).

2. The billboard shown above is an example of
   (A) how an issue became a part of the political agenda as a result of policy entrepreneurs
   (B) a public relations campaign, financed by the federal government, to raise public awareness
   (C) a protest by a public interest group against an unfavorable court decision
   (D) the use of PAC money to influence an election campaign
   (E) how a public interest group attempts to influence the voting records of members of Congress

ANSWER: **A**. Drunk driving was always a problem, but it became a national issue after policy entrepreneurs, such as Mothers Against Drunk Driving (MADD), emphasized it (*American Government*, [not available in 8th ed.] / 9th ed., page 440).

3. Almost everyone has to pay Social Security taxes, but almost everyone will receive Social Security benefits when they retire. This is an example of
   (A) interest group politics, in which a single group benefits most from the policy-making process
   (B) majoritarian politics, in which the policy-making process benefits large numbers of people who also bear the costs
   (C) client politics, in which small identifiable groups will receive most of the benefits from the policy-making process
   (D) entrepreneurial politics, in which a large number of people benefit from a policy that imposes costs on a small group
   (E) pork-barrel politics, in which pet projects benefit the constituents of a member of Congress

ANSWER: **B**. Most people pay for Social Security, and most people will receive its benefits. This is an example of majoritarian politics (*American Government*, 8th ed., pages 441-445 / 9th ed., pages 441-444).

4. Which of the following policies were adopted because a policy entrepreneur dramatized the issue, galvanized public opinion, and mobilized congressional support?
   I. automobile safety legislation
   II. legislation regulating the meatpacking industry
   III. legislation cutting highway funding for states that did not raise the drinking age
   IV. the creation of the Department of Homeland Defense

   (A) I and II
   (B) I, II, and III
   (C) II and III
   (D) II, III, and IV
   (E) I, II, and IV

ANSWER: **B**. Policy entrepreneurs pursued legislation affecting automobile safety, the meatpacking industry, and highway safety (*American Government*, 8th ed., pages 451-452 / 9th ed., page 451).

5. In the 1980s several industries were deregulated. Why did these industries object to deregulation?
   (A) because detailed regulations enabled them to run their businesses using standard operating procedures
   (B) because once those industries were deregulated, they were no longer able to keep prices low for consumers
   (C) because regulations kept those industries competitive in the market
   (D) because deregulation would lead to competition, lower prices, and lower industry profits
   (E) because deregulation would prevent industries from hiring the skilled labor forces they needed to stay competitive

ANSWER: **D**. Industries, like the airlines, resisted deregulation, because it led to more competition, lower prices, and fewer profits (*American Government*, 8th ed., page 455 / 9th ed., page 454).

6. Which of the following historical events changed the political agenda and widened the scope of government?
   I.   the civil rights movement
   II. the Great Depression
   III. the environmental movement
   IV. World War I

   (A) I and II
   (B) I, II, and III
   (C) II and III
   (D) II and IV
   (E) I, III, and IV

ANSWER: **B**. The Great Depression, civil rights movement, and environmental movement all increased the scope of government policy-making. Wars have always been the subject of policy-making (*American Government*, 8th ed., page 436 / 9th ed., page 436).

7. Sometimes policies not demanded by the public nevertheless become items on the political agenda. What explains this?
   (A) Key people in government, the political elites, become interested in certain problems and try to solve them.
   (B) Policy-makers rather than the public set the agenda, so the public has little impact on the political agenda.
   (C) The public does not pay much attention to the policy agenda.
   (D) Members of Congress are more interested in helping their districts than in making policy for the nation.
   (E) The policy-making process is so complicated that it is difficult to determine what the public wants.

ANSWER: **A**. A policy not demanded by the public can be addressed if someone in government is interested in it (*American Government*, 8th ed., pages 437-438 / 9th ed., pages 437-438).

8. Why has the Senate become a major source of political change?
   (A) Senators frequently run for president, so they seek out issues that will garner attention.
   (B) Senators have more time to deliberate than members of the House of Representatives, so they are more able to introduce policies.
   (C) Senators "fly under the radar" more than the president; as a result, they have become policy innovators.
   (D) The Senate has stricter party discipline than the House; as a result, more policies can be enacted.
   (E) Senators are held more accountable to their constituents than representatives are.

ANSWER: **A**. Senators are more visible than representatives, and so more of them run for the presidency. They want to be policy innovators on attention-grabbing issues (*American Government*, 8th ed., page 439 / 9th ed., page 439).

9. Every policy-making decision involves balancing what competing interests?
   (A) the balance between who will write the laws and who will implement them
   (B) the balance between the legislative branch and the executive branch
   (C) the balance between judicial activism and judicial restraint
   (D) the balance between who will benefit and who will bear the costs
   (E) the balance between the powers of the state and federal government

ANSWER: **D**. Under cost-benefit analysis, every policy involves a group that will be helped and a group that will bear the expense. The interests of both groups are considered as part of the policy-making process (*American Government*, 8th ed., page 443 / 9th ed., page 442).

10. What kinds of projects typically are the subject of "logrolling" (exchanging votes on bills)?
   (A) bills that will create new nationwide social programs
   (B) bills involving controversial issues, such as abortion
   (C) bills for funding the military and defense
   (D) bills funding "pork-barrel" projects
   (E) bills regulating the environment

ANSWER: **D**. Logrolling occurs when members of Congress agree to vote for one another's bills. These bills usually contain several projects to benefit specific district and are known as "pork-barrel" legislation (*American Government*, 8th ed., page 444 / 9th ed., page 443).

Free-Response Questions

1. Sometimes policies are adopted that provide benefits to most of society and impose substantial costs on a small group. For EACH of the following, identify a policy that has been adopted, and describe who benefits and who bears the costs.
   environmental policy
   consumer protection policy

RESPONSE: Environmental regulations provide widespread benefits for the public and impose substantial costs on a relatively small group—those who pollute the environment. There are thousands of toxic waste sites nationwide. The Superfund program was developed to force owners of toxic waste sites to clean them up. The Environmental Protection Agency was created to identify those sites and develop clean-up plans. Owners of toxic waste dumps who do not comply with clean-up programs can be fined. There are also heavy penalties for the illegal dumping of toxic waste.

As a result of consumer protection policies, the general public is protected from unsafe products. Ralph Nader founded the consumer protection movement. As a result of this movement, cars are crash tested and given safety ratings. Unsafe products, such as flammable clothing and hazardous baby cribs, are subject to specific government laws regulating their safety. The beneficiaries of these policies are consumers, and the manufacturers pay the costs, although these costs are often passed on to consumers in the form of higher prices (*American Government*, 8th ed., pages 445-446 / 9th ed., pages 444-445).

2. Interest groups compete for favorable policies. Even after policies are passed, interest groups continue to compete as they are enforced. For EACH of the following, identify the major interest groups involved in policy-making and explain how they compete in the process of policy implementation.

                National Labor Relations Board (NLRB)
                Occupational Health and Safety Administration (OSHA)

RESPONSE: The National Labor Relations Board adjudicates disputes between management and labor unions. The president appoints its members. One of the ways management and labor compete is by trying to get their representatives on the NLRB board. Management and labor interpret NRLB decisions differently, and when either side receives an unfavorable ruling, it may decide to take the issue to the courts, where the issue is fought out again.

There is similar competition involving the Occupational Health and Safety Administration, which sets standards for workplace safety. For example, there are limits to how much a worker may be exposed to chemicals. OSHA inspects thousands of workplaces. Companies have criticized the agency for detailed regulations that increase the costs of doing business and result in unnecessary red tape. One struggle between management and labor concerned who would supervise OSHA. It ended up in the Department of Labor, as workers had hoped. However, industry pressured the Reagan administration, and during his presidency, OHSA issued fewer citations (*American Government*, 8th ed., pages 448-449 / 9th ed., pages 448-449).

16

Economic Policy and the Budget

Although the federal government has run deficits for most years since 1969, Americans have never liked the idea of the government spending more money than it receives. Deficits occur when the government spends more than it takes in during a given year. The national debt is the accumulation of deficits over the years. The public is split over two broad philosophies of economic management: manipulating supply or controlling demand. Policy-makers face two big issues: the tax burden, which includes deficits and debt; and economic health.

Key Terms

appropriations bills

budget

budget resolution

Congressional Budget Act of 1974

Council of Economic Advisors (CEA)

deficit

economic planning

entitlements

Federal Reserve Board

Gramm-Rudman Act

Inflation

income tax

Keynesianism

monetarism

Office of Management and Budget (OMB)

pocketbook issue

progressive tax structure

Reaganomics

secretary of the Treasury

Sixteenth Amendment

supply-side tax cut

surplus

tax cut

tax loopholes

Tax Reform Act of 1986

unemployment

KEY CONCEPTS

- Economic health depends on many complex and often unpredictable factors.
- Politicians and economists have conflicting views on how to regulate the economy.
- Economic policy-making involves several parts of the government.
- The budget indicates how much the government will collect in taxes, spend in revenues, and allocate among various programs.

For a full discussion of economic policy and the budget, see *American Government,* 8th ed., Chapter 16 / 9th ed., Chapter 16.

ECONOMIC HEALTH

The deficits of the past thirty-five years have raised ongoing policy debates, yet the surpluses of 1999 and 2000 created controversy as well. Republicans wanted to return the 1999 surplus to the public, while Democrats wanted to use it for new programs. Both sides got some of what they wanted in 2001. Republicans enacted one of three large tax cuts since World War II. Democrats received the assurance that tax cuts would end in 2010, and spending on federal programs was increased.

In the best of times, economic forecasts are uncertain. When the unexpected occurs, they are more uncertain. The past few years have brought the September 11 attacks and subsequent military actions, both of which had significant economic implications. These were followed by a recession, in which tax revenues were sharply reduced and social and military programs required more spending. Economic forecasts made before September 11, 2001, had no chance of being accurate.

Voters see connections between their own economic circumstances, the president, and the nation as a whole. Politicians, especially presidential candidates, worry about the so-called pocketbook issue just before an election. Congressional candidates, especially challengers, can easily evade responsibility for economic conditions, but presidents are the ones who get the blame or the credit for the economy. Voters tend to reelect incumbents if their economic fortunes are good and vote them out of office if their economic fortunes have worsened. Yet voting behavior and economic conditions are not always correlated at national and individual levels. People do not *always* vote their pocketbooks because they understand the government cannot be held accountable for everything.

The reactions of politicians to the pocketbook issue vary. While candidates might take strong stances favoring benefits, such as veterans' pensions and Social Security, in order to gain more votes, incumbents do not always know how to produce desirable economic outcomes. Ideology can play a large role in shaping policy choices, with Democrats favoring a reduction in unemployment and Republicans favoring a reduction in inflation. Republicans tend to manipulate supply in dealing with the economy. Democrats tend to control demand.

THE POLITICS OF TAXING AND SPENDING

> **AP Tip**
>
> Various views of how government can influence the economy are fundamental to understanding economic policy-making and are likely to appear on the AP exam.

When struggling over the politics of taxing and spending, competing politicians offer conflicting recommendations. These include lowering or raising taxes, reducing or increasing the federal debt, and introducing new programs or eliminating old ones that are often costly.

Some of the most prominent economic theories can be summarized as follows:

- **Monetarism** Advocated by the famous economist Milton Friedman, monetarism posits that inflation occurs when there is too much money in the economy chasing after too few goods. Monetarism advocates increasing the money supply at a rate about equal to economic growth, then letting the free market operate. This theory answers the traditional concern that libertarians, conservatives, and Republicans have with inflation.
- **Keynesianism** Derived from the work of the English economist John Maynard Keynes, Keynesianism holds that government should create the right level of demand. The theory assumes that the health of the economy depends on how much of their incomes people save or spend. When demand is too low, government should pump money into the economy by spending more than it collects in taxes. When demand is too high, government should take money out of the economy by increasing taxes or cutting expenditures. This theory answers the traditional concern with unemployment among liberals and Democrats.
- **Economic planning** Some view the free market as too undependable to ensure healthy economic activity. They argue that government should plan parts of a country's economic activity when markets fail to account for the public good. For instance, the prominent economist John Kenneth Galbraith advocated wage and price controls when markets are unable to constrain inflation. Others have argued that government should direct some investments to needed industries that are unable to attract private investment. This is not a popular view in the United States, but it is often found in European, Asian, and African economies.
- **Supply-side tax cuts** Advocates of supply-side tax cuts stress that there is a need for less government interference in the

market and for lower taxes—that lower taxes create incentives for investment, and the greater economic productivity that results will produce more tax revenue. This theory fits with traditional libertarian and conservative political values but ignores political concerns about both inflation and unemployment.

■ **Reaganomics** Set in motion by President Reagan in 1981, Reaganomics is a combination of monetarism, supply-side tax cuts, and domestic budget cutting. The goals sought by Reagan were not entirely consistent. He wanted to reduce the size of the federal government, to stimulate economic growth, and to increase military strength. The inconsistencies in Reaganomics were the result of trying to combine concerns about inflation, economic freedom, unemployment, and increasing military spending. The effects of Reaganomics included the following:

  ■ The economy was stimulated.
  ■ Government spending continued to increase, but at slower rates than before.
  ■ Military spending increased sharply.
  ■ The money supply was controlled, cutting inflation but allowing interest rates to rise.
  ■ Personal income taxes were cut, but Social Security taxes were increased.
  ■ Large deficits were incurred, dramatically increasing the size of the national debt.
  ■ Several important industries, such as the airlines and telephone companies, were deregulated.

THE MACHINERY OF ECONOMIC POLICY-MAKING

Economic policy-making is complicated, and it is conducted by several actors:

■ **Congress** As the most important player in economic policy-making, Congress approves all taxes and almost all expenditures. It consents to wage and price controls when appropriate. It is also internally fragmented, with numerous committees setting economic policy.

■ **Council of Economic Advisers (CEA)** Part of the Executive Office, the CEA includes professional economists sympathetic to the president's view of economics. It forecasts economic trends and analyzes issues. It also prepares the annual economic report that the president sends to Congress.

■ **Office of Management and Budget (OMB)** Also part of the Executive Office, the OMB prepares estimates of amounts to be spent by federal government agencies, as well as negotiates department budgets. It also ensures that the departments' legislative proposals are compatible with the president's program by creating the budget the president submits to Congress.

■ **Secretary of the Treasury** As a member of the president's cabinet, the secretary, often close to or drawn from the world of business and finance, is expected to argue the point of view of the financial community. The secretary provides estimates of the government's revenues and represents the nation with bankers and other nations.

- **The Federal Reserve Board (The Fed)** Members of the Fed are appointed by the president, confirmed by the Senate, and serve nonrenewable fourteen-year terms. Members are removable for cause. The chairman of the Fed serves for four years. The Fed is independent of both the president and Congress. Its most important function is to regulate, insofar as it can, the supply of money (both in circulation and through reserve rates) and the price of money (in the form of interest rates).

Voters and interest groups may lobby for policies that might help only a specific sector. For instance, some interest groups support free trade because free trade makes it easier to sell their goods abroad. Other groups seek subsidies and nontariff trade restrictions because they find it hard to compete with foreign imports.

THE BUDGET

A budget is a policy document that announces how much the government expects to collect in taxes, spend in revenues, and how those expenditures will be allocated among various programs. There was no federal budget before 1921 and no overall presidential budget until the 1930s. Even after presidents began submitting budgets to Congress, congressional committees continued to act on the budget independently.

The Congressional Budget Act of 1974 established procedures to standardize the budgeting process:

- The president submits the budget.
- The House and Senate budget committees study the budget after receiving an analysis from the Congressional Budget Office (CBO).
- Each committee proposes a budget resolution that sets a total budget ceiling, as well as ceilings for each of several spending areas.
- Congress is expected to adopt these resolutions in order to guide its budget debates.
- Congress considers appropriations bills (bills that actually fund programs within established limits) and sees whether they are congruent with the budget resolution.

Big changes in the budget are not possible because approximately two-thirds of government spending is tied up in entitlements (federal programs like Medicare and Social Security that provide benefits to people who meet stipulated criteria). Several efforts have been made to reduce federal spending. The passage of the Gramm-Rudman Balanced Budget Act (1985) was the first to place a cap on spending. It called for automatic cuts from 1986 to 1991 until the federal deficit disappeared. If the president and Congress disagreed on the total spending level, automatic across-the-board cuts would be made. Nevertheless, the president and Congress still found ways to increase spending.

A second attempt was made with the Budget Enforcement Act of 1990. Congress voted a tax increase, and the Budget Enforcement Act capped discretionary funding. If entitlement spending increased, either discretionary spending had to be cut or taxes had to be raised.

Current tax policy reflects a blend of majoritarian and interest group politics. The tax burden is kept reasonably low (Americans pay less than citizens of most other democratic nations do). Most Americans are required to at least pay something. A progressive tax structure in the United States requires higher-income people to pay taxes at rates higher than those for lower-income residents. In addition, tax loopholes (deductions, exemptions, and exclusions) favor certain groups and usually reduce the progressivism of the tax structure. The extent to which taxes are progressive is a matter of dispute. The economic and political results of taxes on income have also been questioned by politicians and economists who think taxes on consumption are fairer and easier to collect.

Income taxes are the major source of federal revenues. Most revenue was derived from tariffs until ratification of the Sixteenth Amendment (1913), which authorized income taxes. For many years tax rates varied, being high during wars and low during peacetime. A sweeping tax reform act (the Tax Reform Act of 1986) lowered rates and decreased deductions. Presidents in the last two decades have often advocated increasing rates while keeping deductions low. The desire to balance the budget has switched policy debates to the issue of tax cuts, but entitlement programs such as Social Security and Medicare remain a challenge to fund.

Attaining national economic health is difficult. While the government can influence the economy's performance through tax policy, monetary policy, the budget, and spending on social programs, a healthy economy requires considerable cooperation across branches of government, accurate economic forecasts, and the right psychology to bring about investment and consumer spending.

Multiple-Choice Questions

1. What is the relationship between voting behavior and economic conditions?
   (A) People who are unemployed are less likely to vote for an incumbent, but voting behavior and economic conditions are not correlated for those who have jobs.
   (B) There is a strong correlation between economic conditions and voting behavior, with people less likely to vote for incumbents in poor economic times.
   (C) Most voters do not believe that the president has much impact on economic conditions, so there is little correlation between voting behavior and the economy.
   (D) Most voters blame Congress when the economy is poor, so incumbent congressmen are more likely than an incumbent president to lose their jobs.
   (E) In poor economic times, incumbents are more likely to be reelected because the public is hesitant to change leadership in hard times.

ANSWER: **B**. Incumbents are less likely to be reelected in hard times (*American Government*, 8th ed., page 461 / 9th ed., page 461).

2. When does a surplus occur?
   (A) when revenues in a given year exceed expenditures
   (B) when expenditures in a given year exceed revenues
   (C) when income tax revenues exceed the revenues from excise taxes
   (D) when the government has excess funds because the national debt has been eliminated.
   (E) when payments have reduced the national debt to a level at which the government can give money to the states in the form of revenue sharing.

ANSWER: **A**. A surplus occurs when revenues exceed expenditures in a given year (*American Government*, 8th ed., page 460 / 9th ed., page 460).

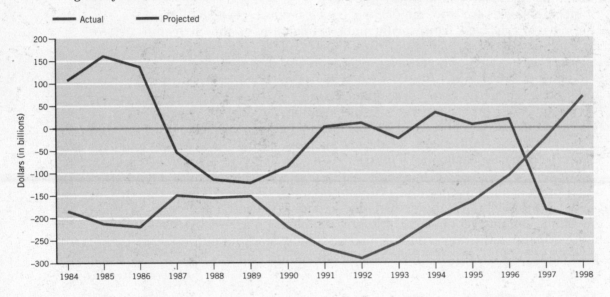

3. The figure above supports which of the following conclusions?
   (A) There were budget deficits from 1984 until 1998.
   (B) The difference between actual and projected deficits and surpluses was greater in 1991 and 1992 than at any other time shown on the chart.
   (C) President Clinton's economic policies resulted in budget surpluses in 1997 and 1998.
   (D) The smallest differences between projected deficits and surpluses and the actual amounts occurred from 1987 to 1989.
   (E) Actual and projected surpluses and deficits have differed more than $75 billion for all the years shown.

ANSWER: **D**. Between 1987 and 1989, budget projections were more accurate (*American Government*, 8th ed., page 460 / 9th ed., page 461).

4. Which of the following statements best reflects the traditional budget ideology of Democrats and Republicans?
    (A) Democrats are more worried about inflation, and Republicans are more worried about unemployment.
    (B) Democrats are more worried about interest rates, and Republicans are more concerned with the money supply.
    (C) Democrats are more worried about unemployment, and Republicans are more worried about inflation.
    (D) Both Democrats and Republicans are more worried about inflation than unemployment.
    (E) It is difficult to determine a particular budget ideology for the political parties because these beliefs change with changing economic conditions.

ANSWER: **C**. Republicans concentrate more on keeping inflation low. Democrats concentrate on lowering unemployment (*American Government*, 8th ed., page 462 / 9th ed., page 462).

5. An economist believes that inflation is caused when there is too much money chasing too few goods. This theory can best be described as
    (A) Keynesianism
    (B) supply-side economics
    (C) Reaganomics
    (D) monetarism
    (E) fiscal conservatism

ANSWER: **D**. Monetarists believe that the government should have a steady and predictable increase in the money supply that is equal to the rate of economic growth (*American Government*, 8th ed., pages 463-464 / 9th ed., page 464).

6. Which of the following is consistent with Reaganomics?
    I.   reduce the size of the federal government
    II. cut social programs
    III. lower taxes
    IV. decrease the money supply

    (A) I and II
    (B) I, II, and III
    (C) II and III
    (D) II, III, and IV
    (E) I, II, III, and IV

ANSWER: **B**. Reaganomics included reducing the size of the federal government, cutting social programs, and lowering taxes. The money supply was held steady to prevent inflation (*American Government*, 8th ed., pages 465-466 / 9th ed., page 465).

7. All of the following are responsibilities of the Federal Reserve Board EXCEPT
   (A) buying and selling federal government securities
   (B) regulating the amount of money a member bank must keep on hand as reserve
   (C) reviewing the federal budget and making recommendations to prevent deficits
   (D) changing the interest rates charged to banks that borrow from the Fed
   (E) setting monetary policy and making predictions about the economy

ANSWER: **C.** The Federal Reserve Board makes economic forecasts and sets monetary policy. This includes establishing the amount of money a bank must keep on reserve and setting the interest rates charged to banks that borrow from the Fed (*American Government*, 8th ed., page 467 / 9th ed., page 467).

8. Which of the following best describes the federal budget?
   (A) It is a document that announces how much the government expects to collect in taxes and how expenditures will be allocated on various programs.
   (B) It is a document that just predicts a bottom line, including the dollar amount of a projected surplus or deficit.
   (C) It is a document that describes the federal debt and proposes a payment plan.
   (D) It is a document that changes over the course of a year, as revenue and expenditures change with the times.
   (E) It is a general policy statement outlining the economic goals of the federal government for the upcoming year.

ANSWER: **A.** The budget is a document announcing proposed revenue collections and explaining how the money will be spent (*American Government*, 8th ed., page 469 / 9th ed., page 469).

9. How do most voters view budget deficits?
   (A) Voters are willing to accept deficits because they are not sophisticated enough to understand the federal budget.
   (B) Voters understand that the federal government runs budget deficits, but they simply do not care.
   (C) Voters are concerned about deficits, but they also want the government to spend money on important public services.
   (D) Voters want money for pet projects that will benefit their states, and they do not care if these projects result in budget deficits.
   (E) The budget deficits were caused by crises that the government could not predict or control.

ANSWER: **C.** Voters are worried about deficits. However, they still want the government to spend money on services, such as schools and health care (*American Government*, 8th ed., page 469 / 9th ed., page 469).

10. What is the viewpoint of the political cartoon above?
    (A) The Internal Revenue Service is making every effort to simplify the tax code.
    (B) Despite the public's desire that the tax code be simplified, this has not happened; it would take a magician to figure it out.
    (C) The Internal Revenue Service has no real incentive to simplify the tax code.
    (D) The tax code can be deciphered, but it takes some research.
    (E) The federal government has not made any effort to simplify the tax code.

ANSWER: **B.** The IRS "sorcerer" is trying to figure out the tax code. Despite efforts to simplify the tax laws, their complexity makes this difficult (*American Government*, 8th ed., page 476 / 9th ed., page 476).

Free-Response Questions

1. Identify and explain three reasons why it is difficult for the government to control the economy.

RESPONSE: One reason it is difficult for the government to control economic outcomes is foreign competition. In many countries labor costs are less than they are in the United States. As a consequence goods made in those countries are less expensive to produce than goods made here. One result of this is that American companies may move their plants overseas, reducing the number of industrial jobs available in the United States and raising unemployment levels. The government can try to control this through our trade policies, but industries that sell goods abroad want free trade. Thus it is difficult for the government to control international trade.

Another reason it is difficult for the government to control the economy is that some decisions affect the economy in both positive and negative ways. For example, decisions to reduce inflation can require the government to raise interest rates. It becomes more expensive for new businesses to get start-up loans. It is also more expensive for ongoing businesses to borrow the money they need to expand their productivity. The result might be a slower economy.

Finally, unexpected events, such as terrorist attacks, can make it difficult for the government to control the economy. After the attacks of September 11, 2001, the airline industry lost passengers and revenues because some people were afraid to fly. The wars in Afghanistan and Iraq that followed the attacks were expensive, and the government had not budgeted for them. The result was a deficit that the government had not anticipated just a year earlier (*American Government*, 8th ed., page 460, 462, 468-469 / 9th ed., pages 460, 462, 468-469).

2. Identify and explain how Keynesianism, monetarism, and supply-side economics have been used to make economic policy.

RESPONSE: Keynesianism is the idea that during tough economic times the government should raise the demand for goods and services. This will increase production and the employment rate. Under this theory, the government should pump money into the economy, often by creating public works projects. The best examples of the use of Keynesian economics are the programs of the New Deal, such as the Works Progress Administration. While these programs did not end the Great Depression, they did lessen unemployment and reduce the depression's effects.

Monetarism is the theory that the government should increase the money supply to keep up with economic growth and limit other kinds of regulations so that the market can operate freely. This policy was used by the Reagan administration, along with supply-side economics. The money supply was controlled in order to combat inflation. Because of this, interest rates were allowed to rise.

Supply-side economics was also used during the Reagan administration. This is the theory that fewer government regulations, less government planning, and tax cuts will stimulate the economy. Regulations put forth by administrative agencies, such as OHSA, were streamlined, domestic spending was cut, and tax rates were lowered. This stimulated the economy. However, this policy was coupled with an increase in defense spending that resulted in a deficit (*American Government*, 8th ed., pages 463-466 / 9th ed., pages 464-465).

17

DOMESTIC POLICY: SOCIAL WELFARE AND THE ENVIRONMENT

The politics of social welfare and the environment are controversial, largely because they often create winners and losers.

KEY TERMS

acid rain

Aid to Families with Dependent Children (AFDC)

bubble standards

Clean Air Act of 1970

Clean Air Act of 1990

Endangered Species Act

entitlements

environmental impact statements (EIC)

Environmental Protection Agency (EPA)

food stamps

global warming

means test

Medicaid

Medicare

Medicare Act of 1965

offsets

pollution allowances

Social Security

Social Security Act of 1935

Temporary Assistance for
    Needy Families (TANF)

KEY CONCEPTS

■ The cornerstones of social welfare policy in the United States are Social Security and Medicare.

■ Environmental policy illustrates the various forms of policy-making in the United States.

For a full discussion of domestic policy as it pertains to social welfare and the environment, see *American Government,* 8th ed., Chapters 17 and 21 / 9th ed., Chapters 17 and 21.

SOCIAL WELFARE POLITICS AND POLICY

The United States has two types of social welfare programs. The first includes programs that are available to everyone regardless of income, such as Social Security and Medicare. These programs are known as entitlements because Congress has obligated itself to pay these benefits to all those old enough to receive them. The second type includes programs that are available only to those whose income falls below a certain level, such as Medicaid and the Food Stamps program. In these programs, means tests are applied to determine if incomes are below a certain level.

Social welfare policy in the United States has developed differently than it has in most other nations. There are several reasons for this. First, many Americans have taken a restrictive view of who deserves to benefit from social welfare. The public often insists that only those who cannot help themselves should benefit. Second, the United States has been slower than most countries in embracing welfare policy. When Congress passed the Social Security Act in 1935, twenty-two European nations already had similar programs. It was not until the reinterpretation of the Constitution in the 1930s that the federal government was allowed to enact social welfare policy. Third, state governments and private enterprises play a significant role in administering programs in the United States.

Two significant acts are the cornerstone of social welfare programs:

■ **The Social Security Act of 1935** When the Great Depression struck in 1929, private charities and city relief programs were overwhelmed. The election of 1932 brought Franklin Roosevelt to the presidency and a wave of Democrats to Congress. Roosevelt's cabinet created two kinds of programs. The first would provide insurance for the unemployed and elderly, to which workers would contribute and from which they would benefit when they became unemployed or retired. The second would provide assistance for dependent children, the blind, and the elderly. The federal government would use its power to tax to provide the funds, but except for old-age insurance, all of the programs would be administered by the states. Everyone would be eligible for the insurance programs. Means tests would be used to measure those eligible for assistance programs.

■ **The Medicare Act of 1965** Medical benefits were omitted from the Social Security Act in 1935 in order to ensure its passage. For thirty years various policy entrepreneurs lobbied for a national health care plan that would win a congressional majority. The 1964 elections brought a huge Democratic majority to Congress. A new Medicare bill applied only to the aged (those over the age of sixty-five), so that the costs of the program would be limited. The program would cover only hospital bills and not doctors' bills so that doctors would not be regulated. The original proposal was broadened to include Medicaid for the poor and payment of doctors' bill for the elderly.

AP Tip

Both Social Security and Medicare are controversial policies in the United States. The problems of funding them cut across several aspects of the policy-making process and will likely appear in some form on the AP exam.

Both Social Security and Medicare are currently under scrutiny because of potential problems some see on the horizon. There will soon be an insufficient number of people paying Social Security taxes to provide benefits for every retired person. Several solutions have been offered, but they are opposed by the public and therefore politically dangerous. These include:

- raising the retirement age to seventy, freezing retirement benefits, and raising Social Security taxes
- privatizing Social Security
- combining the first two reforms and allowing citizens to invest a portion of their Social Security taxes in mutual funds

One part of the Social Security Act received enough negative attention to force its demise. The Aid to Families with Dependent Children (AFDC) was scarcely noticed when it was enacted in the 1930s. Initially the AFDC involved giving federal aid to existing state programs. It allowed states to determine what constituted need, to set benefit levels, and to administer the program.

The program became less acceptable to the public over the years. Many viewed the recipients as undeserving. States became constrained by increasing numbers of federal regulations. Expensive programs were added, such as Food Stamps and Earned Income Tax Credit (a cash grant to poor parents who work). Increasingly, the recipients of aid were unwed mothers who had been assisted for more than eight years. The AFDC increasingly lost political legitimacy until it was abolished in 1996. The abolition of the AFDC is an excellent example of how public perceptions can change policy. During the Great Depression more people were seen as deserving of aid. Perceptions changed in the 1980s and recipients were viewed as undeserving.

In its place the Temporary Assistance for Needy Families (TANF) program was established. Each state is allocated a federal block grant to help pay the costs of providing TANF. Adults can receive TANF benefits for only five years. Aid is reduced to women who do not help identify the fathers of their children. Unmarried mothers under age eighteen are eligible for benefits only if they live with their parents and attend school.

Medicare is also very costly and has the potential to encourage waste and fraud. One possible solution is to nationalize health care, but national health care plans have always faced resistance in the policy-making process. Alternatives to Medicare include having the elderly locate their own health maintenance organization (HMO) coverage and diverting any budget surpluses to the program. Health care issues will remain on the political agenda because the baby boomer population is aging and government health care expenditures continue to grow. The issue is also important to powerful interest groups, such as the American Association of Retired Persons (AARP) and the American Medical Association (AMA).

Social welfare policy is an excellent example of the different patterns of policy-making that exist in the United States. Policies that benefit most or all Americans, such as Social Security and Medicare, are widely supported and amended only with great difficulty. These are examples of majoritarian politics. Policies that benefit relatively few Americans but are paid for by many, such as AFDC, are constantly in jeopardy of being reduced or even abolished. These typify a pattern of client politics.

THE POLITICS OF ENVIRONMENTAL PROTECTION

Environmental policy is very controversial. Environmental issues almost always create those who benefit and those who pay. Those who pay are generally indignant. Another reason environmental policy is controversial is that environmental issues are shrouded in scientific uncertainty, making problems and their solutions uncertain. The United States has a number of political features that make its environmental policy different from policies found in other countries. These include an adversarial political culture, conflict between government and business, and the distribution of monitoring standards to the states.

Environmental issues illustrate all of the styles of policy-making in the United States, including entrepreneurial politics, majoritarian politics, interest group politics, and client politics.

ENVIRONMENTALISM AND ENTREPRENEURIAL POLITICS

In entrepreneurial politics, an unorganized public benefits from the efforts of a well-organized group. The issues of global warming and endangered species reveal the workings of entrepreneurial politics.

Global warming refers to the theory that gases produced when people burn fossil fuels get trapped in the atmosphere, causing the earth's temperature to rise. When the temperature goes up, negative consequences may follow. Floods on coastal areas may occur as polar ice camps melt, and severe weather may produce more destructive storms. There is no consensus in the scientific community regarding the consequences of global warming. Activists, motivated by information provided by scientists, have had great influence regarding global warming. By mobilizing the media, dramatizing the issue, and convincing members of Congress that their reputations will suffer if they do not cast the right vote, activists have provoked action. In 1997 the Kyoto Protocol was signed by the United States, pledging the nation to lower emissions of greenhouse gases such as carbon dioxide by 30 percent. Some fear that complying with the Kyoto Protocol could have severe negative effects on the economy. Others have suggested that the research and innovation necessary to meet the Kyoto goals would spark economic growth, as the space race did. President Bush has opposed the treaty, primarily because the burdens of meeting the Kyoto goals fall more heavily on industrialized nations like the United States and are more forgiving to industrializing countries with which our businesses compete.

Another example of entrepreneurial politics is the Endangered Species Act of 1973. Passed as the result of the efforts of well-organized environmentalists, the act forbids killing a protected species and adversely affecting its habitat. Firms and government agencies that want to build a dam, bridge, or factory in an area where an endangered species lives must comply with federal regulations protecting the endangered plants or animals.

ENVIRONMENTALISM AND MAJORITARIAN POLITICS

In majoritarian politics, the public benefits but also incurs the costs of a policy. One example of environmental policy that illustrates majoritarian politics is the Clean Air Act of 1970, which imposed tough restrictions on automobile emissions. At first the public supported it. However, one provision changed the initial support to opposition: any area where smog was a problem (for example, New York, Denver, Los Angeles), even after emission controls, would have to restrict the public's use of cars. Efforts to enforce these rules failed. This issue illustrates that the public will support tough environmental laws when somebody else pays or when the costs are hidden, but not when they have to pay for it themselves—especially when the payment takes the form of changing how and when to use the family car.

A second example of environmentalism and majoritarian politics is the National Environmental Policy Act of 1969 (NEPA). This legislation contained a provision requiring that an environmental impact statement (EIS) be filed before any government agency or private entity undertakes an activity that will significantly affect the quality of the human environment. Opponents of virtually any government-backed project have used environmental impact statements to block, change, or delay the project. Despite the grumbling of many people adversely affected by fights over these impact statements, popular support for the law remains strong because the public at large does not believe that it is paying a high price and does believe that it is gaining a significant benefit.

Majoritarian politics can also be seen in the public's general opposition to proposals to raise gasoline taxes. Although higher taxes would discourage driving and reduce smog, people are hesitant to embrace the policy because they would pay the tax first and benefit only much later.

ENVIRONMENTALISM AND INTEREST GROUP POLITICS

Interest group politics occur when two organized groups with a stake in the outcome fight over who will pay and who will benefit. The issue of acid rain is a good example of interest group politics. Acid rain is rain, snow, or dust particles that are acidic when they fall to the ground. One source of acid rain is coal, which contains sulfur. When several eastern lakes were acidified and several eastern forests were destroyed by acid in the 1970s, midwestern steel mills and electric power plants that burn high-sulfur coal were blamed because prevailing winds tend to carry the sulfur eastward. Two well-organized groups emerged to fight over the issue. Residents of Canada and New England sought to reap financial benefits from the midwestern businesses, which feared the potential costs. One solution called for the mills to burn low-sulfur coal. This might have been effective but also expensive because low-sulfur coal comes from the West, increasing transportation costs. Another alternative was to install smokestack scrubbers. This is also costly and not always effective. When confronted with the issue, Congress voted for scrubbers on all new plants. This policy protected jobs and pleased environmentalists as well. When the scrubbers did not work, a stalemate took hold for thirteen years. Eventually a two-step regulation was proposed that became part of the Clean Air Act of 1990. Before 1995 some plants could choose their approach to reducing emissions by a fixed amount. After 1995 sharper emission reductions for many more plants would be imposed, requiring the use of some scrubbers. When confronted with interest group politics, Congress tends to find workable compromises, rather than pass sweeping legislation.

ENVIRONMENTALISM AND CLIENT POLITICS

Client politics occur when an organized group gets a benefit and an unorganized public must pay. Farmers have successfully resisted efforts to sharply restrict the use of pesticides. American farmers are the most productive in the world, and most of them believe that they cannot achieve that output without using pesticides. Although often attacked by environmental organizations, farm groups have generally been successful at practicing client politics. Very few pesticides have been taken off the market, and those that have been removed tend to be ones clearly harm the environment—for example, the effect of DDT on birds. One reason few pesticides have been removed from the market is that they have undetermined effects on long-term human health problems, such as cancer. Another reason is that farm groups have very powerful supporters in Congress.

Formulating consistent environmental policies has proven difficult. One problem is that environmental problems are not clear-cut—even scientists often differ in their opinions about environmental matters. Another problem is that public opinion changes, sometimes altering the goals of environmental policy. A third problem is deciding on how goals should be achieved. Issuing rules and enforcing them in court (command-and-control strategy) is not always the wisest policy; this strategy falsely assumes that rule-makers and rule-enforcers know how to achieve the greatest environmental gain at the least cost.

All of these uncertainties have become part of the political controversies surrounding the Environmental Protection Agency (EPA), which is responsible for administering pollution and environmental programs. The EPA must try to identify problems and develop regulations. Congressional demands sometimes intervene and shift priorities. The EPA must also determine the costs and benefits of a policy, even when the public does not distinguish between realistic and unrealistic threats. Then the EPA must set goals, which are often unrealistic and require extensions and revisions. The method of achieving goals has changed from command-and-control strategy to offering incentives, which include the following:

- **Offsets** If a company wants to open a new plant in an area with polluted air, it can do so if the pollution it generates is offset by a reduction in pollution from another source in that area. To achieve this reduction, the new company may buy an existing company and close it down.
- **Bubble standard** A bubble is the total amount of air pollution that can come from a given factory. A company is free to decide which specific sources within that factory must be reduced and how to meet the bubble standard.
- **Pollution allowances, or banks** If a company reduces its polluting emissions by more than the law requires, it can either bank this excess to cover a future plant expansion or sell it to another company as an offset.

Although Americans think that their environment has degenerated, some aspects of it have in fact improved. In particular, progress has been made with air standards. Improvements in water quality are less certain. Hazardous waste and pesticide reduction remain major problems.

Multiple-Choice Questions

1. All of the following statements about America's social welfare policy-making are true EXCEPT
   (A) Americans would prefer that the needy be given services rather than money
   (B) Americans believe in help for the "deserving poor."
   (C) the United States did not provide social welfare benefits until relatively late, in comparison with much of Europe
   (D) Americans support redistribution of wealth to provide everyone with a fair share
   (E) Americans are uncomfortable giving money to people who are already working or could work if they wanted to

ANSWER: **D**. American social welfare policies were created long after those in most European countries. Americans believe that welfare should be given to the deserving poor and favor giving services rather than money (*American Government*, 8th ed., pages 481-482 / 9th ed., pages 481-482).

2. Which of the following are major social welfare programs?
   I.   Medicare and Medicaid
   II. Social Security
   III. national health care
   IV. unemployment insurance

   (A) I and II
   (B) I, II, and III
   (C) II and III
   (D) III and IV
   (E) I, II, and IV

ANSWER: E.   Major   social   welfare   programs   include   Medicare, Medicaid, Social Security, and unemployment insurance. Americans do not have national health care (*American Government*, 8th ed., page 483 / 9th ed., page 483).

3. Why did Social Security meet popular demands and fit within the framework of American beliefs about social welfare?
   (A) because it was viewed as an insurance program that would be available to all Americans who contributed, whether rich or poor
   (B) because it was an insurance program that would be available to all Americans on a voluntary basis
   (C) because it would be available to middle-class and poor Americans as a kind of retirement savings account
   (D) because it was a means-tested program to help those who could not afford retirement
   (E) because it was a means of redistributing wealth, and that philosophy had great popular appeal during the Great Depression

ANSWER: **A**. Social Security is available to all Americans, rich or poor, who contribute. It was viewed as an insurance program (although it has become more of an inter-generational contract) (*American Government*, 8th ed., page 484 / 9th ed., page 484).

4. All of the following solutions have been proposed to make sure there is enough Social Security when future generations retire EXCEPT
   (A) raise the retirement age
   (B) freeze the level of retirement benefits
   (C) end the program entirely by the year 2040
   (D) privatize Social Security so that people could invest those funds in the stock market
   (E) permit citizens to invest some of their Social Security taxes in carefully chosen mutual funds

ANSWER: **C**.   There   are   several   proposals   to   save   Social   Security, including raising the retirement age, freezing benefits, and privatizing all or part of the system (*American Government*, 8th ed., page 486 / 9th ed., page 486).

5. In 1996 Aid to Families with Dependent Children (AFDC) was abolished. Why did support for AFDC weaken?
   (A) Many recipients were unwed mothers who had been on the program for more than eight years.
   (B) Many recipients were children in families in which both parents were working.
   (C) Many recipients were widows who did not obtain employment upon the death of their husbands.
   (D) Many recipients were disabled and were unable to work full-time.
   (E) Support for the program did not weaken, but the government was unable to continue the program in the face of a weak economy.

ANSWER: **A.** Support for AFDC weakened because the public became less sympathetic to the recipients. Many were unwed mothers who had been receiving assistance for more than eight years (*American Government*, 8th ed., pages 487-488 / 9th ed., page 488).

6. What is the impact of filing an environmental impact statement (EIS)?
   (A) None. It is merely a statement and does not require any specific action.
   (B) The statement notifies federal authorities of the potential environmental damage caused by a project, and the government may file an injunction to block the project.
   (C) Opponents have used the EIS as a way of blocking, changing, or delaying projects.
   (D) The EIS notifies the public of the impact of a project and outlines specific steps the builder will take to prevent environmental damage.
   (E) The EIS must show that environmental damage will be minimal, or the federal government will not approve the project.

ANSWER: **C.** The EIS is a statement of the probable impact of a project on the environment. Environmental interest groups can then mobilize to block, change, or delay the project (*American Government*, 8th ed., page 591 / 9th ed., page 591).

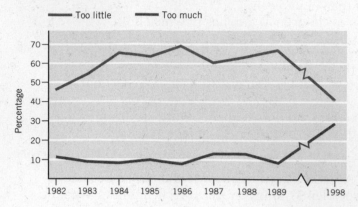

QUESTION *In general do you think there is too much, too little . . . government regulation and involvement in the area of environmental protection?**

7. The chart above supports which of the following conclusions?
   (A) From 1982 until 1998 most Americans believed that the government was doing too little to protect the environment.
   (B) The number of environmental regulations increased from 1989 to 1998.
   (C) Most Americans believe there is too much government regulation of the environment.
   (D) In 1986 almost 70 percent of Americans believed that the government was not doing enough to regulate the environment.
   (E) There is no correlation between the percentage of Americans who believe the government is regulating the environment too much and those who think there is not enough regulation.

ANSWER: **D.** In 1986 nearly 70 percent of Americans thought the government was not involved enough in environmental protection (*American Government,* 8th ed., page 594 / 9th ed., page 594).

8. When is a pesticide most likely to be taken off the market?
   (A) when independent scientists determine that it harms the environment
   (B) when the National Institute of Health finds that it might cause cancer
   (C) when there has been an incident that caused heavy media coverage
   (D) when a manufacturer voluntarily decides to remove it because of the research of the company's scientists
   (E) when farmers protest the use of the pesticide

ANSWER: **C.** A pesticide is most likely to be taken off the market when there is well-publicized environmental harm, such as the impact of DDT on birds (*American Government,* 8th ed., pages 595-596 / 9th ed., page 595).

9. Issuing environmental regulations and then enforcing them in court is an example of which kind of regulatory policy?
   (A) command and control
   (B) incentive
   (C) responsible use
   (D) discretionary
   (E) cost-benefit analysis

ANSWER: **A.** Command-and-control strategy seeks to improve air and water quality by setting detailed pollutions standards and rules and enforcing them in court (*American Government*, 8th ed., page 597 / 9th ed., page 597).

10. All of the following are used by the Environmental Protection Agency (EPA) in regulating pollution EXCEPT
    (A) offsets, by which a company can open a new plant if it reduces pollution from another source in that area
    (B) bringing lawsuits to impose fines and penalties for noncompliance
    (C) bubble standards, by which a factory is allowed a total amount of pollution and can determine how to meet that standard
    (D) pollution allowances, by which companies who reduce pollution may sell credits to other companies
    (E) standardization, by which the pollution levels for industries throughout the country are set at similar levels.

ANSWER: **E.** The EPA provides for offsets, bubbles, and pollution credits. When businesses fail to comply with environmental regulations, they may be taken to court (*American Government*, 8th ed., page 598 / 9th ed., page 598).

Free-Response Questions

1. Social Security and Medicare are badly in need of reform if they are to continue for future generations. For each program, identify the problem it is facing and explain one possible solution to that problem.

RESPONSE: Social Security is facing a crisis. Rather than being an individual retirement fund, as was originally envisioned, it is now an intergenerational contract. The problem is that soon there will not be enough people working to support the people who have retired. This is because new groups, such as the disabled, have been added to the program. In addition the retirement of the baby boomers will add millions of new recipients. Furthermore, the amounts contributed to the system are not enough to make ends meet with inflation. One proposal to alleviate this problem is to allow people to invest their Social Security funds in the stock market. The market usually performs better than mutual funds or savings accounts in the long run. However, there is the risk that people will lose their retirement funds in unsafe investments.

Medicare pays for the health care costs of those who qualify for Social Security benefits. With an aging population and expensive life-saving technologies, the costs of medical care have skyrocketed. Because people can go to the doctor whenever they want, sometimes they visit the doctor when it is not necessary. Although the vast majority of doctors are honest, some have overcharged Medicare patients because the government is picking up the tab. One possible solution would be to nationalize health care, although Clinton's plan to provide national health care coverage failed in Congress. Another potential solution would be for the government to provide Medicare money that could be used to purchase private health insurance (*American Government*, 8th ed., pages 486-487 / 9th ed., pages 486-487).

2. For TWO of the issues below, identify two competing interests and explain how the policy-making process has addressed those issues:
   endangered species
   acid rain
   automobile emissions

RESPONSE: The Endangered Species Act forbids any action that would harm a plant or animal on the endangered list. This list consists of species whose population has diminished so much that they need special protection. The two competing interests involved in making this policy are developers and environmentalists. The Endangered Species Act has prevented the building of dams, industrial buildings, and residential housing and altered farming. Developers complain that their property interests are being sacrificed. Sometimes the species being protected—for example, the snail darter—are obscure. The public as a whole, however, supports protecting endangered species.

Acid rain is created when the runoff from factories is turned into precipitation that contains sulfur and other acidic compounds. Steel mills and electric power plants, large sources of acid rain, have an interest in keeping their plants running. Acid rain has spoiled lakes and killed trees in New England and Canada. The residents of these areas, along with the fishing and logging industries, are affected. The first solution that was tried was the addition of scrubbers to clean the air, but they didn't work very well. The 1990 Clean Air Act contained provisions that gave something to each of the interest groups. Power plants are required to reduce sulfur emissions. Coal miners who were laid off as a result of their employers' compliance with the new limits were provided with some compensation.

The Clean Air Act regulates automobile emissions. People who drive cars, as well as automobile manufacturers, have an interest in both car prices and gas prices. Everyone has an interest in breathing clean air. Automobile engines were designed to pollute less and be more fuel efficient, but they were more expensive. States had to design programs, including rapid transit, to reduce air pollution. The deadlines of the Clean Air Act were hard to meet for both states and automobile manufacturers, and they were extended several times. States like California and Colorado continue to work on plans to reduce smog (*American Government*, 8th ed., pages 588, 590-594 / 9th ed., pages 588, 590-594).

18

FOREIGN AND MILITARY POLICY

The terrorist attacks of September 11, 2001, created a new focus and a new set of problems for American foreign policymakers. Yet dealing with foreign terrorists still involves many traditional questions: How great are the powers of the president? What role should Congress play? How important is public opinion?

KEY TERMS

chain of command

commander in chief

containment

disengagement

human rights

"imperial presidency"

isolationism

Joint Chiefs of Staff

military-industrial complex

national security adviser

National Security Council (NSC)

State Department

War Powers Act

KEY CONCEPTS

- The Constitution creates a power struggle between the president and Congress over foreign policy.
- World War II created a need to coordinate foreign policy in new ways.
- Differing worldviews among the political elites have dominated the nation's foreign policy.
- The defense budget creates controversies regarding military expenditures.

- Military decision-making involves a structure that starts with the president and moves through the various services of the military.

For a full discussion of foreign and military policy, see *American Government,* 8th ed., Chapter 20 / 9th ed., Chapter 20.

THE CONSTITUTIONAL AND LEGAL CONTEXT

The Constitution's ambiguous definition of the foreign policy powers of the president and Congress invites conflict:

- The president is the commander in chief, but Congress appropriates money for foreign and military operations.
- The president appoints ambassadors, but the Senate confirms them.
- The president negotiates treaties, but the Senate must ratify them with a two-thirds vote.
- Although Americans often think the president is in charge of foreign policy, only Congress can regulate commerce with other nations and declare war.

Presidents seem to have great power when they deploy American troops or engage in international diplomacy. Critics of a president's policies have referred to the "imperial presidency"—the tendency for the president to act unilaterally in foreign affairs. By the standards of others nations, however, the ability of an American president to act decisively often appears modest.

The Supreme Court has ruled that the federal government has foreign policy powers beyond those specifically mentioned in the Constitution. The Court has been reluctant to intervene in disputes between the president and Congress over war powers. Therefore the actions taken by presidents during wartime that have struck many as unconstitutional have generally been allowed by the Court (for example, Japanese-American relocation camps during World War II).

Checks on presidential power in regards to foreign policy are chiefly political rather than constitutional. Congress controls appropriations and can resist funding a president's policy. Congress can also limit the president's ability to give military or economic aid to other countries.

AP Tip

The War Powers Act represents the ongoing struggle between the president and Congress for control of foreign policy and is often on the AP exam.

Congress tried to limit the president's control of the use of military force by passing the War Powers Act in 1973. It contained a couple of important provisions:

- The president must report all commitments of troops in hostile situations within forty-eight hours.
- The president may make only a sixty-day commitment of troops, unless there is a declaration of Congressional approval.

The War Powers Act has had very little influence on American military actions. Every president since its passage has sent troops abroad without congressional approval. Presidents believe the act is unconstitutional. Furthermore, Congress has been reluctant to cut off appropriations for popular military actions.

One other check that Congress has on the president's foreign policy powers is oversight of intelligence committees. House and Senate intelligence committees must be fully informed of all intelligence activities, including any covert operations. Committees have no authority to disapprove of any covert actions, but Congress as a whole has attempted to block covert actions (for example, military aid to the Nicaraguan contras).

Important military interventions since 1960 include the following:

- 1961: U.S.-sponsored invasion of Cuba at Bay of Pigs, which failed
- 1961-1975: U.S. troops in Vietnam
- 1962: U.S. naval blockade of Cuba to prevent installation of Soviet missiles
- 1965: U.S. occupying troops in the Dominican Republic to block takeover by communist regime
- 1980: Unsuccessful military effort to rescue U.S. hostages in Iran
- 1981: U.S. military advisers in El Salvador to help the government
- 1982-1989: CIA support for antigovernment guerrillas in Nicaragua
- 1983: U.S. Marines in Lebanon as peacekeeping force (withdrawn in 1984)
- 1983: U.S. invasion of Grenada to oust pro-Cuba government
- 1984: U.S. minesweepers in the Red Sea to clear mines
- 1987: U.S. Navy to escort tankers through Persian Gulf
- 1989: U.S. invasion of Panama to oust dictator Manuel Noriega
- 1991: U.S. troops, together with those from other countries, to force Iraq to end its invasion of Kuwait
- 2001: U.S. attacks in Afghanistan to end Taliban regime
- 2003: U.S. attacks in Iraq

FOREIGN POLICY-MAKING SINCE WORLD WAR II

The United States emerged from World War II as the most powerful country in the world, and this status has created several consequences. The president has become more involved in foreign affairs, and the size of the government has expanded considerably. More agencies are needed to shape foreign policy, not just the State Department, which had traditionally fulfilled this role. Most of the agencies that now influence foreign affairs owe no political or bureaucratic loyalty to the State Department.

The National Security Council (NSC) was created to coordinate all departments and agencies that play a role in foreign policy. The NSC is chaired by the president and includes the vice president and the secretaries of state and defense. The director of the Central Intelligence Agency (CIA), the chairman of the Joint Chiefs of Staff, and the attorney general are usually included as well. The national security adviser heads the staff of the NSC. The goal of the staff is to present various perspectives, facilitate presidential decision-making, and implement presidential decisions. The NSC has grown in influence since the 1960s, and the national security adviser often rivals the secretary of state in influencing policy.

Public opinion and elite opinion are the most important factors in making foreign policy. Prior to World War II the general public often opposed U.S. involvement in world affairs. World War II changed this because the war was popular, successful, and created a position of world leadership for the United States. Support for active involvement in foreign affairs persisted until Vietnam. Since Vietnam, popular support for active involvement has been inconsistent. The public usually backs the president in times of crisis, but it is not as prone to be supportive at other times.

THE FOREIGN POLICY ELITE

The general public is often poorly informed about foreign policy. Therefore the views of the political elites tend to dominate opinions on foreign affairs. Four worldviews have dominated the political elites since the 1920s:

- **Isolationism** During the 1920s and 1930s, most elites were opposed to getting involved in wars. This view was adopted after World War I because the war accomplished little while causing many American deaths.
- **Containment** Pearl Harbor ended isolationist views for most in the United States. After the success of World War II, most elites reacted strongly to the mistake of appeasing Hitler before the war. Postwar policy centered on resisting Soviet expansionism.
- **Disengagement** As a reaction to the failures in Vietnam during the 1960s and 1970s, many political elites sought disengagement from heavy American involvement in international affairs. This was a new isolationism.
- **Human rights** The 1990s brought the view that the nation's foreign policy must assure human rights internationally. In particular, the prevention of genocide has become a foreign policy goal because of the mass murders in Bosnia during the 1990s. However the policy has been applied unevenly, as African genocides persist.

A different post-Cold War view seemed to be driving the Bush administration as it responds to the 9/11 attacks. This includes policies that advocate unilateral and preemptive actions to protect the United States and its allies.

THE DEFENSE BUDGET

There are two prevailing views regarding military expenditures. Some see military spending as an example of majoritarian politics—every taxpayer pays for military expenditures, but everyone also receives protection. Others view military spending as an example of client politics—every taxpayer pays, but it is the generals, defense contractors, and members of Congress who benefit from large military expenditures. In this view, the military budget reflects the lobbying skills of the military-industrial complex, which is made up of the Defense Department and the industries that build military weapons. To sort out these competing claims, it is necessary to understand how America raises and spends its defense dollars.

The peacetime military was very small until 1950. Then, because of the Soviet threat, there was no disarmament after the Korea War. The Cold War military was designed to repel Soviet invasions around the world. Current levels of military spending reflect the public's general support of a large military in the postwar period.

The demise of the Soviet Union in the late 1980s and early 1990s generated a debate about the peacetime military. Liberals wanted sharp defense cuts. Conservatives wanted moderate cuts but a well-funded military to protect against a still dangerous world. Military actions in the Middle East and Bosnia during the 1990s demonstrated that military force was still an important option for American foreign policy. Escalating tensions around the world (for example, Iran and North Korea) provide evidence that a strong military may still be necessary.

When Americans pay taxes that fund the military, they finance a force designed to meet the needs of the new century. The war on terrorism has already been fought very differently from the massive land wars of World War I and World War II. The modern military relies on special forces, allies itself with guerrilla fighters, and demands that all services of the military work in close coordination. The Defense Department faces the challenge of meeting these new needs while still being prepared for traditional threats. The United States needs a state-of-the-art military for the nation's ongoing protection.

Those who see the military as a bastion of client politics cite many controversies and inconsistencies within the military and its budget that spring from self-interest:

■ The purchase of "big-ticket items," such as submarines, airplanes, or missiles, has led to enormous cost overruns. The main reasons for these include unpredictability of cost, the tendency of contractors to underestimate cost, the desire for the best weaponry (termed gold plating), a lack of competitive bids, and the stretching out of production deadlines by Congress over several years.

- "Small-ticket items" sometimes have seemingly outrageous price tags. Coffee makers, especially made to function on a military plane, cost $7,600.
- Privatization of some functions previously handled by the military (like feeding and housing troops) has saved money in peacetime, but it is very costly during conflicts. Eyebrows are raised when profits go to American companies with connections to political leaders.
- Readiness and training of personnel are often the favorite areas for short-term budget cuts, though many argue that these should be the highest priority. Cuts in other areas of the defense budget are bound to hurt a geographic area and are resisted by congressmen representing that area.
- The threat to close military bases is controversial. For many years bases were often opened but seldom closed. A congressional commission issued a report in 1988 that led to extensive closings in 1989 and 1991. A new commission is in the process of evaluating further closings, but congressmen from the areas affected know that the local economy could be harmed, and they fight to keep the bases open.

THE STRUCTURE OF MILITARY DECISION-MAKING

The formal structure for military decision-making has in large part been created since World War II. The structure reflects some concerns that go back to the time of the Founders, particularly the desire to ensure civilian control over the military. The president is commander in chief under the Constitution. The chain of command runs from him to the secretary of defense and then to the various unified and specified commands of each service.

The Joint Chiefs of Staff (JCS) is composed of the uniformed heads of each service of the military. The JCS chair and vice chair are appointed by the president and confirmed by the Senate. The JCS does not have command authority over troops, but it does play a key role in defense planning.

The president and the secretary of defense must find ways to transform the military into an organization that will be effective at fighting terrorists while maintaining its traditional roles. Design of the armed services and the delegation of new tasks and challenges will be large issues in the coming years. This is likely to produce an increase in military expenditures.

Multiple-Choice Questions

1. All of the following are struggles over foreign policy between the president and Congress EXCEPT
    (A) the president is commander in chief, but Congress must authorize funding for the armed forces
    (B) the president appoints ambassadors, but the Senate must confirm them
    (C) the president negotiates treaties, but the Senate must ratify them with a two-thirds vote
    (D) the president declares war, but Congress must authorize troop deployments
    (E) the president appoints ambassadors, but the Senate must confirm them

ANSWER: **D**. Congress has the power to declare war, although the War Powers Act allows the president to commit troops for sixty days (*American Government*, 8th ed., pages 554-555 / 9th ed., page 555).

2. Which of the following statements best describes the "imperial presidency"?
    (A) The president can overstep his constitutional powers by making unilateral foreign policy decisions that create an "empire" in foreign affairs.
    (B) Presidents have used their powers in foreign policy to create empires overseas.
    (C) Presidents must rely on Congress for funding and troops, so they cannot act unilaterally.
    (D) Presidents have only those powers specifically given to them in the Constitution, yet they are still able to influence foreign policy in significant ways.
    (E) Presidents are given more power over domestic affairs, allowing them to create an empire at home.

ANSWER: **A**. Arthur Schlesinger, Jr. used the term "imperial presidency" to criticize presidents who, in his opinion, overstepped their constitutional authority by acting unilaterally in foreign affairs (*American Government*, 8th ed., page 557 / 9th ed., page 557).

3. What position has the Supreme Court generally taken regarding foreign affairs?
    (A) The Court has intervened to prevent the president from committing troops without congressional approval.
    (B) The Court has been reluctant to intervene in disputes over the conduct of foreign affairs.
    (C) The Court has made decisions to protect civil rights, especially during wartime.
    (D) The Court has supported the decisions of Congress but has overturned executive orders.
    (E) The Court has rarely deferred to presidential power for fear of upsetting the balance of powers.

ANSWER: **B.** The Supreme Court is reluctant to make decisions involving foreign affairs (*American Government*, 8th ed., page 557 / 9th ed., page 558).

4. What has been the presidential response to the War Powers Act?
   (A) The War Powers Act has had little impact on presidents' decisions regarding military actions.
   (B) Because of the War Powers Act, Congress has consistently refused to appropriate funds for troops once they have been deployed.
   (C) The War Powers Act has been used successfully by Congress to prevent troop commitments.
   (D) The War Powers Act has encouraged every president since Nixon to consult with Congress before taking military action.
   (E) The War Powers Act was challenged in court by President Nixon and found to be unconstitutional.

ANSWER: **A**. Many presidents believe that the War Powers Act is an unconstitutional infringement on their powers as commander in chief. As a result, it has had little impact (*American Government*, 8th ed., page 559 / 9th ed., page 559).

5. What is the role of Congress with regard to intelligence gathering?
   (A) Committees have an oversight function and can block proposed actions by the intelligence community.
   (B) Committees are informed of proposed covert activities, but they do not have the authority to prevent action by the intelligence services.
   (C) Committees are informed of covert activities after they take place.
   (D) The Congress as a whole is informed of proposed covert activities during a special session.
   (E) Congress has no role regarding the gathering of intelligence; this is an executive function.

ANSWER: **B.** Both the House and Senate have intelligence committees, which are informed of proposed covert actions, but they do not have the authority to block those actions (*American Government*, 8th ed., pages 559-560 / 9th ed., page 560).

Table 20.2	How the Public and the Elite See Foreign Policy, 1999	
	Percentage Agreeing	
	Public	Leaders
Tariffs are necessary to protect American jobs	60%	36%
Oppose giving economic aid to foreign countries	49	10
Russia should solve its problems alone, without U.S. aid	42	18
Oppose U.S. troops helping South Korea if North Korea invades	66	25
Reducing illegal immigration is very important	57	21
Oppose an independent Palestinian state in Israel	42	19
Support assassinating terrorist leaders to combat terrorism	61	35

Source: John E. Rielly, *American Public Opinion and U.S. Foreign Policy, 1999* (Chicago: Chicago Council on Foreign Relations, 1999).

6. The table above supports which of the following conclusions?
   (A) Most Americans support the creation of an independent Palestinian state.
   (B) There is widespread agreement between leaders and the public about most areas of foreign policy.
   (C) Most Americans would support using troops to protect South Korea in the event of an invasion by North Korea, but most leaders would not support it.
   (D) Most Americans favor assassinating terrorist leaders, while most leaders disagree with this position.
   (E) More than half of all Americans oppose giving economic aid to foreign countries.

ANSWER: **D**. There is a difference between the views of the public and the views of leaders on many foreign policy matters. For example, 60 percent of Americans support assassinating terrorists, while only 35 percent of leaders agree (*American Government*, 8th ed., page 565 / 9th ed., page 565).

7. A person who objects to U.S. involvement in other countries has a worldview of "no more Vietnams." What is the best description of this belief about foreign policy?
   (A) containment
   (B) big-stick diplomacy
   (C) disengagement
   (D) appeasement
   (E) humanitarianism

ANSWER: **C**. Disengagement is the new isolationism that followed the Vietnam War. According to this paradigm, America's foreign policy was based on inaccurate assumptions and we should not have become involved in the conflict in Vietnam (*American Government*, 8th ed., pages 565-569 / 9th ed., pages 566-569).

8. The military paid $435 for hammers that could have been purchased at any local hardware store. This is blamed on
   (A) the military-industrial complex
   (B) inaccuracies in estimating budgetary expenditures
   (C) the expenses associated with conflicting regulations
   (D) the failure of the military to communicate effectively with defense contractors
   (E) the ability of defense contractors to overcharge the military without any oversight

ANSWER: **A**. The military-industrial complex is the cozy relationship that has developed between defense contractors and the military. Costs are higher because the military equipment must meet tougher standards, because it operates under extreme conditions. Another reason for higher costs is strict standards, and manufacturers often have a say in drafting those standards. This benefits big corporations and the members of Congress whose districts benefit from defense projects (*American Government*, 8th ed., page 572 / 9th ed., page 572).

9. Despite the end of the Cold War, most Americans still consider it important to have a strong military. This is because of hostile nations including
   I. Iran
   II. North Korea
   III. Saudi Arabia
   IV. Afghanistan

   (A) I and II
   (B) I, II, and III
   (C) I and IV
   (D) I, II, and IV
   (E) I, II, III, and IV

ANSWER: **A**. Iran and North Korea are hostile to the United States. Both countries are suspected of trying to develop nuclear weapons (*American Government*, 8th ed., pages 573-574 / 9th ed., page 574).

10. Why would a member of Congress, even one who strongly believes that military spending should be reduced, fight to keep a military base open?
    (A) Most Americans strongly oppose closing military bases.
    (B) Bases are needed, even when defense spending is cut, to keep the country prepared for war.
    (C) Bases provide important training for both the military and civilian work- forces.
    (D) Members fight to keep bases open in their districts because a base benefits their communities and helps with reelection.
    (E) A member of Congress who strongly believes that military spending should be reduced would not fight to keep bases open.

ANSWER: **D**. Even those members of Congress who fought to reduce military spending during the 1990s wanted to keep bases in their districts open. This is because bases are important to an area's economy, and keeping bases open helps the member at election time (*American Government*, 8th ed., page 580 / 9th ed., page 578).

Free-Response Questions

1. The president's powers in making military and foreign policy are extensive and have expanded over time. Identify and explain two reasons why the president is powerful in military and foreign affairs. Identify and explain one constraint on the president's policy-making in military and foreign affairs.

RESPONSE: Although Congress has the power to declare war, the president is the commander in chief. Presidents have asserted their ability to commit troops on numerous occasions. This gives the president great power in foreign affairs. One example is when both Presidents Kennedy and Johnson sent troops to Vietnam even though there was no official declaration of war. This eventually put half a million troops overseas. The fact that a president can initiate and maintain such a large military action in the absence of a formal declaration of war demonstrates the power of the presidency.

Another reason the president has so much power in foreign affairs is the number of defense and national security agencies under his authority. The Central Intelligence Agency engages in covert activities designed to provide the government with information about threats from abroad. The National Security Council, which coordinates military and foreign policy, includes the secretary of defense, the director of the CIA, the chairman of the Joint Chiefs of Staff, and the attorney general. Because of the wide range of executive agencies that are involved in making foreign and defense policy, the president has considerable power.

One constraint on a president's ability to make foreign policy is that the Senate must ratify treaties. Although the president negotiates treaties, they are no more than a promise until the Senate ratifies them. This means that the Senate has the ultimate authority over agreements made with foreign nations, and the president's power is constrained (*American Government*, 8th ed., pages 555-560 / 9th ed., pages 555-560).

Figure 20.1 Trends in Military Spending (in constant dollars)

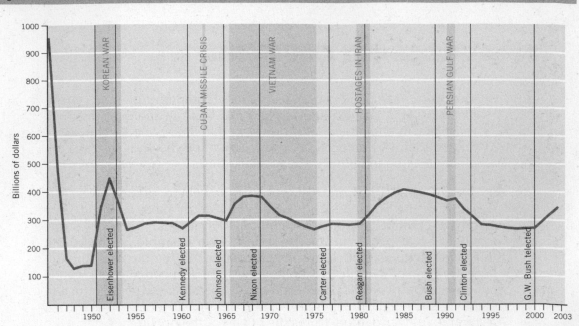

Source: Office of the Under Secretary of Defense (Comptroller), "National Defense Budget Estimates for FY 2003."

2. Using the chart above, complete the following tasks:
   a. Identify two trends in military spending.
   b. Identify one event that increased military spending and explain why.
   c. Identify one event that decreased military spending and explain why.

RESPONSE: Part (a): One trend is that military spending remains stable at about $300 billion during election years. Another trend is that military spending increases during wartime.

Part (b): One event that increased military spending was the election of Ronald Reagan. President Reagan believed in increasing military spending to invest in new defensive technology. Congress approved his proposals, and as a result, military spending increased from $300 billion in 1980 to more than $400 billion in 1985.

Part (c): One event that resulted in a decrease in military spending was the end of the Cold War. In 1991 the Soviet Union broke up. Until that point the USSR was considered one of the major threats to the United States, and much of our military spending was geared toward dealing with that threat. After the end of the Cold War, there was a period of lessened tensions, which resulted in a "peace dividend." As a result military spending declined (*American Government*, 8th ed., page 573 / 9th ed., page 573).

19

CIVIL RIGHTS

Civil rights issues involve discrimination against a group. The government has the authority to treat different people differently—but only if the differences in treatment are reasonable in the view of the courts.

KEY TERMS

affirmative action

Brown v. Board of Education

civil rights

Civil Rights Act of 1964

civil rights movement

de facto segregation

de jure segregation

Fourteenth Amendment

freedom rides

Martin Luther King, Jr.

Montgomery bus boycott

National Association for the Advancement of Colored People (NAACP)

nonviolent civil disobedience

Plessy v. Ferguson

reasonableness standard

Roe v. Wade

Rosa Parks

separate-but-equal doctrine

sit-ins

strict scrutiny standard

Swann v. Charlotte-Mecklenburg Board of Education

Voting Rights Act of 1965

KEY CONCEPTS

- Progress for African Americans in receiving their civil rights was slow.

- African Americans used the federal courts effectively to gain their civil rights.
- Civil rights legislation came as a result of public protest and a change in public opinion regarding the rights of African Americans.
- Women's rights are drawn from different standards than those used for race.
- Affirmative Action is a controversial program to remedy past and present discrimination.

For a full discussion of the topic of civil rights, see *American Government,* 8th ed., Chapter 19 / 9th ed., Chapter 19.

THE BACKGROUND OF THE CIVIL RIGHTS MOVEMENT

Until fairly recently African Americans could not vote, attend integrated schools, sit in the front seats of buses, or buy homes in white neighborhoods. Two main reasons account for the slow pace with which African Americans attained their civil rights. First, politically dominant white minorities in the South feared potential competition for jobs, land, public services, and living space from African Americans. White groups were able to dominate local politics and keep African Americans from organizing politically. Second, the white majority at the national level opposed African American attempts to achieve rights and did not favor federal action to secure those rights.

Progress in achieving civil rights for African Americans depended on either finding more white allies or shifting to new policy-making arenas. Civil rights leaders broadened their base by publicizing the denial to African Americans of essential, widely accepted liberties—for example, voting or organizing. They turned what had been perceived as an interest group set of issues into majoritarian issues. They also moved their legal and political struggle from Congress to the federal courts.

THE CIVIL RIGHTS MOVEMENT IN THE COURTS

The Fourteenth Amendment, adopted in 1868, was both an opportunity and a problem for black activists. It seemed to guarantee equal rights for all. Yet a narrow interpretation of the amendment argued that African Americans had equal legal rights but could otherwise be treated differently than whites. The Supreme Court adopted this narrow view in *Plessy v. Ferguson* (1896), in which it found separate-but-equal facilities to be constitutional.

The National Association for the Advancement of Colored People (NAACP) was established in 1909 to lobby in Washington and publicize black grievances, but its most influential role was played in the courtroom. In fighting the separate-but-equal doctrine, the NAACP established a three-step process to attack school segregation:

- First, persuade the Supreme Court to declare unconstitutional the laws creating schools that were separate but obviously unequal (in regards to funding, facilities, faculty, etc.).
- Second, persuade the Supreme Court to declare unconstitutional the laws creating schools that were separate but not so obviously unequal.
- Finally, have the Supreme Court rule that separate schools are inherently unequal and therefore unconstitutional.

AP Tip

Brown v. Board of Education is one of the most important decisions ever rendered by the Supreme Court and will likely appear on the AP exam.

In a series of court cases that stretched from 1938 to 1954, the NAACP implemented its strategy, culminating in *Brown v. Board of Education* (1954). In the *Brown* case the Supreme Court ruled that separate schools were inherently unequal and overturned *Plessy* in a unanimous decision.

Brown was a landmark decision, and the reasons for it and the means chosen to implement it were important and controversial. Three issues emerged from the decision:

- **Implementation** The *Brown* case was a class action suit that applied to all similarly situated African American students. The Court later ruled that integration should proceed in public schools "with all deliberate speed." In the South, this turned out to be a snail's pace. In 1956 more than one hundred southern members of Congress signed a "Southern Manifesto" that condemned the *Brown* decision as an abuse of judicial power and pledged to use all lawful means to reverse the decision. In the late 1950s and early 1960s, the National Guard and regular army paratroopers were used to escort black students into formerly all-white schools and universities. The collapse of resistance to integration in the 1970s was due to numerous political changes, including the voting power of blacks.
- **Rationale** The decision in *Brown* argued that segregation was detrimental to African American students, creating a sense of inferiority. The Court relied on the findings of social science.
- **Desegregation versus integration** In the South segregation by law (*de jure* segregation) was clearly unconstitutional as a result of *Brown*. In the North segregation was the result of residential segregation (*de facto* segregation). Integration came to be defined by the Court as a "unitary, nonracial system of education." The case of *Swann v. Charlotte-Mecklenburg Board of Education* (1971) set guidelines for all subsequent cases involving school integration:
  - To violate the Constitution, a school system must have intended to discriminate.

- A one-race school creates a presumption of intent to discriminate.
- Remedies for past discrimination can include quotas, busing, and redrawn district lines.
- Not every school must reflect the racial composition of the entire system.

The result of the *Swann* decision was often "white flight" to the suburbs. One issue not settled by *Swann* was whether busing and other remedies should cut across school district lines. The Court later ruled that intercity busing could be authorized only if both the city and the suburbs had practiced segregation. In some cities, the Court believed, there had been intent to segregate and busing was necessary. Busing still remains a controversial issue.

THE CIVIL RIGHTS MOVEMENT IN CONGRESS

Getting Congress to pass new civil rights laws required a far more difficult and decentralized strategy than campaigning in the federal courts. This part of the movement aimed at mobilizing public opinion and overcoming the many congressional barriers to action.

The first strategy was to get civil rights issues on the political agenda by mobilizing public opinion through dramatic events. Sit-ins at segregated lunch counters and "freedom rides" on segregated bus lines made headlines in the newspapers. Efforts were made to get blacks registered to vote in counties where whites had used intimidation and harassment to prevent registration by blacks. Rosa Parks started a bus boycott, organized by a young minister named Martin Luther King, Jr., in Montgomery, Alabama, when she refused to surrender her seat to a white man. Early demonstrations were based on the philosophy of nonviolent civil disobedience—that is, peaceful violation of a law. Later, racial violence and riots erupted when more militant organizations became involved in the civil rights movement.

This mobilization of public opinion had mixed results. It succeeded in getting civil rights on the national political agenda. Yet it set back coalition-building because demonstrations and riots were seen as law breaking by many whites.

In Congress opponents of civil rights had strong defensive positions. Southern Democrats controlled the Senate Judiciary Committee. A southerner controlled the House Rules Committee. A filibuster in the Senate occurred when civil rights legislation came to the floor. President Kennedy was reluctant to submit strong civil rights legislation.

Four developments changed the civil rights movement's chances in Congress:

- Public opinion became more favorable towards the movement as the years wore on.
- Violent reactions by white segregationists received extensive coverage by the media.
- The assassination of President Kennedy, in 1963, gave his successor, President Johnson, a period of strong relations with

Congress and a mythical hero figure to refer to in promoting civil rights.
- The 1964 election was a Democratic landslide that allowed northern Democrats to seize power in Congress.

Five important civil rights bills were passed between 1957 and 1968. Significant voting rights laws were passed in 1957, 1960, and 1965. A housing discrimination law was passed in 1968. The high point of civil rights legislation, however, was the Civil Rights Act of 1964. It assured equality of opportunity in employment, public accommodations, voting, and schools.

The civil rights movement boasted many achievements. Among the most important have been a dramatic rise in African American voting and changes in the opinions of whites regarding civil rights.

WOMEN AND EQUAL RIGHTS

The feminist movement that reappeared in the 1960s questioned the claim that women differed from men in ways that justified differences in legal status. Congress responded by passing laws that required equal pay for equal work, prohibited discrimination on the basis of sex in employment and public education, and banned discrimination against pregnant women on the job.

The Supreme Court had a choice between two standards in considering sex discrimination. The first is the reasonableness standard, which holds that when the government treats some classes of people differently from others, the different treatment must be reasonable and not arbitrary. The second is the strict scrutiny standard, which holds that some instances of drawing distinctions between different groups are inherently suspect. This is the standard used for racial discrimination. Thus the Court will subject those cases to strict scrutiny to ensure that they are clearly necessary to attain a legitimate state goal.

When women complained that some laws treated them unfairly, the Court adopted a mid-level standard somewhere between the reasonable and strict scrutiny tests. For example, the courts prohibit gender-based differences when applied to the age of adulthood, the drinking age, arbitrary employee height and weight requirements, and mandatory pregnancy leaves. Gender-based differences are allowed by the courts in areas such as statutory rape, all-boy/all-girl public schools, and delayed promotions in the Navy.

The rights of women have been determined in three far-reaching areas:

- **The draft** In *Rostker v. Goldberg* (1981), the Supreme Court held that Congress can require men but not women to register for the draft without violating the due-process clause of the Fifth Amendment. In 1993 the secretary of defense allowed women to have air and sea combat positions but not ground combat positions. These decisions remain controversial.
- **Sexual harassment** There are two forms of harassment. The first is quid pro quo, in which sexual favors are expected in return for holding a job or gaining a promotion. Employers are

strictly liable for this form of harassment. The other form is a hostile environment—creating a setting in which harassment impairs a person's ability to work. Employers are liable in this form *if* they are negligent.

- **Abortion** The issue of abortion was left to the states until 1973, when the Supreme Court used *Roe v. Wade* to strike down a Texas ban on abortion and all similar state laws. It holds that a woman's freedom to choose an abortion is protected by the Fourteenth Amendment in the first trimester of pregnancy. Abortion during the second trimester is also left up to a woman, but states are allowed to pass reasonable regulations to protect the mother's health. During the third trimester, states can ban abortion because the fetus is viable. Constitutional amendments to overturn *Roe* have failed. However, there have been successful attempts to restrict abortions:
  - 1976: Congress barred the use of federal funds to pay for abortions except when the life of the mother is at stake.
  - 1989: The Supreme Court first upheld the right of states to impose some restrictions on abortion.
  - 1992: In *Casey v. Planned Parenthood* the Court permitted more restrictions, such as a twenty-four-hour waiting period and parental consent for teenagers. A spousal consent requirement was overturned.

AFFIRMATIVE ACTION

The politics of civil rights are often expressed in one of two views. The first view advocates equality of results. In this view the assumption is that racism and sexism can be overcome only when remedies change the results. Equal rights are not thought to be enough. People need benefits as well. Proponents of this view argue that affirmative action—preferential practices—should be used in hiring and college admissions decisions.

The second view advocates equality of opportunities. Proponents believe that reverse discrimination occurs when race or sex is used as a basis for preferential treatment. Laws should be color-blind and sex neutral.

In the *Bakke* case of 1978, the Supreme Court ruled that numerical minority quotas are not permissible but that race could be considered in admissions policies. In general the Court supports the concept of affirmative action, but it is reluctant to support the use of quotas.

Standards are emerging for quotas and preference systems. They include the following:

- Quota systems are subjected to strict scrutiny, and there must be a compelling state interest to justify quotas.
- Quotas must correct an actual pattern of discrimination.
- Quotas must identify actual practices that discriminate.
- Federal quotas will be given deference because the Constitution gives Congress greater power to correct the effects of racial discrimination.

■ Preferences are acceptable for the purpose of achieving diversity.

The public generally supports compensatory action (helping minorities catch up) but not preferential treatment. This is in line with American political culture, which supports individualism but also those in need.

Conflicts persist in other areas of civil rights. Immigration rights and the rights of enemy combatants are bound to provoke more rulings from the Supreme Court in the future. An area that is already receiving widespread attention is gay rights. In the past, sexual conduct has been regulated by the states. The Supreme Court has overturned some state laws that ban certain sexual practices by citing the privacy rights implied in the Fourth and Fourteenth Amendments. Yet other rulings have not upheld gay rights, such as the Boy Scouts' right to exclude gays. Gay rights remain controversial.

Multiple-Choice Questions

1. Which of the following cases most likely involves a violation of civil rights?
   (A) classifying people into brackets on the basis on income and taxing them at different rates
   (B) conducting a search without a warrant or probable cause
   (C) classifying people using any system that treats one group of people differently than another
   (D) classifying people and treating them differently on the basis of race or gender
   (E) giving adults more rights, such as voting and drinking alcohol, than the rights possessed by minors

ANSWER: **D**. Civil rights laws protect people from being discriminated against if they are in a protected class, such as race or gender (*American Government,* 8th ed., pages 521-522 / 9th ed., pages 523-524).

2. All of the following made it difficult for African Americans to gain equality EXCEPT
   (A) blacks were in the minority population in the states with the most discrimination
   (B) lower income whites were worried that gains by blacks would be at their expense
   (C) because blacks could not vote, they had little influence in policy-making
   (D) racism by whites blocked blacks' efforts to gain equality
   (E) until the early 1960s, most citizens of the North did little to help blacks in the South gain equality

ANSWER: **A**. Although blacks were in a majority in the Deep South, it was difficult for them to gain equality because of fear, racism, and the lack of northern support (*American Government,* 8th ed., pages 522-523 / 9th ed., pages 524-525).

3. The National Association for the Advancement of Colored People (NAACP) developed a strategy to challenge the "separate-but-equal" ruling in *Plessy v. Ferguson*. Put the following tactics in the order in which they were used by the NAACP.
   I. persuade the Court to declare laws unconstitutional if they were separate but unequal in subtle ways
   II. persuade the Court to rule that racially segregated schools were inherently unequal.
   III. persuade the Court to declare laws unconstitutional if they were separate and unequal in obvious ways

   (A) II, III, and I
   (B) I, II, and III
   (C) III, II, and I
   (D) III, I, and II
   (E) II, I, and III

ANSWER: **D**. The NAACP attacked cases of obvious inequality first. Then it pursued cases in which there was subtle inequality. The final step was to argue that all segregation is inherently unequal (*American Government*, 8th ed., page 525 / 9th ed., page 527).

4. The federal government took which of the following measures to end southern resistance to desegregation?
   I. sent in the National Guard to force schools to desegregate
   II. closed southern school systems until they agreed to desegregate
   III. provided financial aid for schools that integrated
   IV. withheld financial aid from schools that refused to desegregate

   (A) I and II
   (B) I, II, and III
   (C) I and III
   (D) III and IV
   (E) I, III, and IV

ANSWER: **E**. The federal government sent troops to desegregate schools, such as Central High School in Little Rock, Arkansas. In addition, financial aid was provided to integrated schools and withheld from segregated schools (*American Government*, 8th ed., page 528 / 9th ed., page 530).

5. In the 1960s, Denver, Colorado, had several racially distinct neighborhoods. Denver Public Schools developed a neighborhood schools plan in which students would attend the school closest to home. On what grounds was this plan challenged?
   (A) that it was *de jure* segregation
   (B) that it was *de facto* segregation
   (C) that the plan did not allow students the freedom to travel to a school of their choice
   (D) that the plan would not allow black students to attend schools with whites
   (E) there was no valid legal basis for challenging this plan

ANSWER: **B**. The neighborhood schools plan was challenged as *de facto* segregation because it resulted in racially separate schools (*American Government,* 8th ed., page 529 / 9th ed., page 531).

6. As a result of desegregation plans that required students to be bused in central-city schools, many whites moved to the suburbs. How did the courts respond to this "white flight"?
    (A) The Supreme Court held that white flight was *de facto* segregation and ordered busing across district lines.
    (B) The Supreme Court ordered central-city schools to develop magnet programs to prevent white flight.
    (C) The Supreme Court ruled that intercity busing could be ordered only if both districts practiced school segregation.
    (D) The Supreme Court refused to take the case on grounds of federalism because school district boundaries are set by the states.
    (E) The Supreme Court refused to order cross-district busing because most of the public opposed it.

ANSWER: **C**. The Supreme Court has refused to order busing across school district lines unless there is a history of segregation by both the city and the suburban school districts (*American Government,* 8th ed., page 530 / 9th ed., page 532).

7. After many delays, all of the following events enabled the passage of the Civil Rights Act of 1964 EXCEPT
    (A) public opinion was changing, and more whites supported civil rights
    (B) the media, making the public aware of the discrimination faced by blacks, showed violence by white segregationists
    (C) President Kennedy, who was a proponent of civil rights, was assassinated
    (D) most southern whites favored desegregation once public schools became integrated
    (E) the government was united, with Democrats controlling the presidency, House, and Senate

ANSWER: **D**. The Civil Rights Act of 1964 was finally passed because of increasing white support and reactions by the public to the violence against civil rights advocates as shown by the media. President Kennedy's assassination led many to support civil rights in his honor, and under the erroneous theory that the right wing was responsible for his death. The law was passed by a Democratic Congress and signed by President Johnson (*American Government,* 8th ed., pages 533-534 / 9th ed., pages 535-536).

8. Why is the all-male draft constitutional even though it is gender discrimination?
   (A) because it meets the standard of strict scrutiny—men are much more effective in combat than women
   (B) because it meets mid-level scrutiny—on average, women have less upper body strength than men
   (C) because there is a rational basis for the law—the nation has never needed so many troops that it required women in combat
   (D) because discrimination against men is legal—they are not in a protected class
   (E) the all-male draft has not been challenged in the Supreme Court because the Court avoids what it considers political questions

ANSWER: **B.** The all-male draft meets the standard of mid-level scrutiny required for gender discrimination cases. In general men are stronger than women (*American Government,* 8th ed., page 538 / 9th ed., page 540).

9. What is overall impact of the Supreme Court's rulings on abortion?
   (A) Abortion is a social, moral, and family issue and is left to the discretion of the states.
   (B) Abortion is prohibited except in cases of rape or incest.
   (C) Abortion may not be prohibited or regulated during the first two trimesters.
   (D) Abortion may not be prohibited during the first two trimesters, but it can be regulated as long as there is no undue burden.
   (E) There is a broad right to abortion throughout pregnancy.

ANSWER: **D.** Abortion may not be outlawed during the first two trimesters of pregnancy, although it may be regulated as long as those regulations do not create an undue burden on the pregnant woman (*American Government,* 8th ed., pages 540-541 / 9th ed., pages 542-543).

10. Which of the following statements best describes the Supreme Court's position on affirmative action?
    (A) Quotas can be used in college admissions to achieve a racially balanced student body.
    (B) Laws should be color-blind and race neutral.
    (C) Quotas can be used in construction contracts, but not in hiring or in college admissions.
    (D) Affirmative actions programs are not legal, because they are reverse discrimination.
    (E) Quotas are viewed with strict scrutiny, but preferences are acceptable for the purpose of achieving diversity.

ANSWER: **E.** The Supreme Court has upheld affirmative action programs but dislikes quotas. Preferences are acceptable to reach a goal of increased diversity (*American Government,* 8th ed., pages 541-548 / 9th ed., pages 544-548).

Free-Response Questions

1. The Supreme Court has decided a number of cases involving civil rights. For TWO of the following issues, identify the legal issue involved and summarize the Court's decisions on the issue:
   - abortion
   - affirmative action
   - homosexual rights

RESPONSE: Abortion is one of the most contentious issues in the United States today. Until the Supreme Court's decision in *Roe v. Wade*, abortion was regulated by the states. Some states allowed unrestricted access to abortion, while other states prohibited it. In the *Roe* case, the Court held that the Fourth and Fourteenth Amendments protect a right of privacy that includes abortion. In that decision the Court said that there was an unrestricted right of abortion during the first trimester. States could regulate abortion in the second trimester and could prohibit it in the third. Subsequent Court decisions have allowed regulations on abortion as long as they do not create an undue burden. For example, parental notification and short waiting periods have been upheld. On the other hand, a spousal consent law was overturned.

Affirmative action programs use preferential practices in hiring and college admissions. The goals of these programs are to foster more diversity and to make up for past and present discrimination. These programs were challenged in *Bakke v. University of California* when a white medical school applicant with good grades and test scores was not admitted because of a quota system. The Court upheld affirmative action plans in general, but it overturned the quota system. The quota system was found to be race discrimination under the equal protection clause of the Fourteenth Amendment. The Court is more willing to accept programs when there has been a history of past discrimination or when the federal government is involved.

Conflicts over homosexuality continue. Sexual conduct has usually been regulated by the states. However, state laws banning certain sexual practices have been overturned by the Supreme Court because of the privacy interests protected by the Fourth and Fourteenth Amendments. When Colorado passed a law banning special protections for gays, the Supreme Court overturned it as a violation of the Equal Protection Clause. However, the Court upheld a rule by the Boy Scouts excluding gays. The Court held that private organizations could choose their own members. Thus the status of gay rights is not clear (*American Government*, 8th ed., pages 540-549 / 9th ed., pages 542-549).

2. Both *Brown v. Board of Education* and *Swann v. Charlotte-Mecklenburg Board of Education* deal with school desegregation. For EACH case,
   a. Discuss the Court's ruling and its impact.
   b. Identify and discuss one limitation on school desegregation.

RESPONSE: Part (a): In *Brown v. Board of Education*, the issue was whether segregation in public schools was constitutional. The NAACP argued that separate educational facilities were unconstitutional, even if funding and facilities were similar in black and white schools. This was the last in a long series of cases designed to chip away at the ruling in *Plessy v. Ferguson*. The Supreme Court held that segregated schools violate the Fourteenth Amendment because they were "inherently unequal." Separate but equal was dead. The immediate impact of the decision was limited because of white resistance. However, over the next decades, public schools were desegregated throughout the South.

The issue in *Swann v. Charlotte-Mecklenburg* was *de facto* segregation. This means that the law did not segregate the school district but that it was segregated in fact. Kids attended the school nearest home, and because neighborhoods were segregated, so were the schools. The Supreme Court ordered a school busing plan to achieve more racial balance within the schools. Because of the *Swann* case, several large metropolitan school districts implemented busing plans to desegregate. However, the Court later ruled that schools could not bus students across district lines.

Part (b): The ruling that school districts could not bus students across district lines to achieve integrated schools limited school desegregation. Following the Court's ruling in *Swann,* many cities experienced "white flight" when white families moved to the suburbs. These areas were predominantly white, and the cities they left behind had a higher percentage of minorities. These areas remained racially imbalanced because busing could not occur across school district boundaries (*American Government,* 8th ed., pages 527-530 / 9th ed., pages 529-532).

20

CIVIL LIBERTIES

Civil liberties are the constitutional protections an individual has against government. In order to understand the nature of civil liberties, it is necessary to understand why the liberties stated in the Bill of Rights are important, how they came to apply to the states, and why they have grown in scope and meaning.

KEY TERMS

Bill of Rights	libel
civil liberties	*Mapp v. Ohio*
clear-and-present danger doctrine	*Miranda v. Arizona*
commercial speech	Patriot Act
due-process clause	obscenity
establishment clause	prior restraint
exclusionary rule	probable cause
free-exercise clause	search warrant
Gitlow v. New York	slander
incorporation doctrine	symbolic speech

KEY CONCEPTS

- Civil liberties have created significant issues because there is often competition among groups and individuals for rights guaranteed in the Constitution.
- First Amendment rights have created several controversial and enduring issues.
- Several rights of the accused are guaranteed in the Bill of Rights.

- The Patriot Act was created as a result of the 9/11 attacks, and many believe that some of its provisions violate the Constitution.

For a full discussion of civil liberties, see *American Government,* 8th ed., Chapter 18 / 9th ed., Chapter 18.

BACKGROUND OF CIVIL LIBERTIES ISSUES

The Framers of the Constitution had three objectives in regards to civil liberties. First, they wanted to limit federal powers and assure the rights and liberties found in the various state constitutions. Second, they meant for the Constitution to be a document proclaiming what the federal government *could* do, not what it *could not* do. Third, any mention of what the government could not do was meant to apply only to the federal government, not to the state governments.

Civil liberties have created major issues in the nation's history for three reasons:

- The Bill of Rights contains competing rights. Often the rights of one group or individual directly conflict with the rights of another. For instance the media may insist on their right to broadcast information about a court case, but that information may compromise an individual's right to a fair trial. The right of a group to protest may be in conflict with the right of citizens to have public order.
- Government officials have often been successful at taking action against the rights of political or religious dissidents. In times of crisis, politicians can convince the public that the liberty of a minority needs to be restricted. For instance congressional acts were passed during World War I that made it a crime to utter statements that would interfere with the draft. During the Cold War a law required members of the Communist party to register with the government.
- Waves of immigrants who are not white and Western European have created cultural conflicts. Conflicts continue to exist about the meaning of constitutionally protected freedoms based on ethnic, cultural, or religious factors. For instance, Jews have been offended by crèches at Christmastime on government property, while some English-speakers press for monolingual schools in Spanish-speaking areas.

FIRST AMENDMENT RIGHTS

Because the First Amendment contains several of our most basic freedoms, it has often been the battleground for civil liberties issues. Interpreting and applying the First Amendment has typically dealt with one of the following issues:

- **Freedom of expression and national security** Early American legal thought set forth the idea that the press should be free of prior restraint—government censorship of the press in advance of publication—even if publication is clearly against the interests or security of the government. The press, however, had to accept the consequence if what was published was inaccurate or illegal. During World War I, Congress defined further some of the limits of expression by passing legislation stating that treason, insurrection, forcible resistance to federal laws, and encouraging disloyalty in the armed services were not protected by the First Amendment. The Supreme Court upheld these limits on free expression in 1919 by issuing the "clear-and-present danger" test: the words used cannot create a clear and present danger to the public, and Congress can prevent such dangers. Later the Court moved towards allowing more freedom of expression but deferred to Congress during times of crisis. For instance, under the Smith Act of 1940, the Court upheld the convictions of communists preaching revolution. In 1969, however, the Court ruled that speech calling for illegal acts is protected if those acts are not imminent. In 1977 an American Nazi march in Skokie, Illinois, an area heavily populated by Jews, was held to be lawful. The general view of the Court has been that hate speech is permissible, but not hate crimes that result in direct physical harm.

AP Tip

Incorporation doctrine is basic to an understanding of civil liberties and will likely appear on the AP exam.

- **Incorporation doctrine** The Fourteenth Amendment (1868) created the possibility that some or all of the Bill of Rights might restrict state government actions based on the amendment's "due-process clause." The Supreme Court initially denied making the Bill of Rights applicable to the states. However, in *Gitlow v. New York* (1925), the Court argued for the first time that fundamental personal rights are protected from infringement by the states because of the due-process clause. Most, though not all, of the Bill of Rights has been incorporated into the states since 1925.
- **Defining speech** Some kinds of speech are not fully protected by the First Amendment:
  - Libel (a written statement defaming another with false information) and slander (a defamatory oral statement) have drawn variable jury awards. The burden of proof in libel and slander cases tends to be higher for public figures because they must also show the words were written with actual malice, with reckless disregard for the truth, and with knowledge that the words were false.
  - The Federal Communications Commission has not created an enduring and comprehensive definition of obscenity. A 1973 definition allowed contemporary community standards to determine what is obscene. The same ruling

created a standard for obscenity based on whether the material in question had "serious literary, artistic, political, or scientific value." The Supreme Court has typically upheld zoning ordinances for adult theaters and bookstores. Pornography on television, video, and the Internet has strained the community standard ruling, and regulation of these has generally been ruled unconstitutional.

- Symbolic speech, or expression through acts rather than words, is not protected when it involves an illegal act (for example, burning a draft card). Symbolic speech is generally protected when no illegal act is involved. For instance, flag burning has been ruled protected speech.

- **Defining a person** Corporations and organizations usually have the same First Amendment rights as individuals. More restrictions can be placed on commercial speech than on individual speech, but the restrictions must be narrowly tailored and serve the public interest. Young people have fewer rights than adults do. For instance, the Supreme Court has ruled that a school newspaper can be censored by the school's administration.

- **Church and state** Religious rights in the First Amendment are protected by two different clauses:

  - *The free-exercise clause* The government cannot interfere with an individual's practice of religion. Furthermore, the law may not impose special burdens on religion. Yet there are no religious exemptions from a law binding all other citizens, even if that law oppresses one's religious beliefs. Some conflict between religious freedom and public policy continues to be problematic, such as conscientious objectors to military service and refusal to work on Saturdays.

  - *The establishment clause* The Supreme Court has traditionally interpreted the establishment clause to mean no government involvement in religion, even if the involvement is not preferential. Yet some kinds of government aid to parochial schools and denominational colleges have been allowed. Aid is allowed if it involves a secular purpose, has an impact that neither advances nor inhibits religion, and does not create "excessive government entanglement with religion." Supreme Court rulings remain complex and shifting in regard to the establishment clause.

RIGHTS OF THE ACCUSED

The Bill of Rights offers several civil liberties that protect the accused. These include the right to exclude evidence improperly obtained from a trial, the right to proper searches and seizures, and the right to avoid self-incrimination.

Evidence gathered in violation of the Constitution cannot be used in trials; this is referred to as the exclusionary rule. The exclusionary rule is derived from both the Fourth Amendment (freedom from unreasonable searches and seizures) and the Fifth Amendment (protection against self incrimination). In *Mapp v. Ohio* (1961), the Supreme Court ruled that the exclusionary rule applies to the states as well as the federal government.

Reasonable searches of individuals can be made only with a properly obtained search warrant, issued when a judge determines that the police have good reason—probable cause—to believe that a crime has been committed and that the evidence bearing on that crime will be found at a certain location. In addition an individual can be searched if that search occurs in the process of a lawful arrest. In general the police can search the individual being arrested, items in plain view, and items under the immediate control of the individual. An arrest made of someone in a car is a constantly changing matter in regards to proper searches. Recent court rulings have tended to allow the police to do more searching of a car upon arrest. Concern for public safety can justify mandatory drug testing, even without a search warrant or individualized suspicion. Lacking the threat to public safety, however, the Supreme Court has been skeptical about drug testing.

The constitutional ban on confessions and self-incrimination was originally intended to prevent torture or coercion. These rights were extended in the 1960s. *Miranda v. Arizona* (1966) set guidelines for police questioning the accused by forcing officers to read suspects their rights. These were designed to protect the accused against self-incrimination and to protect their right to counsel. Police were originally disgruntled by having to follow the guidelines of *Miranda* because they thought that reading suspects their rights would silence them and hinder investigations. Today police accept the reading of rights as a routine part of an arrest.

TERRORISM AND CIVIL LIBERTIES

The attacks of September 11, 2001, raised important questions about how far the government can go in investigating and prosecuting individuals. Congress passed a new law, the Patriot Act, designed to increase federal powers in investigating terrorists. It included these provisions:

- The government may tap any telephone used by a suspect after receiving a court order.
- The government may tap Internet connections with a court order.
- The government may seize voicemail with a court order.
- Investigators can share information learned in grand jury proceedings.
- Any noncitizen may be held as a security risk for seven days, or longer if certified to be a security risk.
- The federal government may track money across U.S. borders and among banks.
- The statute of limitations on terrorist crimes is eliminated, with increased penalties.

An executive order then proclaimed a national emergency so that any noncitizen believed to be a terrorist or to have harbored a terrorist would be tried by a military court. A military court operates with the following provisions:

- The accused are tried before a commission of military officers.
- A two-thirds vote of the commission is needed to find the accused guilty.
- An appeal by the accused may be made only to the secretary of defense or to the president.

The Patriot Act continues to raise issues regarding terrorism and civil liberties. The ability to tap phones and Internet connections is an expansion of police powers that many feel is dangerous and could lead to invasions of privacy against citizens who have no terrorist ties. Government investigations into phone, Internet, voice mail, and even library records can be conducted in secrecy without the knowledge of the person being investigated. Many civil libertarians feel this is a violation of due process of law.

Multiple-Choice Questions

1. All of the following situations involve civil liberties EXCEPT
   (A) an angry protestor burns an American flag
   (B) a burglary suspect is read her rights before questioning
   (C) homosexuals challenge a ban on gay marriage in court
   (D) a group sacrifices a goat as part of a religious ceremony
   (E) a state provides funds to increase salaries of teachers in religious schools

ANSWER: **C.** Civil liberties are protections individuals have from the government. These include free speech, religious freedom, separation of church and state, and defendants' rights. Civil rights include protections for groups, such as homosexuals (*American Government,* 8th ed., pages 495-496 / 9th ed., pages 497-498).

2. The Supreme Court has upheld which of the following limits on free speech?
   I. laws against libel
   II. laws against speech that presents a clear and present danger
   III. laws against flag burning
   IV. laws against obscenity

   (A) I and II
   (B) I, II, and III
   (C) II and IV
   (D) I, II, and IV
   (E) I and IV

ANSWER: **D.** Although the First Amendment protects freedom of speech, this right is not absolute. The Court has upheld laws against libel and obscenity and speech that presents a clear and present danger (*American Government,* 8th ed., pages 500-506 / 9th ed., pages 503-508).

3. What is the "incorporation doctrine"?
   (A) the idea that corporations cannot be held liable for violations of civil liberties because they are nongovernmental entities
   (B) the interpretation of the due-process clause of the Fourteenth Amendment to apply the fundamental rights in the Bill of Rights to protect people from state action
   (C) the interpretation of the due-process clause of the Fourteenth Amendment to apply all of the Bill of Rights to protect people from state action
   (D) the concept that rights must be balanced with liberties and that the rights of the majority generally prevail
   (E) the idea that each state must include the Bill of Rights in its constitution

ANSWER: **B.** In *Gitlow v. New York* the Supreme Court held that the due-process clause of the Fourteenth Amendment protects individuals from state action that violates fundamental rights. Not all of the Bill of Rights has been incorporated (*American Government,* 8th ed., page 502 / 9th ed., page 504).

4. The Ku Klux Klan burns a cross at a rally across the street from a predominantly African American Baptist Church. The members of the church are offended by what they view as a hateful display. How would the courts most likely rule?
   (A) The First Amendment protects hate speech.
   (B) The First Amendment does not protect cross burning because it is intimidating.
   (C) The First Amendment protects hate speech, but burning a cross is not speech and is not protected.
   (D) The First Amendment protects hate speech, unless a community decides to ban it.
   (E) The First Amendment does not protect hate speech.

ANSWER: **A.** The First Amendment protects unpopular and offensive speech, whether verbal or symbolic, such as burning a cross (*American Government,* 8th ed., page 503 / 9th ed., page 505).

5. The First Amendment protects expressions of sexual or erotic interest. However, some restrictions on pornography have been upheld. In what ways can pornography be regulated?
   I. Child pornography can be banned.
   II. Zoning laws can prohibit "adult" businesses in certain places.
   III. The Federal Communications Commission can shut down adult pornographic Web sites.
   IV. Cities can ban all pornographic books and videos.

   (A) I and II
   (B) I, II, and III
   (C) I and III
   (D) I, II, and IV
   (E) II and III

ANSWER: **A.** The First Amendment protects some sexually explicit material. However, child pornography is against the law. Cities may use zoning laws to ban the sale of adult materials in certain areas (*American Government,* 8th ed., pages 504-506 / 9th ed., pages 506-508).

6. Colorado passed a law requiring that all school children say the Pledge of Allegiance every morning. The law was challenged as a violation of which civil liberties?
   I.   free-exercise clause
   II. right to petition
   III. freedom of speech
   IV. freedom of assembly

   (A) I and III
   (B) I, II, and III
   (C) II and III
   (D) II, III, and IV
   (E) I, III, and IV

ANSWER: **A**. A law requiring the Pledge of Allegiance was challenged as a violation of the free-exercise clause, which protects a person's right to practice—or not to practice—religion. It was also challenged as a violation of the First Amendment, which protects the right to speak—or not to speak. The Colorado law was replaced with a statute making the Pledge of Allegiance voluntary (*American Government,* 8th ed., page 508 / 9th ed., page 510).

7. Interact Club is a school-sponsored organization that prays around the flagpole of a public school every morning before school. Is this activity constitutional?
   (A) no, because the prayer takes place on school grounds, which is a violation of the establishment clause
   (B) no, because the prayer is part of a school-sponsored club, which is a violation of the establishment clause
   (C) no, because it is a violation of both the establishment clause and the free- exercise clause to pray on the grounds of a public school
   (D) yes, because the prayer takes place before the school day
   (E) yes, because the prayer is part of a club, not part of a class, and it could take place at any time during the school day

ANSWER: **D.** The establishment clause does not prohibit all religious activity on school grounds. However, the prayer must take place outside of the school building or outside of normal school hours (*American Government,* 8th ed., page 510 / 9th ed., page 512).

8. A house is searched without a valid search warrant, and a dead body is found. What would be the most likely outcome?
   (A) The discovery of the body could be used in court because it is the best evidence that a murder occurred.
   (B) The discovery of the body could not be used as evidence because it was discovered without a warrant, but hair samples on the body could be used in DNA testing.
   (C) The case could not be prosecuted because the exclusionary rule would prevent any evidence of the murder from being presented in court.
   (D) The case could be prosecuted with independent evidence, but the discovery of the body could not be used under the exclusionary rule.
   (E) This case would be decided under state law because many states have passed laws eliminating the exclusionary rule.

ANSWER: **D**. With some exceptions, the exclusionary rule prohibits evidence from an invalid search from being used in court. It also excludes evidence that is "fruit of the poisonous tree"—evidence that stems from an illegal search. However, the case could still be prosecuted with other evidence (*American Government,* 8th ed., page 512 / 9th ed., page 514).

9. What can be searched, without a search warrant, upon a valid arrest?
   I.   the person being arrested
   II. items in the plain view of the arresting officer
   III. items under the immediate control of the person being arrested
   IV. the home of the person being arrested

   (A) I and II
   (B) II and III
   (C) I and III
   (D) II, III, and IV
   (E) I, II, and III

ANSWER: **E**. Upon a valid arrest, an officer may search the person being arrested, items in plain view, and items under the person's immediate control (*American Government,* 8th ed., page 514 / 9th ed., page 516).

10. What is the result of the Supreme Court's ruling in *Miranda v. Arizona*?
    (A) Police officers must read a suspect his or her rights upon arrest; otherwise, the case against the defendant must be dismissed.
    (B) If a police officer fails to read a suspect his or her rights upon arrest, the suspect's confession cannot be used in court.
    (C) This case established the exclusionary rule that any illegally obtained evidence cannot be used in court.
    (D) If a defendant is not read his or her rights upon arrest, a confession cannot be used in court unless it is given voluntarily.
    (E) The confession of a defendant who has not been read his or her rights upon arrest may be used in court, but the defendant may bring a civil suit against the arresting officer.

ANSWER: **B**. Under *Miranda,* if a suspect is not read his or her rights upon arrest, his or her confession cannot be used in court even if that confession was given voluntarily (*American Government,* 8th ed., pages 515-516 / 9th ed., pages 517-518).

Free-Response Questions

1. The First Amendment states, "Congress shall make no law… abridging the freedom of speech." However, freedom of speech is not absolute. Identify and explain two ways freedom of speech is limited.

RESPONSE: Libel laws protect people from written statements that are untrue and damaging, and these laws restrict freedom of speech. If freedom of speech were allowed to operate without restriction, anything, no matter how damaging and untrue, could be printed without penalty. To recover damages for libel, an ordinary citizen must prove the falsehood of the statement and the damage the statement caused. The standard of proof is much higher for public figures. To recover damages for libel, public figures must prove not only that the statement is false, but also that it was made with malice—a reckless disregard for the truth. Although laws against libel infringe on freedom of speech, the courts, to balance protection of free speech and protection of a person's reputation, have upheld them.

Another restriction on freedom of speech pertains to statements that present a "clear and present danger." In *Schenck v. United States,* the Supreme Court upheld Schenck's conviction for making statements that might hinder the military draft. Schenck wrote pamphlets in which he claimed that World War I was being fought to benefit the defense industry, and he urged men to resist the draft. The Court held that the pamphlets created a clear and present danger to the country, because if men had listened to Schenck and avoided the draft, it would have hindered the war effort. What constitutes a clear and present danger is open to interpretation. Speech that is acceptable in peacetime might be limited during war (*American Government,* 8ᵗʰ ed., pages 500-503 / 9ᵗʰ ed., pages 503-505).

2. Civil liberties include the right of criminal defendants to be treated fairly during investigation, arrest, and trial. Rules against illegal search and seizure and self- incrimination protect a defendant's right to due process.
   a. Identify one rule regarding illegal search and seizure, and explain how that rule operates to protect a defendant's right to due process.
   b. Identify one rule regarding self-incrimination, and explain how that rule operates to protect a defendant's right to due process.

RESPONSE: Part (a): One rule that protects a defendant's right to due process is the exclusionary rule. This rule prevents illegally obtained evidence from being used against a defendant at trial. The Supreme Court established the exclusionary rule in *Mapp v. Ohio.* The defendant was suspected of possessing illegal drugs. When police broke into her home, they did not find drugs, but they found obscene pictures. The Court ruled that the pornography could not be used as evidence in court because the police did not obtain a search warrant, even though they had time to do so. The exclusionary rule protects due process, because it encourages authorities to obtain search warrants and discourages illegal searches.

Part (b): Miranda warnings also protect defendants' due-process rights. In *Miranda v. Arizona,* a rape suspect gave a confession after hours of questioning. He had not been read his rights. The Supreme Court held that the confession was inadmissible because Miranda did not know that he had the right to remain silent or to have an attorney present during questioning. Now when police take suspects into custody, they read from a "Miranda card." Miranda warnings protect defendants' rights to due process by ensuring that they understand their legal rights. This prevents uninformed self-incrimination (*American Government,* 8ᵗʰ ed., pages 512-516 / 9ᵗʰ ed., pages 514-518).

Part III

Practice Tests

Practice Test 1

UNITED STATES GOVERNMENT AND POLITICS
Section I
Time—45 minutes
60 Questions

Directions The questions or incomplete statements below are each followed by five suggested answers. Select the best answer.

MULTIPLE-CHOICE QUESTIONS

1. What kind of federal grants are used for building airports, roads, schools, and other specific undertakings?
   (A) formula grants
   (B) block grants
   (C) revenue sharing
   (D) project grants
   (E) broad-based aid

2. Why was the Voting Rights Act successful in meeting its goal of increasing African American voter registration in the South?
   I. because the goal was clear—to increase African American voter registration
   II. because federal officials oversaw the law
   III. because local officials understood the law and were able to carry it out
   IV. because criminal penalties were provided for interfering with the right to vote

   (A) I and II
   (B) I, II, and IV
   (C) II, III, and IV
   (D) I, III, and IV
   (E) II and IV

3. When does a president have the best chance of getting his program enacted?
   (A) during a honeymoon period at the beginning of his term
   (B) halfway through his first term, after he has established himself
   (C) during his second term, after he has had time to develop relationships with members of Congress
   (D) after he holds a press conference and asks the public to support a program during wartime

4. What was the result of the Court's ruling in *Miranda v. Arizona*?
   (A) It established the exclusionary rule.
   (B) It established the good-faith exception to the exclusionary rule.
   (C) If a suspect has not been informed of his rights, his confession cannot be used as evidence.
   (D) If a suspect has not been informed of his rights, the charges against him must be dropped.
   (E) The state must provide an attorney if a defendant cannot afford one.

GO ON TO NEXT PAGE

5. The president has all of the following expressed powers under the Constitution EXCEPT
   (A) to grant reprieves and pardons for federal offenses
   (B) to convene Congress in special sessions
   (C) to exercise the line-item veto
   (D) to appoint ambassadors, subject to Senate confirmation
   (E) to commission officers in the armed forces

6. All of the following statements about voter turnout are true EXCEPT
   (A) voter turnout in presidential elections was at its highest point in the late 1800s
   (B) people ages 18-21 have the lowest voter turnout rates
   (C) voter turnout has dropped in every presidential election since 1960
   (D) voter turnout is higher in federal elections than in state and local elections
   (E) voter turnout is greater in presidential elections than in midterm congressional elections

7. What encourages a two-party system in the United States?
   (A) the inclusion of ballot initiatives and referendums
   (B) the selection of candidates through primaries
   (C) the selection of candidates through caucuses
   (D) ticket-splitting by voters between the Republican and Democratic parties
   (E) the fact that elections are for single-member districts, winner-take-all

8. Which of the following serves as a check by Congress over the executive?
   (A) Congress can change the number and jurisdiction of the lower courts.
   (B) Congress can refuse to confirm a person nominated to be a judge.
   (C) All revenue bills must originate in the House of Representatives.
   (D) Congress can override a presidential veto by a majority vote of both houses.
   (E) Congress can remove cabinet secretaries.

9. What role does political party affiliation play in the selection of federal judges?
   (A) Presidents usually appoint members of their political party, and these people are generally qualified.
   (B) None. Federal judges are appointed based upon their qualifications rather than their party affiliation.
   (C) Some. Federal judges are appointed based upon their qualifications, but equally qualified candidates are judged based upon party affiliation.
   (D) Party affiliation is much more important than qualifications. Many unqualified judges are appointed because they are party faithful.
   (E) Under the merit rules for civil service, presidents are barred from considering party affiliation in appointing federal judges.

10. Why has the custom of senatorial courtesy been criticized?
   (A) because senators block the nomination of judges on the basis of party politics
   (B) because presidents find it difficult to find judicial candidates who would be accepted by their state senators
   (C) because senators from the opposing party use it to block the president's nominations for partisan purposes
   (D) because it results in unqualified candidates being confirmed
   (E) because it amounts to a legislative veto on presidential actions

11. Beginning in 1994, it was difficult for President Clinton to get his domestic program passed. What is the best explanation for this?
    (A) His approval ratings suffered a steady decline.
    (B) The government was divided.
    (C) The poor economy made it difficult for Congress to fund new programs.
    (D) The impeachment process took up the last six years of his presidency.
    (E) He concentrated on foreign affairs and did not put forth a domestic agenda.

12. Why is the threat of a veto a powerful presidential tool?
    (A) because Congress does not want the negative media attention associated with a presidential veto
    (B) because a presidential veto kills a bill until the next session of Congress
    (C) because it is difficult for Congress to obtain the two-thirds vote necessary to override a presidential veto
    (D) because the president can use the line-item veto to cut out pet projects favored by certain members of Congress
    (E) because the public usually supports the president more than it supports Congress

13. What is the basis of James Madison's argument in the *Federalist Paper* No. 10?
    (A) Factions are dangerous and must be destroyed.
    (B) The government can eliminate the causes of faction.
    (C) Political parties should be encouraged to form so that all viewpoints are represented.
    (D) A balanced government can control factions and prevent one faction from gaining too much power.
    (E) State government will prevent factions from forming.

14. Why did many states oppose the Americans with Disabilities Act?
    (A) because it was an unfunded mandate
    (B) because the matching funds provided by the federal government were not enough to pay for compliance with the law
    (C) because they did not agree with the goal of providing the disabled with access to government buildings
    (D) because most states already provided access for the disabled to government buildings
    (E) because helping people with disabilities is a state, rather than federal, issue

15. One criticism of the media is that it does not cover candidates' speeches in depth. This is best illustrated in which of the following?
    (A) the rise of the Internet
    (B) horse-race journalism
    (C) the shrinking sound bite
    (D) the liberal bias in the media
    (E) sensationalism

16. What was the biggest change to campaign financing made by the Campaign Finance Reform Act of 2002 (McCain-Feingold)?
    (A) the elimination of PAC contributions to candidates
    (B) the elimination of "soft money"
    (C) new requirements for full disclosure of campaign contributions
    (D) the creation of a new, nonpartisan, board of directors of the Federal Election Commission
    (E) the banning of all advertising by any political party in the sixty days before an election

GO ON TO NEXT PAGE

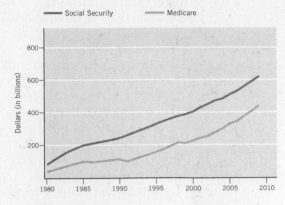

17. The graph above best supports which of the following conclusions?
(A) The federal debt will continue to rise unless income taxes are raised.
(B) Uncontrollable expenditures have resulted in annual deficits since 1980.
(C) Discretionary spending is outpacing spending in all other categories.
(D) The mandatory retirement age will have to be raised in order to balance the budget.
(E) Uncontrollable expenditures have increased since 1990.

18. Under which of the following principles has the due-process clause of the Fourteenth Amendment been applied to protect individuals from violations of fundamental rights by the states?
(A) equal protection
(B) constitutional federalism
(C) the incorporation doctrine
(D) the inclusionary doctrine
(E) the wall of separation

19. What is the primary source of political socialization?
(A) family
(B) peer groups
(C) television
(D) the Internet
(E) public schools

20. The Supreme Court has upheld all of the following restrictions on abortion EXCEPT
(A) a twenty-four-hour waiting period
(B) parental consent
(C) prohibition of abortion after the fetus is viable
(D) spousal consent
(E) required pamphlcts with information about alternatives

21. What was the biggest problem with the Articles of Confederation?
(A) The national government imposed heavy taxes on the wealthy.
(B) The states did not have enough power.
(C) Individual states could not control their economies.
(D) The national government did not have the power to regulate intrastate commerce.
(E) The national government could not lay and collect taxes.

22. A judge who believes that the Constitution should be interpreted according to its literal meaning and in its historical context favors what approach?
(A) judicial activism
(B) original intent
(C) limited jurisdiction
(D) dual federalism
(E) states' rights

23. Which of the following is a difference between the House of Representatives and the Senate?
(A) The Senate has stricter rules for floor debate.
(B) There is no leader in the Senate, except for the vice president in case of a tie vote.
(C) Revenue bills must originate in the Senate.
(D) Floor rules and debate are more casual in the Senate than in the House.
(E) The Senate has standing committees, but the House uses only select committees.

24. All of the following statements about filibusters are true EXCEPT
    (A) either political party may use the filibuster
    (B) senators who vote for cloture risk having their own filibusters ended the same way
    (C) filibusters have been used to block judicial appointments
    (D) cloture votes are rare, because they require seventy-five votes
    (E) both filibusters and cloture votes are becoming more common

25. What are political action committees?
    (A) registered organizations that donate money to campaigns and causes
    (B) committees that work as part of an iron triangle to change bureaucratic regulations
    (C) interest groups that have raised more than $200,000 in a single fiscal year
    (D) groups of people who are interested in a cause and lobby on its behalf
    (E) organizations whose primary purpose is to lobby Congress

26. How does an executive order differ from legislation?
    (A) Executive orders are submitted by the president to Congress for approval; bills are submitted by the Congress to the president for approval.
    (B) Executive orders have the force of law but do not have to be approved by Congress.
    (C) Executive orders expire after five years.
    (D) Executive orders require ratification by the Senate but not the House.
    (E) The Supreme Court cannot rule on the constitutionality of an executive order.

Table 4.1 Responsibility for Success or Failure

Statement	Percentage of High School Students Agreeing	
	1924	1977
It is entirely the fault of the man himself if he cannot succeed.	47%	47%
The fact that some men [in 1977: people] have so much more money than others shows there is an unjust condition in this country that ought to be changed.	30	34

Source: Theodore Caplow and Howard M. Bahr, "Half a Century of Change in Adolescent Attitudes: A Replication of a Middletown Survey by the Lynds," Public Opinion Quarterly 43 (Spring 1979): 1–17, table 1. Copyright © 1979, reprinted by permission of University of Chicago Press.

27. The table above best supports which statement about American core values?
    (A) Most Americans believe that hard work leads to success.
    (B) Americans have become slightly more conservative over time.
    (C) From 1924 until 1977, slightly less than half of all Americans blamed people for their lack of success.
    (D) Most Americans are political moderates.
    (E) Americans are more conservative on economic issues than Europeans.

28. Which of the following are valid criticisms of the Iowa caucus and New Hampshire primary?
    I. Too much attention is paid to them because they are early.
    II. It is difficult for a candidate to gain momentum in either of these states.
    III. These states' populations are not representative of the country as a whole.
    IV. Because these states are small, these contests do not get enough media coverage.

    (A) I and II
    (B) II and III
    (C) I, II, and III
    (D) I and III
    (E) II and IV

GO ON TO NEXT PAGE

29. What is judicial review?
    (A) the review of judicial appointments by members of the Senate, who have the power to confirm nominees
    (B) the ability of the Supreme Court to overturn rulings by federal district court judges
    (C) the power of the Supreme Court to overturn rulings by federal appeals court judges
    (D) the power of the chief justice of the Supreme Court to preside over impeachment hearings
    (E) the power of the Supreme Court to declare acts of Congress or the states unconstitutional

30. Which of the following programs are entitlements?
    I. Medicaid
    II. Medicare
    III. Food Stamps
    IV. Social Security

    (A) I and II
    (B) I, III, and III
    (C) II and IV
    (D) I and IV
    (E) II, III, and IV

31. Some evidence suggests that in the 1980 election, voters did not vote for Ronald Reagan as much as they voted against Jimmy Carter. What best describes this kind of voting behavior?
    (A) prospective voting
    (B) ideological voting
    (C) retrospective voting
    (D) group-benefits voting
    (E) no-issue-content voting

32. What advantage does Congress have by sending bills to the president more than ten days before the end of a congressional session?
    (A) The president will not have much time to write a veto message.
    (B) The bill cannot be pocket vetoed.
    (C) The president cannot use a line-item veto.
    (D) Congress has time to rewrite the bill if the president does not like it.
    (E) Congress will have the time to call a special session if necessary.

33. Which of the following statements best describes the accuracy of public opinion polls?
    (A) Even in a close election, most public opinion polls accurately predict the winner.
    (B) The bigger the sample, the more room there is for sampling error.
    (C) Different polling organizations often have different results, even when they ask the same question.
    (D) The sampling error is usually plus or minus 3 percent.
    (E) Public opinion polls cannot predict elections with any degree of accuracy.

34. All of the following are necessary for an accurate public opinion poll EXCEPT
    (A) the question must be asked in an unbiased manner
    (B) the persons interviewed must be selected based on a random sample
    (C) the questions must be understandable
    (D) the answer categories must offer people a choice between different responses
    (E) the number of people sampled must be at least 10% percent of the population

35. Which constitutional provision gives states most of their powers?
    (A) the Ninth Amendment
    (B) the Tenth Amendment
    (C) the commerce clause
    (D) the necessary and proper clause
    (E) the full faith and credit clause

36. What is the main reason for the shift from dual to cooperative federalism?
    (A) court decisions that required the states and federal government to coordinate policies
    (B) inconsistent welfare policies at the state level, which required national coordination
    (C) the increase in federal grants-in-aid to the states
    (D) the global economy and the importance of improving the trained workforce
    (E) revenue sharing, which occurred during budgetary surpluses

37. What is the role of the federal courts of appeals?
    (A) to send cases to the Supreme Court when there is a constitutional issue involved
    (B) to hear appeals from the federal district courts
    (C) to hear new testimony in cases being retried
    (D) to hear appeals from state supreme courts when there is a constitutional issue involved
    (E) to review acts of Congress before they are sent to the Supreme Court for final judicial review

38. The College Board filed briefs in the affirmative action cases brought by college applicants against the University of Michigan. What is the best description of these briefs?
    (A) amicus curiae
    (B) stare decisis
    (C) per curiam
    (D) reply briefs
    (E) appellate briefs

39. Which of the following is the best example of fiscal federalism?
    (A) the use of the commerce clause to regulate public places and accommodations
    (B) the Court's decision in *United States v. Lopez*
    (C) categorical, project, and block grants
    (D) the Court's decision in *McCulloch v. Maryland*

(E) state budget cuts as a result of rising inflation

40. A state, which is not Maine or Nebraska, has eight members in the House of Representatives. In a presidential election, that state's population votes 40 percent for the Democratic candidate and 60 percent for the Republican candidate. How are that state's electoral votes allocated?
    (A) Eight electoral votes are pledged to the Republican candidate.
    (B) Ten electoral votes are pledged to the Republican candidate.
    (C) Four votes are pledged to the Democrat, and six votes are pledged to the Republican.
    (D) Six votes are pledged to the Democrat and four votes are pledged to the Republican.
    (E) It is impossible to determine the number of electoral college votes from the facts given.

41. When the House and Senate pass different versions of a bill, where is the language of the bill resolved?
    (A) joint committee
    (B) standing committee
    (C) conference committee
    (D) select committee
    (E) in a meeting with the leadership of both houses

42. Which constitutional provision has expanded the power of the federal government in regulating privately owned businesses?
    (A) commerce clause
    (B) Tenth Amendment
    (C) full faith and credit clause
    (D) power to lay and collect taxes
    (E) power to borrow money

43. All of the following are likely to vote for a candidate from the Democratic party EXCEPT
    (A) African Americans
    (B) non-Cuban Hispanics
    (C) union members
    (D) women
    (E) small business owners

GO ON TO NEXT PAGE

44. What is the term for a sharp, lasting shift that occurs in the popular coalitions supporting one or both parties?
    (A) readjustment
    (B) deviating election
    (C) electoral shift
    (D) critical realignment
    (E) party reorganization

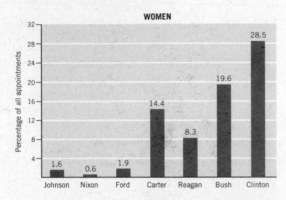

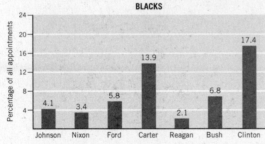

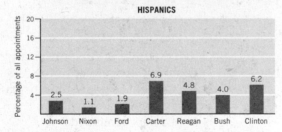

45. The chart above best supports which of the following conclusions?
    (A) From 1963 until 2000, Democratic presidents appointed more blacks to the judiciary than Republican presidents did.
    (B) Blacks being appointed to the judiciary are appointed to the district court level, rather than to the appellate courts.
    (C) Twenty percent of the judges appointed by Clinton were black.

    (D) President George H. W. Bush appointed more black judges than President Johnson did.
    (E) The percentage of black judges appointed by President Carter mirrored the percentage of blacks in the population.

46. When the Supreme Court ruled that laws against flag-burning are unconstitutional, many citizens disagreed with the Court's ruling and wanted Congress to take action. What could Congress do to make flag-burning illegal?
    (A) pass a federal law that bans flag-burning
    (B) pass a constitutional amendment banning flag-burning
    (C) with a two-thirds vote, approve a constitutional amendment, to be ratified by three-fourths of the states
    (D) pressure the president for an executive order banning flag-burning
    (E) there is nothing Congress can do once the Supreme Court rules a law unconstitutional; the Supreme Court is a court of last resort

47. Congressional committees do all of the following tasks EXCEPT
    (A) revise bills
    (B) kill bills
    (C) refer bills to subcommittees
    (D) delay bills
    (E) enact legislation

48. The equal protection clause of the Fourteenth Amendment would be used to decide all of the following types of cases EXCEPT
    (A) school segregation
    (B) affirmative action
    (C) sex discrimination
    (D) abortion
    (E) racial profiling

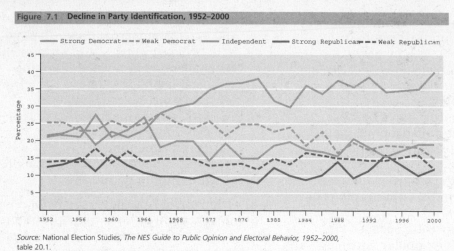

Figure 7.1   Decline in Party Identification, 1952–2000

— Strong Democrat --- Weak Democrat — Independent — Strong Republican --- Weak Republican

Source: National Election Studies, *The NES Guide to Public Opinion and Electoral Behavior, 1952–2000*, table 20.1.

49. The chart above best supports which of the following statements?
   (A) In 2000 there were more Republicans than Democrats.
   (B) The biggest gap between strong Republicans and strong Democrats occurred in 1984.
   (C) In 2000 the number of independent voters was the highest in any year since 1952.
   (D) Since 1980 there has been steady increase in the number of voters who identify themselves as Republican.
   (E) The number of weak Republicans has outnumbered strong Republicans since 1976.

50. What is the typical method for becoming a member of the White House staff?
   (A) be a longtime associate of the president who has served on his campaign staff
   (B) be a longtime member of Congress with substantial experience in policy making
   (C) serve on the staff of the president's predecessor if the former president was a member of the president's political party
   (D) have experience in business and industry and apply for the job based upon qualifications
   (E) have experience in academia, preferably as a professor at an Ivy League college

51. How do delegates to national conventions differ ideologically from most party members?
   (A)   They are more moderate because they represent the interests of an entire state.
   (B)   The Republicans are more right wing, and the Democrats are more moderate.
   (C)   The Democrats are more left wing, and the Republicans are more moderate.
   (D)   The Democrats are more left wing, and the Republicans are more right wing.
   (E) There is no significant difference in the ideology of the delegates and that of party members.

52. The census is important for which of the following purposes?
   I.   to determine the number of representatives a state will have in the House of Representatives
   II. to determine the number of senators each state will have
   III. for the purpose of receiving categorical grant money
   IV. to determine the number of electoral college votes a state will have

   (A) I and III
   (B) I, II, and III
   (C) II, III, and IV
   (D) I and IV
   (E) I, III, and IV

53. All of the following are advantages of incumbency for members of Congress EXCEPT
   (A) the recognition they receive by sitting on oversight committees
   (B) the use of franking privileges to let members of their districts know what they have been doing
   (C) the ability to provide casework
   (D) the ability to bring pork-barrel projects to their states
   (E) name recognition

GO ON TO NEXT PAGE

54. All of the following arguments have been made about the electoral college EXCEPT
   (A) it benefits small states because they receive a disproportionate share of votes
   (B) it benefits large states because they receive a disproportionate share of attention from the candidates
   (C) it benefits third parties because they can control entire regions of the country
   (D) it is undemocratic because the winner of the popular vote may not win in the electoral college
   (E) states with large urban populations get more attention from the candidates

55. What does the above drawing illustrate?
   (A) political machines
   (B) gerrymandering
   (C) aggressive foreign policy
   (D) divided government
   (E) the hostile press

56. A state law that requires posting of the Ten Commandments in all public school classrooms would most likely be challenged as a violation of the
   (A) establishment clause
   (B) free exercise clause
   (C) First Amendment protection of symbolic speech
   (D) Tenth Amendment
   (E) First Amendment protection of the right to petition

57. The Patriot Act allows the federal government to tap a person's phones with a court order without having to get a separate search warrant for each phone. What rights are balanced in this case?
   (A) privacy and the Freedom of Information Act
   (B) expression and information gathering
   (C) privacy and national security
   (D) expression and speech
   (E) this case does not involve balancing competing rights

58. Those who attempt to influence governmental decisions, especially legislation, often on behalf of interest groups, are best described as
   (A) PACs
   (B) influence peddlers
   (C) social movements
   (D) lobbyists
   (E) campaign strategists

59. Which of the following groups voted most heavily in favor of Ronald Reagan?
   (A) moderate conservatives
   (B) pure conservatives
   (C) moderate liberals
   (D) pure liberals
   (E) independent voters

60. In the following scenario, the Senate has fifty Republicans and fifty Democrats and the president is Republican. What would be the result if one Republican senator changed his affiliation to become an independent?
    (A) No major changes would occur in the conduct of the Senate.
    (B) The Senate would have a Democratic majority, and it would become impossible for the president to enact his program.
    (C) The Republican whip would be used to make sure the independent senator voted with the Republicans.
    (D) The Republican committee heads would be replaced with Democrats.
    (E) The vice president would no longer be the president of the Senate.

STOP

END OF SECTION I

IF YOU FINISH BEFORE TIME IS CALLED, YOU MAY CHECK YOUR WORK ON THIS SECTION. DO NOT GO ON TO SECTION II UNTIL YOU ARE TOLD TO DO SO.

UNITED STATES GOVERNMENT AND POLITICS
Section II
Time—100 minutes

Directions You have 100 minutes to answer all four of the following questions. Unless the directions indicate otherwise, respond to all parts of each question. It is recommended that you take a few minutes to plan and outline each answer. <u>Spend approximately 25 minutes on each question.</u> Support your essay with specific examples where appropriate. Be sure to number each of your answers.

1. Civil rights have expanded over time, and new groups continue to ask the federal government for protection from discrimination.
   a. Identify and explain one decision made by the Supreme Court that expanded civil rights.
   b. Identify and explain one law passed by Congress that expanded civil rights.
   c. Identify a group that has encountered roadblocks in obtaining civil rights protection, and explain two reasons for these roadblocks.

2. The federal government cannot control the economy, but it can take measures to improve the health of the American economy.
   a. Identify and explain one way that the government uses monetary policy to influence the economy.
   b. Identify and explain one way that the government uses the budget to influence the economy.
   c. Identify and explain one way Congress can influence the economy.
   d. Identify and explain one way the president can influence the economy.

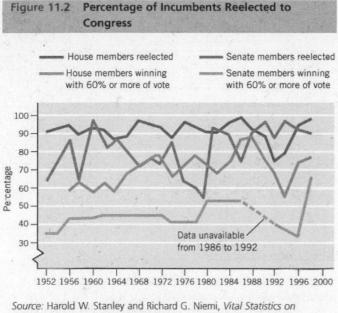

Figure 11.2 **Percentage of Incumbents Reelected to Congress**

House members reelected — Senate members reelected

House members winning with 60% or more of vote — Senate members winning with 60% or more of vote

Data unavailable from 1986 to 1992

Source: Harold W. Stanley and Richard G. Niemi, *Vital Statistics on American Politics, 1999–2000* (Washington, D.C.: Congressional Quarterly Press, 2000), table 1-18.

3. Using the data in the graph above and your knowledge of United States politics, perform the following tasks:
   a. Identify one trend shown in the graph as it relates to members of the House of Representatives, and explain one reason for this trend.
   b. Identify one trend shown in the graph as it relates to senators, and explain one reason for this trend.
   c. Identify one trend that relates to the differences in the graph between members of the House of Representatives and senators, and explain one reason for this trend.

4. The power of the president is the power to persuade rather than the power to command.
   a. Identify and explain one formal power and one informal power used by the president to influence domestic policy.
   b. Identify and explain one formal power and one informal power used by the president to influence foreign policy.

END OF EXAMINATION

GO ON TO NEXT PAGE

Answer Key for Multiple-Choice Questions

1. D	11. B	21. E	31. C	41. C	51. D
2. B	12. C	22. B	32. B	42. A	52. E
3. A	13. D	23. D	33. D	43. E	53. A
4. C	14. A	24. D	34. E	44. D	54. C
5. C	15. C	25. A	35. B	45. D	55. B
6. C	16. B	26. B	36. C	46. C	56. A
7. E	17. E	27. C	37. B	47. E	57. C
8. B	18. C	28. D	38. A	48. D	58. D
9. A	19. A	29. E	39. C	49. C	59. B
10. E	20. D	30. C	40. B	50. A	60. D

ANSWERS TO MULTIPLE-CHOICE QUESTIONS

1. Answer: **D**. Project grants are based on competitive applications for specific undertakings (*American Government*, 8th ed., pages 62-64 / 9th ed., page 62).

2. Answer: **B**. The Voting Rights Act of 1965 had a clear goal of increasing registration and voting by blacks. Federal officials oversaw its implementation, and criminal penalties were provided for interfering with voting rights (*American Government*, 8th ed., page 133 / 9th ed., page 135).

3. Answer: **A**. A president's popularity tends to be highest right after he is elected, and this is the best time for him to get programs enacted (*American Government*, 8th ed., page 357 / 9th ed., page 354).

4. Answer: **C**. In *Miranda v. Arizona*, the court held that suspects must be read their rights. Otherwise, their confessions are not admissible in court (*American Government*, 8th ed., page 515 / 9th ed., page 517).

5. Answer: **C**. While the president may veto a bill in its entirety, he cannot veto a portion of a bill (*American Government*, 8th ed., page 344 / 9th ed., page 340).

6. Answer: **C**. The turnout in the 2000 election was slightly above 50 percent, while turnout in 1996 was slightly above 49 percent (*American Government*, 8th ed., pages 135-136 / 9th ed., page 137).

7. Answer: **E**. Single-member districts with winner-take-all elections favor two parties and make it difficult for third parties to compete (*American Government*, 8th ed., pages 165-168 / 9th ed., pages 171-173).

8. Answer: **B**. Congress can refuse to confirm a judge nominated by the president. This is a check on both the executive and judicial branches (*American Government*, 8th ed., page 29 / 9th ed., page 29).

9. Answer: **A**. Presidents usually appoint judges from the ranks of their political party. These candidates are also chosen based upon their qualifications (*American Government*, 8th ed., page 413 / 9th ed., page 413).

10. Answer: **E**. Senatorial courtesy allows a senator to block the nomination of a federal district judge from his or her home state. This has been criticized as a legislative veto, which reverses the balance of powers (*American Government*, 8th ed., pages 412-413 / 9th ed., pages 412-413).

11. Answer: **B.** Beginning in 1994, Clinton faced divided government, in which the party opposing the president holds one or both houses of Congress. This makes it difficult for a president to get programs passed (*American Government*, 8th ed., page 335 / 9th ed., page 331).

12. Answer: **C.** It is difficult for Congress to obtain the two-thirds vote necessary to override a presidential veto (*American Government*, 8th ed., pages 358-360 / 9th ed., pages 356-357).

13. Answer: **D.** Madison believed that a balanced government (including separation of powers, checks and balances, and federalism) could eliminate "the mischiefs of faction" (*American Government*, 8th ed., pages 32-33 / 9th ed., pages 32-33).

14. Answer: **A.** Many states opposed the Americans with Disabilities Act because it created an unfunded mandate (*American Government*, 8th ed., pages 66-68 / 9th ed., pages 65-67).

15. Answer: **C.** The sound bite dropped from about 42 seconds in 1968 to 7.3 seconds in 2000. As a result, candidates' speeches are not covered in depth (*American Government*, 8th ed., page 250 / 9th ed., page 256).

16. Answer: **B.** The McCain-Feingold law bans soft-money contributions—these were unlimited contributions to political parties that were considered the largest loophole in previous campaign finance reform laws (*American Government*, 8th ed., pages 194-195 / 9th ed., pages 205-206).

17. Answer: **E.** Social Security and Medicare are uncontrollable expenditures. They have increased since 1990 (*American Government*, 8th ed., page 471 / 9th ed., page 471).

18. Answer: **C.** In *Gitlow v. New York*, the Supreme Court held that the due-process clause of the Fourteenth Amendment protects individuals from state action that violates fundamental rights. This is known as the incorporation doctrine (*American Government*, 8th ed., page 502 / 9th ed., page 504).

19. Answer: **A.** Families have the most influence in political socialization (*American Government*, 8th ed., pages 106-109 / 9th ed., pages 106-109).

20. Answer: **D.** Abortion may be banned during the third trimester. The court has upheld parental consent laws, a twenty-four-hour waiting period, and a requirement that women be given information about alternatives. The Court struck down a spousal consent requirement (*American Government*, 8th ed., pages 540-541 / 9th ed., pages 542-543).

21. Answer: **E.** Under the Articles of Confederation, the national government did not have the power to tax (*American Government*, 8th ed., pages 21-22 / 9th ed., pages 21-22).

22. Answer: **B.** Strict constructionists use original intent to interpret the Constitution in a narrow manner, using the document's expressed language and in light of its historical context (*American Government*, 8th ed., page 404 / 9th ed., page 404).

23. Answer: **D.** Because the House is larger than the Senate, it is more difficult to control. The House is more formal and has more rules in the conduct of its business (*American Government*, 8th ed., pages 316-317 / 9th ed., pages 316-317).

24. Answer: **D.** Sixty votes are required to end a filibuster by cloture (*American Government*, 8th ed., page 317 / 9th ed., page 317).

GO ON TO NEXT PAGE

25. Answer: **A**. PACs are committees set up to raise and spend campaign contributions on behalf of one or more candidates or causes (*American Government*, 8th ed., pages 236-238 / 9th ed., pages 241-243).

26. Answer: **B**. Executive orders are presidential directives that have the force of law but do not need to be approved by Congress (*American Government*, 8th ed., pages 345-346 / 9th ed., pages 340-341).

27. Answer: **C**. In both 1924 and 1977, 47 percent of Americans polled believed that it was entirely the fault of the man himself if he cannot succeed (*American Government*, 8th ed., page 84 / 9th ed., page 82).

28. Answer: **D**. Iowa and New Hampshire are not demographically representative of the country as a whole. Yet they receive a disproportionate share of attention because they hold the first caucus and primary (*American Government*, 8th ed., pages 183-187 / 9th ed., pages 192-194).

29. Answer: **E**. Judicial review was established in *Marbury v. Madison*. It is the power of the Supreme Court to declare state or federal laws unconstitutional (*American Government*, 8th ed., page 403 / 9th ed., page 403).

30. Answer: **C**. Medicare and Social Security are entitlement programs. They have been promised to people once they meet certain qualifications. They are not based on financial need (*American Government*, 8th ed., page 483 / 9th ed., page 483).

31. Answer: **C**. Retrospective voting means looking at how things have gone in the recent past. Voters were not happy with the track record of the Carter administration, and he lost the 1980 election (*American Government*, 8th ed., page 202 / 9th ed., pages 210-211).

32. Answer: **B**. A pocket veto occurs when a president does not sign a bill within ten days and Congress has adjourned. A pocket veto cannot occur if Congress sends the president a bill more than ten days prior to adjournment (*American Government*, 8th ed., pages 358-360 / 9th ed., pages 356-357).

33. Answer: **D**. Normal sampling error is plus or minus 3 percent. This makes it difficult to predict the winner in a close election (*American Government*, 8th ed., pages 114-115 / 9th ed., pages 116-117).

34. Answer: **E**. For any population over 500,000, at least 1,065 people need to be polled to achieve a sampling error of plus or minus 3 percent, 95 percent of the time (*American Government*, 8th ed., pages 114-115 / 9th ed., pages 116-117).

35. Answer: **B**. The Tenth Amendment reserves powers not delegated to the national government, nor prohibited to the states, to the states and the people. It is the main basis for state power (*American Government*, 8th ed., pages 53-54 / 9th ed., pages 53-54).

36. Answer: **C**. Federal grants-in-aid often come with strings attached. This was a major reason for the move from dual to cooperative federalism (*American Government*, 8th ed., pages 59-61 / 9th ed., page 59-61).

37. Answer: **B**. The federal courts of appeals hear appeals from the federal district courts. If a litigant is unhappy with an appeals court decision, the final level of appeal is the Supreme Court, which may or may not grant a writ of certiorari to decide the case (*American Government*, 8th ed., page 411 / 9th ed., page 411).

38. Answer: **A**. An amicus curiae brief is filed by an interested party not directly involved in the lawsuit (*American Government*, 8th ed., page 421 / 9th ed., page 421).

39. Answer: **C**. Fiscal federalism involves using federal money to pay for state and local programs through project, categorical, and block grants (*American Government*, 8th ed., pages 59-64 / 9th ed., pages 59-63).

40. Answer: **B**. In all states except Maine and Nebraska, a winner-take-all system is used. The state will have ten electoral college votes (eight for its members in the House of Representatives and two for its senators), all of which will be pledged to the Republican candidate (*American Government*, 8th ed., pages 340-341 / 9th ed., pages 336-337).

41. Answer: **C**. Conference committees with members of both houses work on the language of bills that were passed in different versions (*American Government*, 8th ed., pages 306-307 / 9th ed., page 305).

42. Answer: **A**. The commerce clause, in conjunction with the necessary and proper clause, allows the federal government to regulate private businesses (*American Government*, 8th ed., pages 446-448 / 9th ed., pages 446-448).

43. Answer: **E**. African Americans, Jews, and union members tend to vote for Democrats. In addition, there is a gender gap, with women favoring the Democrats and men favoring the Republicans (*American Government*, 8th ed., pages 109-110, 209-210 / 9th ed., pages 109, 160).

44. Answer: **D**. A critical or realigning period occurs when there is a major and permanent shift in the groups supporting the political parties (*American Government*, 8th ed., page 208 / 9th ed., page 158).

45. Answer: **D**. Blacks accounted for 6.8 percent of President George H. W. Bush's appointments. This is greater than the 4.1 percent appointed by President Johnson (*American Government*, 8th ed., page 413 / 9th ed., page 413).

46. Answer: **C**. An amendment to the Constitution can, in effect, overturn a Supreme Court decision. An amendment requires the approval of two-thirds of both houses of Congress and ratification by three-fourths of the states (*American Government*, 8th ed., pages 427-428 / 9th ed., page 428).

47. Answer: **E**. Congressional committees revise, delay, and kill bills. The can also refer bill to subcommittees for further review (*American Government*, 8th ed., pages 306-309 / 9th ed., pages 304-309).

48. Answer: **D**. The Fourteenth Amendment's equal protection clause prohibits race and gender discrimination. It applies in cases involving school segregation, affirmative action, sex discrimination, and racial profiling. Abortion cases are decided under the due process clause (*American Government*, 8th ed., pages 527-541 / 9th ed., pages 529-543).

49. Answer: **C**. In 2000, 40 percent of the electorate identified themselves as independent. This is the highest percentage shown on the table (*American Government*, 8th ed., page 150 / 9th ed., page 152).

50. Answer: **A**. Senior White House staff members are typically drawn from the ranks of the president's campaign staff and are longtime associates of the president (*American Government*, 8th ed., page 348 / 9th ed., page 344).

51. Answer: **D**. Delegates are more extreme in their ideology than average party members are. This means that Republican delegates are more right wing, and Democratic delegates are more left wing (*American Government*, 8th ed., page 160 / 9th ed., page 166).

52. Answer: **E**. The census determines the number of representatives a state will have in the House of Representatives. This also impacts the number of electoral college votes. Census data are also important for receiving formula grant money (*American Government*, 8th ed., pages 27, 66-67 / 9th ed., pages 27, 65).

53. Answer: **A**. Incumbent members of Congress benefit from name recognition, the use of franking privileges, casework, and by bringing pork-barrel projects to their states. Sitting on oversight committees usually does not bring much attention (*American Government*, 8th ed., pages 287-289 / 9th ed., pages 291-293)

54. Answer: **C**. The electoral college hurts third parties because it is difficult for them to get a majority in any state. It is difficult for third parties to get any electoral college votes (*American Government*, 8th ed., pages 340-341 / 9th ed., pages 336-337).

55. Answer: **B**. The drawing shows gerrymandering, whereby districts are malapportioned (*American Government*, 8th ed., page 290 / 9th ed., page 189).

56. Answer: **A**. A law requiring the posting of the Ten Commandments in public schools could be challenged under the establishment clause as violating the separation between church and state (*American Government*, 8th ed., pages 508-511 / 9th ed., pages 511-513).

57. Answer: **C**. The Patriot Act balanced privacy rights with national security (*American Government*, 8th ed., page 517 / 9th ed., page 519).

58. Answer: **D**. Lobbyists, often working for interest groups, attempt to influence legislation (*American Government*, 8th ed., page 218 / 9th ed., page 224).

59. Answer: **B**. Pure conservatives strongly supported Ronald Reagan's philosophy of tax cuts and decreased social spending (*American Government*, 8th ed., pages 122-123 / 9th ed., page 121).

60. Answer: **D**. The majority party in the Senate appoints committee heads (*American Government*, 8th ed., pages 306-307 / 9th ed., page 305).

ANSWERS TO FREE-RESPONSE QUESTIONS

QUESTION 1 Sample answer for Part (a): The Supreme Court decision in *Brown v. Board of Education* expanded civil rights. The plaintiffs claimed that separate schools for blacks and whites violated the Fourteenth Amendment. The Court agreed, ruling that segregated schools were inherently unequal. This overturned the separate but equal doctrine established in *Plessy v. Ferguson*. The *Brown* case paved the way for more equal educational opportunities for black children.

Sample answer for Part (b): The Voting Rights Act of 1965 also expanded civil rights. Although blacks were given the right to vote in the Fifteenth Amendment, southern states used several tactics to block this right, including grandfather clauses, literacy tests, and terrorism. Under the Voting Rights Act, federal marshals were sent to the offending states to register blacks and protect them at the polls. The result was increased registration and turnout by blacks.

Sample answer for Part (c): One group that has encountered roadblocks in obtaining civil rights protection is homosexuals. For example, some states have expressly prohibited gay marriage, and some favor passing a constitutional amendment to ban gay marriage. One reason for this roadblock is that the language of the Fourteenth

Amendment does not expressly protect gay people. Another reason for the roadblock is that some religions oppose homosexuality, and this opposition is a part of many Americans' beliefs. As a result, it is difficult for gay people to get widespread support for civil rights protections (*American Government*, 8th ed., pages 527-537, 548-549 / 9th ed., pages 529-539, 548-549).

SCORING This essay is worth 7 points. Part (a) is worth 2 points—1 point for identifying a case (*Brown v. Board of Education*), and 1 point for explaining how the case expanded civil rights (it ended segregation and provided educational opportunities). There are a number of civil rights cases that could be identified and explained in this section.

Part (b) is worth 2 points—1 point for identifying a law (the Voting Rights Act of 1965), and 1 point for explaining how the law expanded civil rights (it sent federal marshals to enable blacks to register and vote). Other laws could be identified, such as the Civil Rights Act of 1964.

Part (c) is worth 3 points—1 for identifying a group that has faced roadblocks (homosexuals), and 1 point for each of two obstacles identified (the Fourteenth Amendment does not mention gays, and homosexuality is opposed by some religious groups). Other groups could be identified as well, including the disabled and minors under age eighteen.

QUESTION 2 Part (a): One way that monetary policy is used to influence the economy is by changing interest rates. The Federal Reserve Board sets the interest rates it charges banks to borrow from the federal government. This is called the discount rate. If the Fed raises the discount rate, banks pay more to borrow money, and they pass these higher interest rates on to their customers. This makes money more expensive to borrow and slows the rate of inflation.

Part (b): One way the budget is used to influence the economy is through taxation policy. Based on supply-side economics, the Reagan and George W. Bush administrations wanted to stimulate economic growth by cutting taxes. Supporters of supply-side economics believe that high taxes (often coupled with numerous government regulations) hinder the growth of businesses. Under this theory, the money that would have been spent on taxes might be spent by businesses to increase production and hire more workers. As a result, unemployment would drop and production would increase.

Part (c): One way Congress can influence the economy comes from its role in approving all taxes and almost all expenditures. Appropriations committees in both houses must approve all spending. Budget committees, assisted by the Congressional Budget Office, make recommendations about the budget submitted by the president.

Part (d): The president has some influence over the economy because he appoints the members of the Federal Reserve Board (subject to Senate confirmation). This board sets monetary policy, and the president appoints candidates who share his philosophy about regulating the money supply. Members serve for a nonrenewable term of fourteen years, and this gives them significant influence over the economy (*American Government*, 8th ed., pages 463-473 / 9th ed., pages 464-473).

SCORING This essay is worth 8 points. Part (a) is worth 2 points—1 point for identifying a monetary tool (interest rates), and 1 point for explaining how this tool influences the economy (higher interest rates control inflation). Points would be awarded for other identifications and explanations, such as changing the amount of reserves a bank must keep on hand.

Part (b) is worth 2 points—1 point for identifying a budgetary tool (taxation), and 1 point for explaining how this tool influences the economy (lower taxes may stimulate growth). Points would be awarded for identifying and explaining other budgetary tools, such as using government spending to stimulate the economy.

Part (c) is worth 2 points—1 point for identifying a way Congress influences the economy (by approving taxing and spending) and 1 point for the explanation (Congress can influence the budget by proposing its own plan with the assistance of the CBO). Points would be awarded for identifying other ways Congress influences the economy, such as Senate confirmation of members of the Federal Reserve Board.

Part (d) is worth 2 points—1 point for identifying a way the president influences the economy (by appointing members of the Federal Reserve Board), and 1 point for the explanation (members are appointed for long terms and share the president's monetary philosophy). Points would be awarded for identifying other ways the president can influence the economy, such as by proposing an annual budget.

QUESTION 3 Part (a): One trend is that members of the House of Representatives are reelected at high rates. Most years, the rate is reelection is around 90 percent, and it has never fallen below 70 percent. One reason for this trend is that most members of the House of Representatives do not represent an entire state but represent a district. They can do casework for constituents in their districts, and satisfied constituents will vote for their reelection.

Part (b): One trend shown is that the reelection rate for senators drops during hard economic times and periods of instability. For example, during the mid to late 1960s, the Vietnam War caused national discontent. The reelection rate for senators dropped. During the early 1970s in the period following Watergate, the reelection rate for senators also dropped. The reason for this is that senators are visible and represent an entire state. They are held accountable for the performance of the federal government.

Part (c): One trend shown is that members of the House of Representatives are elected at higher rates than senators are. This is because House members are elected every two years and are therefore constantly campaigning. Also, House members represent smaller constituencies than most senators do, and it is easier for them to stay in touch with their constituents. (*American Government*, 8th ed., pages 284-287 / 9th ed., pages 289-291).

SCORING This essay is worth 6 points. Part (a) is worth 2 points—1 point for identifying a trend (incumbents in the House are elected at high rates), and 1 point for the explanation (casework encourages voters to reelect them). Points would be awarded for identifying other trends, such as a fairly stable reelection rate over time, and for other explanations, such as the use of franking privileges or bringing in pork barrel projects.

Part (b) is worth 2 points—1 point for identifying a trend (fewer incumbent senators are reelected during hard times), and 1 point for giving an explanation (senators represent larger areas that are harder to please). Points would be awarded for identifying other trends, such as volatility, and for other explanations, such as the diversity of interests within a state.

Part (c) is worth 2 points—1 point for identifying a trend (more House incumbents are reelected), and 1 point for an explanation (House members are accountable to fewer people). Points would be awarded for identifying other trends, such are more volatility in the Senate, and for other explanations, such as the shorter term of office for the House.

QUESTION 4 Part (a): One formal power of the president in influencing domestic policy is the power to appoint cabinet secretaries. For example, President George W. Bush appointed Tom Ridge to head the Department of Homeland Security. These appointments are subject to Senate confirmation. Presidents try to select candidates who agree with their domestic agendas and will carry out their wishes. For example, President Bush wanted some system to warn people of impending dangers and to plan a preparedness program. Tom Ridge has developed programs to address these issues, although some of his proposals have been questioned.

One informal power the president has to influence domestic policy is the power to call a press conference and ask for the public's support for a program. President Reagan did this with his first set of tax cuts. In a television address, Reagan asked the public to contact Congress in support of the cuts. Congress was inundated with calls, and the tax cuts became law.

Part (b): One formal power of the president in foreign affairs is the power as commander in chief to commit troops. Although the War Powers Act allows presidents to do so for only sixty days, most presidents have ignored this. For example, President Clinton sent troops into Bosnia and Somalia.

One informal power of the president in foreign affairs is the power to address international organizations, such as the United Nations. For example, President George W. Bush recently addressed the United Nations and defended the war in Iraq. Although these addresses may or may not convince other countries that our actions were justified, they do give the president the power to send his message to people throughout the world who have an opportunity to see the addresses on television (*American Government*, 8th ed., pages 375-376, 554-562 / 9th ed., pages 375-376, 554-564).

SCORING This essay is worth 8 points. Part (a) is worth 4 points—1 point for the formal power identified (presidents appoint cabinet secretaries) and 1 point for the explanation (they set policy in accordance with his wishes), 1 point for an informal power (the power to use the media) and 1 point for the explanation (the public supports the president's program). Points would also be awarded for identifying and explaining other formal powers, such as the power to approve laws, and other informal powers, such as the power to offer a member of Congress support with his or her campaign in exchange for favorable legislation.

Part (b) is worth 4 points—1 point for the formal power identified (commander in chief) and 1 point for the explanation (commit troops), 1 point for identifying an informal power (speaking to the United Nations) and 1 point for the explanation (influencing citizens of other countries). Points would also be awarded for identifying and explaining other formal powers, such as the power to appoint the secretary of defense, and other informal powers, such as the ability to form relationships with world leaders, such as Tony Blair.

Calculating your score on the AP Exam

SECTION 1: MULTIPLE-CHOICE QUESTIONS

_____ Minus (1/4 X _____) Equals _____
correct   wrong   score

Rounded to nearest whole number _____
                                      **adjusted
                                      score**

SECTION II: FREE-RESPONSE QUESTIONS

Question 1 _____ X 1.875 equals _____
           Out of 8   do not round

Question 2 _____ X 2.5   equals _____
           Out of 6   do not round

Question 3 _____ X 3.0   equals _____
           Out of 5   do not round

Question 4 _____ X 2.5   equals _____
           Out of 6   do not round

TOTAL FOR SECTION II   _____

COMPOSITE SCORE:

_____ + _____ = _____
Section I   Section II   Composite Score

Student scores are weighted a differently each year to determine the final AP score. The conversion chart below is according to the weighing on the 2002 exam:

COMPOSITE SCORE RANGE	AP GRADE
94-120	5
79-93	4
61-78	3
35 60	2
0-34	1

Practice Test 2

UNITED STATES GOVERNMENT AND POLITICS
Section I
Time—45 minutes
60 Questions

Directions The questions or incomplete statements below are each followed by five suggested answers. Select the best answer.

MULTIPLE-CHOICE QUESTIONS

1. How can the executive branch check the judicial branch?
   (A) by approving the nomination of federal judges
   (B) by nominating federal judges, subject to senate approval
   (C) by issuing an executive order overturning a court's decision
   (D) by firing a federal judge for cause
   (E) by reducing the number of federal courts

2. A conservative is likely to support all of the following EXCEPT
   (A) increased military spending
   (B) tax cuts
   (C) prayer in schools
   (D) affirmative action
   (E) restrictions on abortion

3. How do voters in closed primaries differ from voters in general elections?
   I. They must be registered to a party.
   II. They are leaders in their party.
   III. They are stauncher in their ideology.
   IV. They are more active in politics.

   (A) I and II
   (B) I, II, and III
   (C) I, II, and IV
   (D) I, III, and IV
   (E) I, II, III, and IV

4. Which statement best describes the importance of the vice president?
   (A) He checks on the health of the president daily and attends the funerals of Third World dictators.
   (B) He has an important role as the president of the Senate.
   (C) His importance depends on his relationship with the president and the duties the president asks him to assume.
   (D) He is a lightening rod for criticism that would be otherwise directed at the president.
   (E) He does not have an important role; his function is largely ceremonial.

5. Which of the following candidates would most likely receive the most money from a PAC?
   (A) an incumbent who has consistently supported the PAC's positions
   (B) a challenger whose viewpoints are unknown
   (C) a challenger whose viewpoints are opposed to the PAC's
   (D) an incumbent who has not voted consistently to support the PAC's positions in the past
   (E) any candidate who is likely to win

6. All of the following are true of Reaganomics EXCEPT
   (A) there was a large deficit at the end of Reagan's term
   (B) the income gap widened
   (C) tax cuts increased profits for most businesses
   (D) the largest tax cuts were for the wealthiest Americans
   (E) domestic spending and military spending were reduced to offset the decrease in federal revenue

7. Why was the election of 2000 significant?
   (A) because there was no winner in the electoral college, and the election was decided by a majority vote in the House of Representatives
   (B) because there was no winner in the electoral college, and the election was decided by one vote per state in the House of Representatives
   (C) because for the first time in more than a century, the winner in the electoral college lost the popular vote
   (D) because a third party, the Green party, won electoral college votes in three states
   (E) because the Supreme Court overturned the electoral college's decision

8. The House Armed Services Committee is best described as
   (A) standing
   (B) conference
   (C) select
   (D) joint
   (E) appropriations

9. What is the best rationale for allowing Supreme Court justices to serve for life terms?
   (A) It takes time for a justice to gain experience in decision making, so they serve for life to make sure the judiciary is experienced.
   (B) They protect the rights of the minority, and the protection of life tenure allows them to make legally correct, but unpopular, decisions.
   (C) Congress should not be able to remove them, because the average member of Congress does not have a legal background.
   (D) Their salaries are so low that it is difficult to attract good candidates; job security makes their positions more attractive.
   (E) They serve for life terms so that they may develop a body of consistent and understandable law over time.

10. In what respects is the Senate more powerful than the House of Representatives?
    I. It has the power to ratify treaties.
    II. It has the power to confirm judicial appointments.
    III. All revenue bills must originate there.
    IV. Each senator represents an entire state rather than a congressional district.

    (A) I and II
    (B) I, II, and III
    (C) II and III
    (D) I, II, and IV
    (E) III and IV

11. Which of the following cases falls under the original jurisdiction of the Supreme Court?
    (A) cases involving a state law that is alleged to violate the United States Constitution
    (B) cases involving a federal law that is alleged to violate the United States Constitution
    (C) controversies between two or more states
    (D) cases where the amount in controversy exceeds $50,000
    (E) conflicts between the president and Congress

GO ON TO NEXT PAGE

12. The president can influence legislation in all of the following ways EXCEPT
   (A) by having his staff write a legislative program that is then introduced by a member of his party in Congress
   (B) by asking the public to call Congress and express support for his legislative agenda
   (C) by threatening to veto a bill when there is not enough likely support in Congress to override the veto
   (D) by personally contacting members of Congress and asking for their support
   (E) by rewriting a portion of a bill and then signing the amended bill into law

13. What do the decisions of the Court led by Chief Justice Earl Warren illustrate about the relationship between the Court and the presidency?
   (A) Supreme Court justices closely follow the views of the presidents who appointed them, and try to use those views in making decisions.
   (B) Supreme Court justices stay in close contact with the presidents who nominate them, and they often become close friends.
   (C) Supreme Court justices are independent. You can never predict with certainty what they will do once in office.
   (D) Supreme Court justices are more likely to consider the opinions of the public if the president supports those beliefs.
   (E) Supreme Court justices are hesitant to lose the political support of the party that nominated them.

14. Which of the following have been used to expand civil rights?
   I.   commerce clause
   II. due process clause
   III. full faith and credit clause
   IV. equal protection clause

   (A) I, II, and IV
   (B) I and IV
   (C) II and IV
   (D) I and II
   (E) II, III, and IV

15. Two students who attended a public high school were suspended because they wore black armbands to protest the war in Vietnam. Their clothing might have caused a disruption, but no disruption occurred. They challenged the suspension, arguing that their First Amendment rights were violated. What is the most likely outcome of their case?
   (A) It will be dismissed, because wearing an armband is not speech protected by the First Amendment.
   (B) It will be dismissed, because students do not have free speech rights while they are in school.
   (C) It will be dismissed, because students to not have a right to be disruptive in school.
   (D) The students will win, because wearing an armband is protected symbolic speech.
   (E) The students will win, because teenagers have the same free speech rights as adults.

16. The House Rules Committee has all of the following powers EXCEPT
   (A) the power to make revisions to bills
   (B) the power to set strict time limits for debate
   (C) the power to specify the kinds of amendments that can be added to bills
   (D) the power to govern the procedures under which the bill will be considered by the house
   (E) the power to forbid amendments to bills

17. What has been the impact of the War Powers Act on American military actions?
    (A) Presidents have carefully followed the law and have asked Congress for permission before committing troops.
    (B) Presidents have committed troops and then asked for Congress to continue the troop commitments beyond sixty days.
    (C) Presidents have generally ignored the law because they believe it violates their powers as commander in chief.
    (D) Congress has used the law to call troops home once they have been committed for more than sixty days.
    (E) None. The Supreme Court ruled the War Powers Act unconstitutional under the political questions doctrine.

18. When Newt Gingrich became Speaker of the House in 1995, what changes were made to House rules?
    I.   He passed over some senior members in picking committee chairs.
    II. He did not want committee chairs to serve for more than six years.
    III. He eliminated the practice of making party membership on committees proportional to membership in the House as a whole.
    IV. He abolished some committees.

    (A) I and II
    (B) II and III
    (C) I, II, and III
    (D) I, II, and IV
    (E) II, III, and IV

19. The Civil Rights Act of 1964 did all of the following EXCEPT
    (A) barred race discrimination in public accommodations
    (B) banned discrimination in housing
    (C) outlawed race discrimination in hiring and firing
    (D) barred race discrimination in movie theaters, stadiums, and arenas
    (E) authorized the attorney general to bring suit to enforce school desegregation

20. What is the incorporation doctrine, first established in *Gitlow v. New York?*
    (A) The Bill of Rights protects individuals from the federal government but not from state government.
    (B) The Fourteenth Amendment protects individuals from state violations of all of the rights in the Bill of Rights.
    (C) The Fourteenth Amendment protects individuals from state violations of all of the rights in the Bill of Rights plus other fundamental rights.
    (D) The First Amendment protects individuals from state violations of free speech rights.
    (E) The Fourteenth Amendment protects individuals from state violations of fundamental personal rights.

21. What case established that the necessary and proper clause could be used to extend the national government's power beyond its expressed authority?
    (A) *McCulloch v. Maryland*
    (B) *Marbury v. Madison*
    (C) *Gitlow v. New York*
    (D) *Gibbons v. Ogden*
    (E) *Barron v. Baltimore*

22. Which of the following most accurately describes the origins of political attitudes (political socialization).
    (A) The media has the biggest influence on the political attitudes of people ages eighteen to twenty-one.
    (B) Teenagers aged eighteen to twenty-one tend to vote opposite of their parents because they want to rebel against their parents.
    (C) The family usually plays the largest role in political socialization, and people tend to vote the same way as their parents vote.
    (D) Schools play a large role in socialization, and high school students tend to follow the ideology of their social studies teachers.
    (E) There are so many influences on political socialization that no single factor determines ideology.

23. Which statement describes the "swing voter," who often decides elections?
    (A) prospective
    (B) no issue content
    (C) group benefits
    (D) retrospective
    (E) ideological

24. Which of the following candidates is most likely to get elected to Congress?
    (A) an incumbent senator
    (B) an incumbent member of the House of Representatives
    (C) a challenger for a seat in the Senate
    (D) a challenger for a seat in the House of Representatives impossible to tell from this scenario who is more likely to be reelected
    (E) because reelection depends mostly on party affiliation

25. Why is the filibuster criticized as being undemocratic?
    (A) because it allows a member of the House of Representatives to block legislation that has substantial popular support
    (B) because it can be used in the Senate but not in the House of Representatives
    (C) because it can be used by a member of either house to block legislation that has substantial popular support
    (D) because it allows a senator to block legislation that has substantial popular support
    (E) because there is no procedure for ending a filibuster once it has started

26. Which of the following accurately describes the outcome of impeachment in United States history?
    (A) President Nixon was impeached, but he resigned before he was removed from office.
    (B) Nixon and Clinton are the only presidents who have faced impeachment.
    (C) Articles of impeachment were approved against President Clinton, but he was not impeached.
    (D) Bill Clinton and Andrew Johnson were impeached but not convicted or removed from office.
    (E) Andrew Johnson is the only president to have been impeached and removed from office.

27. Iron triangles have weakened, and some have been replaced by groups of people in interest groups, on congressional staffs, in universities, from the media, and in other interested organizations who debate policies. These are known as
    (A) policy entrepreneurs
    (B) policy allies
    (C) issue networks
    (D) PACs
    (E) social movements

28. The Supreme Court is most likely to issue a writ of certiorari in which of the following cases?
    (A) a conflict between two circuits that have issued opposite rulings about the constitutionality of a federal law
    (B) a conflict between the president and Congress over the War Powers Act
    (C) a criminal case from a state court in which the defendant proclaims his innocence
    (D) a conflict between a federal agency and a state government
    (E) a conflict over the meaning of an unclear regulation issued by an administrative agency

29. How are congressional district boundaries determined?
    I. They are redrawn every ten years according to census data.
    II. They are drawn so that they are roughly equal in square miles.
    III. They are drawn so that, as much as possible, one person's vote will be worth the same as another person's vote.
    IV. They are drawn to favor minority racial groups.

    (A) I and II
    (B) III and IV
    (C) I and III
    (D) II, III, and IV
    (E) II and IV

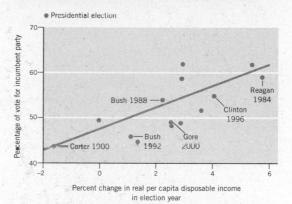

Figure 8.3 Economic Performance and Vote for the Incumbent President's Party

• Presidential election

Percentage of vote for incumbent party

Percent change in real per capita disposable income in election year

Bush 1988
Reagan 1984
Clinton 1996
Carter 1980
Bush 1992
Gore 2000

Note: Each dot represents a presidential election, showing the popular vote received by the incumbent president's party; 1992 data do not include votes for independent candidate H. Ross Perot.

Source: From Robert S. Erikson and Kent L. Tedin, *American Public Opinion*, 5th ed., p. 271. Copyright © 1995 by Allyn & Bacon/Longman. Reprinted by permission of Pearson Education, Inc.

30. The above graph supports which of the following conclusions?
    (A) There is no relationship between an increase in per capita income and the percentage of voters supporting an incumbent president.
    (B) There is an inverse relationship between an increase in per capita income and the percentage of voters who support an incumbent president.
    (C) When per capita income drops, incumbent presidents are not reelected.
    (D) The percent change in per capita income is the same percentage of vote for the incumbent party.
    (E) There is a direct relationship between a rise in per capita income and the percentage voting for an incumbent president.

GO ON TO NEXT PAGE

31. There are 538 total votes in the electoral college. The Democrat receives 265, the Republican receives 255, and an Independent candidate receives 18. How will the election be decided?
    (A) The Democrat will win because he received the most electoral college votes.
    (B) The Democrat will win because no candidate received the majority of the electoral votes and the Democrat won the popular vote.
    (C) There will be a runoff election between the Democrat and the Republican.
    (D) The House of Representatives will decide, with each representative casting one vote.
    (E) The House of Representatives will decide, with each state casting one vote.

32. Which statement best describes the media's coverage of presidential campaigns?
    (A) The media focus primarily on the issues and platforms.
    (B) The media focus primarily on the differences between the candidates.
    (C) The media focus primarily on the horse-race aspects of the campaign.
    (D) Sensational or unusual aspects of the campaigns are the focus of most reports.
    (E) Each candidate is given significant free media time to address the issues.

33. What has been the impact of the Twenty-sixth Amendment?
    (A) People between eighteen and twenty-one years of age are now an important demographic group that significantly influences national policy.
    (B) This group of voters is leading a campaign to lower the drinking age to eighteen.

(C) This group of voters is important at election time, and as a result of their efforts, the move to reinstate the military draft was defeated.
    (D) This group of voters has the lowest turnout rate of any age category.
    (E) More people in this age group are running for office.

34. Which of the following was a critical election?
    (A) the 1996 presidential election, because the vote fell below 50 percent
    (B) the 2000 presidential election, because the electoral college vote did not mirror the popular vote
    (C) the 1932 presidential election, because African Americans made a permanent shift to the Democratic party
    (D) the 1972 reelection of Richard Nixon, because he won in a landslide
    (E) none of these elections meet the criteria for being a critical election

35. Which of the following constitutional provisions has been used to strengthen state powers?
    (A) Tenth Amendment
    (B) full faith and credit clause
    (C) necessary and proper clause
    (D) privilege and immunities clause
    (E) commerce clause

36. All of the following were problems under the Articles of Confederation EXCEPT
    (A) Shays's Rebellion
    (B) state constitutions did not contain bills of rights
    (C) the national government was in debt
    (D) inflation
    (E) states fought over western lands

37. Which of the following is an advantage of a federal system?
    (A) Local governments are more likely to be dominated by factions.
    (B) It is easy to determine which level of government is responsible for a particular problem.
    (C) States can experiment with programs, and the successful ones can be adopted on the national level.
    (D) A federal system is less expensive than a unitary system because there are fewer national government entities.
    (E) States have traditionally protected the rights of minority groups more than the national government has.

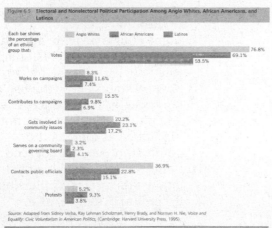

Figure 6.5 Electoral and Nonelectoral Political Participation Among Anglo Whites, African Americans, and Latinos

Each bar shows the percentage of an ethnic group that:

	Anglo Whites	African Americans	Latinos
Votes	76.8%	69.1%	53.5%
Works on campaigns	8.3%	11.6%	7.4%
Contributes to campaigns	15.5%	9.8%	6.9%
Gets involved in community issues	20.2%	23.1%	17.2%
Serves on a community governing board	3.2%	2.3%	4.1%
Contacts public officials	36.9%	22.8%	15.1%
Protests	5.2%	9.3%	3.8%

Source: Adapted from Sidney Verba, Kay Lehman Scholzman, Henry Brady, and Norman H. Nie, Voice and Equality: Civic Voluntarism in American Politics, (Cambridge: Harvard University Press, 1995).

38. The above graph supports which of the following statements?
    (A) Anglo whites participate more in all kinds of political activities than African Americans or Latinos.
    (B) Voting patterns are a result more of income and social class than of race.
    (C) More than half of all Latinos do not vote.
    (D) Protest is the least frequent form of participation for all groups.
    (E) African Americans get more involved in community issues than either Anglo whites or Hispanics do.

39 The above picture best illustrates which of the following?
    (A) a member of an interest group who received an incentive to join
    (B) how the rapidly aging population will strain Social Security and Medicare
    (C) the increased literacy rate
    (D) the power of PACs in influencing legislation to provide prescription drug benefits
    (E) an ideological voter

40. How do political parties choose their presidential nominee?
    (A) by a majority vote in the primaries
    (B) by a majority vote in the caucuses
    (C) through a majority vote of delegates at the national convention
    (D) through a vote of party leaders at the national convention
    (E) through a primary runoff election between the top two candidates

GO ON TO NEXT PAGE

41. In studying government and politics, what does the term "political agenda" mean?
    (A) the scope of government regulation in a particular policy area
    (B) a set of issues that is important to the public and the government
    (C) the platform set forth by the president's political party
    (D) the issues that are subject to legislation currently pending in Congress
    (E) the list of issues determined by the media as meriting public attention

42. Which statement best describes how presidential power has changed over time since ratification of the Constitution?
    (A) Presidential power over foreign affairs has increased, but power over the bureaucracy has decreased over time.
    (B) Presidential power over foreign affairs has decreased because the War Powers Act requires presidents to consult with Congress.
    (C) Presidential power over the legislation has decreased because of negative press coverage of presidential proposals.
    (D) Presidential power over foreign affairs has increased, along with power over the bureaucracy.
    (E) Presidential power has not changed significantly since the Constitution was ratified.

43. All of the following are ways that Congress oversees the bureaucracy EXCEPT
    (A) it can fire agency heads
    (B) the Senate confirms the appointment of cabinet heads
    (C) Congress can submit legislation to the president that cuts an agency's budget
    (D) congressional committees can hold oversight hearings.

(E) Congress can write legislation to clarify agency regulations and procedures.

44. Which statement best describes the Warren Court?
    (A) It made decisions to increase personal liberties, including abortion.
    (B) It made decisions that ended school segregation and restricted defendants' rights.
    (C) It frequently used judicial restraint.
    (D) It made decisions that expanded civil rights and civil liberties.
    (E) It supported affirmative action.

45. Which of the following has been used to weaken the exclusionary rule?
    (A) Several states have passed laws ending the use of the exclusionary rule.
    (B) Some courts provide a good faith exception to the exclusionary rule.
    (C) Several states allow the use of confessions as evidence, even when the defendant was not read his rights, as long as the confession was not coerced.
    (D) Some states now allow civil suits against the police, rather than excluding evidence, as a deterrent to illegal searches.
    (E) States cannot weaken the exclusionary rule because the Supreme Court settled the matter.

46. All of the following features of elections in the United States favor a two-party system EXCEPT
    (A) winner-take-all in the electoral college
    (B) single-member districts
    (C) a plurality vote determines the winner
    (D) one member of Congress is elected from each district
    (E) proportional representation

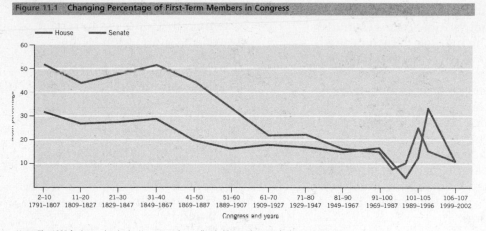

Figure 11.1   Changing Percentage of First-Term Members in Congress

Notes: The 1989 freshman class in the House was the smallest in history. The 1993 freshman class in the House was the largest since 1949.

Sources: Data for 90th through 103rd congresses are from *Congressional Quarterly Weekly Reports.* Data for 69th through 89th congresses are adapted from Nelson W. Polsby, "The Institutionalization of the U.S. House of Representatives," *American Political Science Review* (March 1968): 146. Data for 1st through 68th congresses are from Stuart A. Rice, *Quantitative Methods in Politics* (New York: Knopf, 1928), 296–297, as reported in Polsby, 146. Data for Senate are from N. J. Ornstein, T. J. Mann, and M. J. Malbin, *Vital Statistics on Congress, 1989–1990* (Washington, D.C.: Congressional Quarterly Press, 1990), 56–57, 59–60; and Stanley Harold and Richard Niemi, *Vital Statistics on American Politics* (Washington, D.C.: Congressional Quarterly Press, 2001).

47. What checks does Congress have over the judiciary?
  I.   The Senate confirms federal judges.
  II. Senatorial courtesy can be used to block a nomination.
  III. Congress can overcome an unpopular court decision by proposing a constitutional amendment, subject to ratification.
  IV. Congress can rewrite legislation to overcome a negative court ruling.

  (A) I and II
  (B) I, II, and III
  (C) II and III
  (D) II, III, and IV
  (E) I, II, III, and IV

48. The House of Representatives and Senate pass different versions of a bill. What happens next?
  (A) The bill is sent to a conference committee, then back to both houses for final approval, and then to the president.
  (B) The bill is sent to a conference committee, then back to its original committees for approval, and then to the president.
  (C) The bill is sent to a conference committee, and if the changes are not significant, it is sent directly to the president.
  (D) Both versions of the bill are sent to the president, who signs the version that he prefers.
  (E) The bill is sent to the Speaker of the House and the president pro tempore of the Senate, who agree on common language and then send the bill to the president for signature.

49. The chart above best supports which of the following conclusions?
  (A) The percentage of first-time members in the House of Representatives is always higher than the percentage in the Senate.
  (B) By the 1950s serving in Congress had become a career.
  (C) It is easier for an incumbent in the House of Representative to be reelected than it is for a senator.
  (D) In the period from 1849 to 1991 there was a public backlash against "professional politicians."
  (E) From 1791 until 2002 there was a steady decline in the percentage of first-term members in the House of Representatives.

GO ON TO NEXT PAGE

50. The Food and Drug Administration decides whether new drugs should be put on the market. Which of the following presents the potential for undue influence?
    (A) Pharmaceutical companies are asked to write the new legislation, subject to agency approval.
    (B) Pharmaceutical PACs contribute to the campaigns of members of Congress who support their industry with favorable legislation.
    (C) If a new drug is approved, leaders within the FDA might be offered lucrative positions with a pharmaceutical company.
    (D) An issue network may form to advocate for the availability of prescription drugs from Canada.
    (E) The FDA may ask for more funding from Congress to keep up with its increased workload.

51. How can Congress check the executive branch?
    I. by overriding a presidential veto
    II. by rejecting the president's proposed budget
    III. by refusing the confirm a president's choice for vice president
    IV. the Senate can refuse to approve the president's nomination for a position as cabinet secretary

    (A) I and II
    (B) II and III
    (C) I, II, and III
    (D) III and IV
    (E) I, II, and IV

52. What is the most important factor in predicting the winner in congressional elections?
    (A) the amount of casework done for a district
    (B) the number of pork-barrel projects brought to a district
    (C) incumbency
    (D) the number of times franking privileges have been used to contact constituents
    (E) whether the economy is doing well or poorly

53. Which of the following represent attempts by Congress to regain power in comparison to the president?
    I. the Budget Reform Act (Impoundment and Control Act) of 1974
    II. the Patriot Act
    III. creation of the Office of Independent Counsel
    IV. the War Powers Act

    (A) I and II
    (B) I, III, and III
    (C) II and IV
    (D) II, III, and IV
    (E) I, III, and IV

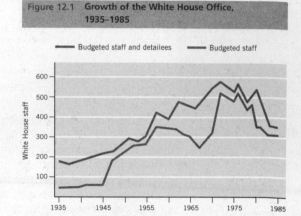

Figure 12.1   **Growth of the White House Office, 1935–1985**

Note: Detailees are people who are employed by and paid by another federal agency but are assigned to work in the White House. Number of detailees for 1981 unavailable.
Sources: For 1935–1977: *Congressional Record* (April 13, 1978), 10111; for 1979–1985: annual reports filed by the White House with the House of Representatives Committee on Post Office and Civil Service, titled "Aggregate Report on Personnel; Pursuant to Title 3, United States Code, Section 113"; and *Budget of the United States Government.* From Samuel Kernell and Samuel Popkin, eds., *Chief of Staff* (Berkeley: University of California Press, 1986), 201.

54. Which of the following statements is best supported by the above graph?
    (A) Since 1935 presidential staffs have grown at a steady rate.
    (B) Democratic presidents have larger staffs than Republican presidents.
    (C) Ronald Reagan decreased the size of the White House staff.
    (D) The size of the White House staff decreased during the Great Depression.
    (E) The size of the White House staff is greater for presidents who use a wheel-and-spokes (circular) structure.

55. Sometimes members of Congress form groups based upon their characteristics or interests. Which term best describes these groups?
    (A) interest groups
    (B) committees
    (C) PACs
    (D) caucuses
    (E) issue networks

56. Which of the following form an iron triangle?
    I.   congressional committees and subcommittees
    II. issue networks
    III. bureaucratic agencies
    IV. interest groups

    (A) I, II, and III
    (B) II, III, and IV
    (C) I, III, and IV
    (D) I, II, and IV
    (E) I and IV

Table 8.1   Changes in State Representation in the House of Representatives

States	Before 1990 Census	After 1990 Census	After 2000 Census	Change
Number of Seats				
Gained Seats **After Both 1990 and 2000 Census**				
Arizona	6	8	10	+4
California	45	52	53	+8
Florida	15	23	25	+10
Georgia	10	11	13	+3
North Carolina	11	12	13	+2
Texas	27	30	32	+5
Lost Seats **After Both 1990 and 2000 Census**				
Illinois	22	20	19	-3
Michigan	18	16	15	-3
New York	34	31	29	-5
Ohio	21	19	18	-3
Pennsylvania	23	21	19	-4

Source: U.S. Bureau of the Census.

57. The table above best supports which of the following statements?
    (A) Most states that lost representatives after the 1990 census regained some of those seats after the 2000 census.
    (B) The states that are gaining in population are the "sunbelt" states in the South and West.
    (C) The states that are losing representatives do not have big cities.
    (D) The states that are gaining in populations all have coastlines.
    (E) There is no geographical pattern to explain why some states are growing in population and other states are decreasing.

58. If voting patterns among African Americans and non-Cuban Hispanics continue, what is the likely implication of having a minority-majority?
    (A) More Republicans will be elected.
    (B) More Independents will be elected.
    (C) Voter turnout will decrease.
    (D) More Democrats will be elected.
    (E) There are so many minorities that having a minority-majority is unlikely to affect elections.

GO ON TO NEXT PAGE

59. All of the following provisions
    govern how states deal with one
    another EXCEPT
    (A) extradition clause
    (B) full faith and credit clause
    (C) supremacy clause
    (D) privileges and immunities clause
    (E) Article I, Section 10 (states may
    not place tariffs on one another)

60. *Griswold v. Connecticut*, in which the
    Supreme Court held that the Fourth
    Amendment includes a right to
    privacy, is an example of what
    judicial philosophy?
    (A) original intent
    (B) judicial activism
    (C) judicial restraint
    (D) statutory construction
    (E) political questions doctrine

STOP

END OF SECTION I

IF YOU FINISH BEFORE TIME IS CALLED, YOU MAY CHECK YOUR WORK ON THIS SECTION. DO NOT GO ON TO SECTION II UNTIL YOU ARE TOLD TO DO SO.

UNITED STATES GOVERNMENT AND POLITICS
Section II
Time—100 minutes

Directions You have 100 minutes to answer all four of the following questions. Unless the directions indicate otherwise, respond to all parts of each question. It is recommended that you take a few minutes to plan and outline each answer. <u>Spend approximately 25 minutes on each question.</u> Support your essay with specific examples where appropriate. Be sure to number each of your answers.

1. Congress exercises control over both the judiciary and the bureaucracy.
   a. Identify and explain two checks that Congress has over the judiciary.
   b. Identify and explain two checks that Congress has over the bureaucracy.

2. Identify, explain, and give a specific example of two changes in the media's coverage of United States government and politics since 1960.

3. Interest groups and PACs have several ways to influence the political process. However, several factors limit their ability to influence the political process.
   a. Identify and explain two ways interest groups or PACs attempt to influence the political process.
   b. Identify and explain one factor that limits interest groups or PACs.

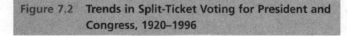

Figure 7.2 **Trends in Split-Ticket Voting for President and Congress, 1920–1996**

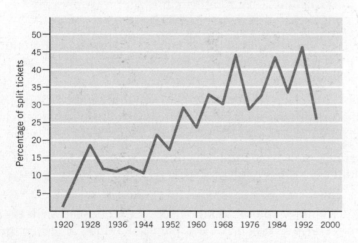

Note: The figure is the percentage of congressional districts carried by presidential and congressional candidates of different parties in each election year.

4. Using the information from the figure above and your knowledge of United States government and politics, complete the following tasks:
   a. Define split-ticket voting.
   b. Identify and explain one trend in split-ticket voting.
   c. Identify and explain one reason for split-ticket voting.

END OF EXAMINATION

Answer Key for Multiple-Choice Questions

1. B	11. C	21. A	31. E	41. B	51. E
2. D	12. E	22. C	32. C	42. D	52. C
3. D	13. C	23. D	33. D	43. A	53. E
4. C	14. A	24. B	34. C	44. D	54. C
5. A	15. D	25. E	35. A	45. B	55. D
6. E	16. A	26. D	36. B	46. E	56. C
7. C	17. C	27. C	37. C	47. E	57. B
8. A	18. D	28. A	38. E	48. A	58. D
9. B	19. B	29. C	39. A	49. B	59. C
10. D	20. E	30. E	40. C	50. C	60. B

ANSWERS TO MULTIPLE-CHOICE QUESTIONS

1. Answer: **B**. The executive has a check on the judiciary by nominating federal judges, subject to Senate confirmation (*American Government*, 8th ed., page 29 / 9th ed., page 29).

2. Answer: **D**. Conservatives tend to support tax cuts, increased military spending, and prayer in schools. They oppose abortion and affirmative action (*American Government*, 8th ed., pages 120-121 / 9th ed., pages 118-119).

3. Answer: **D**. Voters in closed primaries must be registered to a party, are stauncher in their ideology, and are more active in politics (*American Government*, 8th ed., pages 183-185 / 9th ed., pages 192-193).

4. Answer: **C**. Vice presidents have varied in their duties and importance, depending on their relationship with the president and the duties the president wants them to assume (*American Government*, 8th ed., page 367 / 9th ed., page 363).

5. Answer: **A**. Most PAC money goes to incumbents because they are more likely to win. Money goes to candidates who support a PAC's position (*American Government*, 8th ed., pages 236-238 / 9th ed., pages 241-243).

6. Answer: **E**. Under Reagan, military spending increased. This, coupled with tax cuts, resulted in a deficit (*American Government*, 8th ed., pages 465-466 / 9th ed., page 465).

7. Answer: **C**. In the 2000 presidential election, for the first time since 1888, the winner of the popular vote lost the election because of the electoral college vote (*American Government*, 8th ed., pages 340-341 / 9th ed., pages 336-337).

8. Answer: **A**. The House Armed Services Committee is a standing committee because it is permanent (*American Government*, 8th ed., pages 307-308 / 9th ed., pages 307-308).

9. Answer: **B**. Supreme Court justices serve for life to enable them to protect unpopular views and minority rights without fear of reprisal (*American Government*, 8th ed., pages 411, 420-424 / 9th ed., pages 411, 420-424).

10. Answer: **D**. The Senate is the upper house, and it ratifies treaties and confirms judicial nominations. Each senator represents an entire state, which means senators usually represent a bigger constituency than members of the House. Revenue bills

must originate in the House (*American Government*, 8th ed., pages 27-29, 279-282 / 9th ed., pages 27-29, 286-287).

11. Answer: **C**. The Supreme Court has original jurisdiction over controversies between states. There are a few other kinds of cases in which the Court has original jurisdiction; most of the Court's jurisdiction is appellate (*American Government*, 8th ed., pages 414-417 / 9th ed., pages 414-417).

12. Answer: **E**. The president does not have a line-item veto power (*American Government*, 8th ed., pages 358-360 / 9th ed., pages 356-357).

13. Answer: **C**. Chief Justice Earl Warren presided over a liberal court. Eisenhower, a Republican, nominated him. This shows that justices can be very independent once in office (*American Government*, 8th ed., pages 410-411 / 9th ed., pages 410-411).

14. Answer: **A**. The due process and equal protection clauses of the Fourteenth Amendment have been used by the courts to protect groups from discrimination by the states. Congress used the commerce clause to pass the Civil Rights Act of 1964, which prohibits racial discrimination (*American Government*, 8th ed., pages 527-537 / 9th ed., pages 529-539)

15. Answer: **D**. Wearing an armband is symbolic speech that is protected by the First Amendment, as long as it does not cause a substantial disruption in the learning environment (*American Government*, 8th ed., page 497 / 9th ed., page 499).

16. Answer: **A**. The House Rules Committee adopts a rule that governs procedures for considering the bill in the House. It sets time limits on debates, and it can specify the kinds of amendments allowed or prohibit amendments entirely (*American Government*, 8th ed., page 315 / 9th ed., page 315).

17. Answer: **C**. Presidents have generally ignored the War Powers Act and committed troops for more than sixty days without congressional approval (*American Government*, 8th ed., page 559 / 9th ed., page 559).

18. Answer: **D**. Gingrich passed over some senior members as committee heads, abolished three committees, and wanted to limit the committee chairs' terms to six years (*American Government*, 8th ed., page 301 / 9th ed., page 300).

19. Answer: **B**. The Civil Rights Act of 1964 banned discrimination in public places and employment. It authorized the attorney general to bring suits to desegregate schools. A similar law passed in 1968 banned racial discrimination in housing (*American Government*, 8th ed., page 535 / 9th ed., page 537).

20. Answer: **E**. Under the incorporation doctrine, the Fourteenth Amendment protects individuals from state violations of "fundamental personal rights" (*American Government*, 8th ed., page 405 / 9th ed., page 405).

21. Answer: **A**. In *McCulloch v. Maryland*, the Supreme Court held that the necessary and proper clause enabled the federal government to establish a bank because such a power was implied in the power to regulate the currency (*American Government*, 8th ed., pages 55-56 / 9th ed., pages 55-56).

22. Answer: **C**. The family plays the largest role in political socialization (*American Government*, 8th ed., pages 106-107 / 9th ed., pages 106-107).

23. Answer: **D**. Retrospective voters vote based upon how things have gone in the recent past (*American Government*, 8th ed., pages 201-203 / 9th ed., pages 210-213).

24. Answer: **B**. Incumbent members in the House of Representatives have the highest reelection rates (*American Government*, 8th ed., pages 286-287 / 9th ed., page 291).

25. Answer: **E.** A filibuster, which takes place only in the Senate, has been criticized as being undemocratic because one senator can talk a popular bill to death (*American Government*, 8th ed., page 283 / 9th ed., page 288).

26. Answer: **D.** Presidents Johnson and Clinton were impeached. Impeachment is a process in which a president is charged by the House and tried by the Senate. Neither president was convicted or removed (*American Government*, 8th ed., pages 369-370 / 9th ed., page 365-366).

27. Answer: **C.** Issue networks are groups of people from interest groups, congressional staffs, universities, and the media who debate specific issues, like health care (*American Government*, 8th ed., page 391 / 9th ed., page 391).

28. Answer: **A.** The Supreme Court is most likely to take a case when two different circuit courts make opposite rulings over the constitutionality of a federal law. The Court would take the case to clarify the meaning of the Constitution (*American Government*, 8th ed., page 416 / 9th ed., page 416).

29. Answer: **C.** Congressional district boundaries are drawn every ten years, following the census. As much as possible, they are drawn so that every person's vote counts equally (*American Government*, 8th ed., pages 290-291 / 9th ed., page 190)

30. Answer: **E.** The more per capita income rises, the higher the percentage of vote for the incumbent party (*American Government*, 8th ed., page 203 / 9th ed., page 213).

31. Answer: **E.** If no candidate receives a majority vote (270 votes) in the electoral college, the House of Representative decides, with each state casting one vote (*American Government*, 8th ed., pages 340-341 / 9th ed., pages 336-337).

32. Answer: **C.** The media focuses primarily on the horse race—who is winning in the polls and by how much (*American Government*, 8th ed., pages 253-255 / 9th ed., pages 259-260).

33. Answer: **D.** Voters ages eighteen to twenty-one have the lowest turnout of any age group (*American Government*, 8th ed., pages 139-140 / 9th ed., page 142).

34. Answer: **C.** A critical election occurs when there is a major and permanent electoral shift. In 1932 African Americans began voting for the Democratic party (*American Government*, 8th ed., pages 210-211, 204-207 / 9th ed., pages 158-161, 214-216).

35. Answer: **A.** The Tenth Amendment reserves for the states and the people those powers that are not expressly given to the national government or prohibited to the states (*American Government*, 8th ed., page 58 / 9th ed., page 58).

36. Answer: **B.** Under the Articles of Confederation, there was inflation, the nation was in debt, and states fought over western lands. Shays's Rebellion illustrated the weaknesses of the national government. Most state constitutions contained bills of rights (*American Government*, 8th ed., pages 21-23 / 9th ed., pages 21-23).

37. Answer: **C.** Under federalism, states can become laboratories for experimental programs and policies (*American Government*, 8th ed., page 51 / 9th ed., page 51).

38. Answer: **E.** The graph shows that 23.1 percent of African Americans get involved in community issues compared to 20.2 percent of Anglo whites and 17.2 percent of Latinos (*American Government*, 8th ed., page 144 / 9th ed., page 146).

39. Answer: **A.** The American Association of Retired Persons is an interest group that provides its members with a magazine as an incentive to join (*American Government*, 8th ed., page 223 / 9th ed., page 229).

40. Answer: **C**. Delegates are pledged to candidates during state primaries and caucuses. The candidate is formally selected by a vote of the delegates at the national convention (*American Government*, 8ᵗʰ ed., pages 183-185 / 9ᵗʰ ed., pages 192-194).

41. Answer: **B**. The political agenda is a set of issues thought by the public or those in government to merit action by the government (*American Government*, 8ᵗʰ ed., pages 424-426 / 9ᵗʰ ed., page 426).

42. Answer: **D**. Presidential power over foreign affairs has increased along with military technology and sophisticated weaponry. In addition, the bureaucracy has increased to fifteen cabinet departments from the three originally established (*American Government*, 8ᵗʰ ed., pages 349-353, 571-572 / 9ᵗʰ ed., pages 345-350, 571-572).

43. Answer: **A**. Congress can rewrite agency regulations, propose cuts in their budgets, and hold oversight hearings. The Senate confirms the appointments of cabinet secretaries (*American Government*, 8ᵗʰ ed., pages 393-395 / 9ᵗʰ ed., pages 391-395).

44. Answer: **D**. The Warren Court used judicial activism to expand civil rights and civil liberties (*American Government*, 8ᵗʰ ed., pages 410-411, 527 / 9ᵗʰ ed., pages 410-411, 529).

45. Answer: **B**. Some courts allow a good faith exception to the exclusionary rule; evidence obtained under the good faith belief that the search was legal can be used in court (*American Government*, 8ᵗʰ ed., page 516 / 9ᵗʰ ed., page 518).

46. Answer: **E**. The winner-take-all, single-member district, and plurality vote favor a two-party system. In proportional systems used in some European countries and elsewhere, smaller parties benefit by being allocated a proportional amount of seats in the legislature (*American Government*, 8ᵗʰ ed., pages 166-167 / 9ᵗʰ ed., page 173).

47. Answer: **E**. Congress can check the judiciary by approving nominations, rewriting legislation, and proposing a constitutional amendment. Senatorial courtesy allows a senator from the president's party to block the nomination of a district judge from his or her home state (*American Government*, 8ᵗʰ ed., pages 426-429 / 9ᵗʰ ed., pages 427-429).

48. Answer: **A**. When the House and Senate pass different versions of a bill, it is sent to a conference committee to work out the language. Both houses must approve it before the bill is sent to the president (*American Government*, 8ᵗʰ ed., pages 311-312 / 9ᵗʰ ed., pages 312-313).

49. Answer: **B**. The table shows that since 1950 serving in Congress has become a career. Since that time the percentage of first-term members has been below 33 percent (*American Government*, 8ᵗʰ ed., page 286 / 9ᵗʰ ed., page 290).

50. Answer: **C**. Private industry often recruits people from the agencies that once regulated them. This enables them to lobby the agency more effectively (*American Government*, 8ᵗʰ ed., pages 238-239 / 9ᵗʰ ed., page 244).

51. Answer: **E**. Congress can check the executive by vetoing legislation and rejecting the president's budget. The Senate can refuse to confirm the appointment of a cabinet secretary (*American Government*, 8ᵗʰ ed., page 29 / 9ᵗʰ ed., page 29).

52. Answer: **C**. Incumbency is the most important factor in congressional elections (*American Government*, 8ᵗʰ ed., pages 287-289 / 9ᵗʰ ed., pages 291-293).

53. Answer: E. The War Powers Act, Office of Independent Counsel, and Budget Control Act are all attempts by Congress to reassert power over the presidency (*American Government*, 8ᵗʰ ed., pages 361-362, 369-371, 558-559 / 9ᵗʰ ed., pages 358, 365-368, 559-560).

54. Answer: **C**. The White House staff decreased under President Reagan (*American Government*, 8th ed., page 346 / 9th ed., page 342).

55. Answer: **D**. A congressional caucus is a group formed by members of Congress who share characteristics (for example, women's caucuses) or interests (for example, mushrooms) (*American Government*, 8th ed., pages 306-307 / 9th ed., pages 305-306).

56. Answer: **C**. A congressional committee or subcommittee, a bureaucratic agency, and an interest group form an iron triangle (*American Government*, 8th ed., page 455 / 9th ed., pages 454-455).

57. Answer: **B**. States that gained in population and representation in 1990 and 2000 are in the sunbelt in the South and West (*American Government*, 8th ed., page 291 / 9th ed., page 190).

58. Answer: **D**. African Americans and non-Cuban Hispanics are the largest ethnic groups. They tend to vote for the Democratic party. The most likely outcome of having a minority-majority is that more Democrats will be elected (*American Government*, 8th ed., pages 114-118 / 9th ed., pages 113-115).

59. Answer: **C**. The extradition clause, the full faith and credit clause, and the privileges and immunities clause are provisions of the Constitution governing states' relationships with one another. In addition, Article I, Section 10 prohibits interstate tariffs (*American Government*, 8th ed., page 54 / 9th ed., page 55).

60. Answer: **B**. The Supreme Court found a right to privacy implied in the language of the Fourth Amendment. This is a case of judicial activism (*American Government*, 8th ed., pages 404-405 / 9th ed., pages 404-405).

Answers to Free-Response Questions

QUESTION 1 Part (a): One check that Congress has over the judiciary is that the Senate must confirm the president's judicial nominees. Of course, presidents nominate candidates for the federal bench who support the president's judicial philosophies. However, these candidates must face the scrutiny of the Senate. In addition, they might face a filibuster by a senator from the opposing party to block their nomination. This means that the Senate has the final say over who is appointed to the federal bench.

Another check that Congress has over the judiciary is the power to propose a constitutional amendment, approved by a two-thirds vote in each house, if it does not agree with a decision reached by the Supreme Court. For example, the Supreme Court once ruled that the income tax was unconstitutional. This ruling was overcome with a constitutional amendment. Recently, a constitutional amendment was proposed to ban gay marriage that, if ratified, would overcome court rulings to the contrary. Of course, amendments must be approved by three-fourths of the states in order be ratified.

Part (b): One check that Congress has over the bureaucracy is the power of the purse. Appropriations bills start in the House and are required for funding all government programs. Authorizations bills set limits on what agencies can spend. Because Congress can cut or increase an agency's budget, the activities of federal agencies are under congressional scrutiny, and they must justify their budgets.

Another check that Congress has over the bureaucracy is oversight hearings. Congressional committees can hold hearings in which agency heads and personnel are required to testify. Congress investigates whether agencies are operating efficiently and effectively. If necessary, committees can recommend legislation that changes the agency's procedures (*American Government*, 8th ed., pages 394-395, 426-428, 473 / 9th ed., pages 393-395, 427-428, 473).

SCORING This essay is worth 8 points. Part (a) is worth 4 points—1 point is awarded for each identification of a check Congress has over the judiciary (the Senate confirms appointments, and Congress can propose an amendment), and 1 point is awarded for each explanation (the Senate has the final say over who sits on the federal bench, and amendments can overturn a court decision). Points would be awarded for identifying and explaining other powers Congress has over the judiciary, such as enlarging or reducing the number of courts.

Part (b) is worth 4 points—1 point is awarded for each identification of a check Congress has over the bureaucracy (power of the purse and oversight hearings), and 1 point is awarded for each explanation (Congress can cut or increase an agency's budget and Congress can determine how well an agency is operating). Points would be awarded for other checks Congress has over the bureaucracy, such as confirming the appointment of cabinet heads.

QUESTION 2 One change in the way the media report issues is that press coverage of the government is more adversarial. Following the Vietnam War and revelations that the government was not honest with the press about the war's progress, the relationship between the media and the government became more mistrustful. Because of this mistrust, and because scandalous stories sell papers, reporters now investigate potential government wrongdoing and report on it. The best example of this is the Watergate scandal. Two reporters from the *Washington Post* investigated a burglary at Democratic party headquarters and discovered that the Nixon administration tried to cover up the break-in.

Another change in the media's coverage of government and politics is increased sensationalism. The major news networks are now competing with cable stations for viewers. Furthermore, fewer people are watching news programs. This gives networks a big financial incentive to rely on sensationalized news stories involving violence, sex, and intrigue. An example of this is the scandal involving President Clinton and his relationship with a White House intern, Monica Lewinsky (*American Government*, 8th ed., pages 266-269 / 9th ed., pages 271-274).

SCORING This essay is worth 6 points—1 point is awarded for identifying each change in the media's coverage of government and politics (a more adversarial relationship between the media and the government, and increased sensationalism), 1 point for explaining each change (reporters investigate the government looking for wrongdoing, and networks have an incentive to produce scandalous stories), and 1 point for each specific example (Watergate and the Lewinsky scandal). Points would be awarded for identifying other changes, such as the increasing use of sound bites; for identifying other changes, such as the increasing use of sound bites; and for citing other examples, such as the Whitewater scandal.

QUESTION 3 Part (a): One way that PACs attempt to influence the political process is by spending money to help candidates they favor get elected. This spending can take two forms—campaign contributions and independent expenditures. Donations usually go to candidates who are already sympathetic to the PAC's positions. Congressional candidates do not get any federal money to run their campaigns. By giving money to campaigns, PACs hope that a candidate will be elected and will pursue policies favored by the PAC. In addition, through independent expenditures, PACs may spend money on their own advertising campaigns.

One way that interest groups can influence the political process is by providing credible information to members of Congress. Members of Congress are policy generalists who must make decisions in very specific and often technical policy areas. Interest groups can provide congressmen with the kind of detailed, specific, and up-to-date information politicians need. By presenting organized and persuasive information to Congress, lobbyists can develop and maintain the confidence of a legislator and further their group's policy interests.

Part (b): One constraint on PACs is campaign finance reform. Although there is no limit on independent expenditures, PACs are limited to $5,000 in the amount they can contribute to a particular candidate. In addition, advertisements run by PACs may not refer to a specifically identified candidate in the sixty days prior to a general election (*American Government*, 8th ed., pages 192-195, 232-233 / 9th ed., pages 201-204, 237-238).

SCORING This essay is worth 6 points. Part (a) is worth 4 points—1 point is awarded for each identification of a way that PACs or interest groups influence the political process (giving money), and 1 point is awarded for the explanation (money helps sympathetic candidates get elected). You would receive 1 point for identifying a second way that PACs or interest groups influence the political process (giving needed information) and 1 point for an explanation (persuasive information helps congressmen further the group's interests). Points would be awarded for identifying and explaining other ways interest groups or PACs influence the political process, such as hiring the former heads of agencies to help them lobby current members of the agency.

Part (b) is worth 2 points—1 point is awarded for identifying a constraint on interest group influence (campaign finance reform laws), and 1 point is awarded for an explanation (PACs are limited in how much they can give and in the kinds of ads they can run before an election). Points would be awarded for identifying and explaining other constraints on PACs and interest groups, such as the harm that is caused to the group's reputation if it acts in a heavy-handed fashion or exaggerates the facts.

QUESTION 4 Part (a): Split-ticket voting occurs when a person votes for a president from one political party and votes for a member of either house of Congress from the opposing political party. The result of split-ticket voting is divided government.

Part (b): One trend in split-ticket voting is that it increased in frequency from 1920, when less than 5 percent of voters split their tickets, until 1992, when more than 45 percent of voters did so. An explanation for the increase in split-ticket voting over time is that political parties no longer give voters preprinted ballots with only that party's candidates—all voters had to do was mark the top of the ballot and drop it intact into the ballot box. Today, ballots list all candidates for office, allowing voters to split their tickets.

Part (c): One explanation for ticket splitting is that fewer voters identify with a political party and more people consider themselves to be independent. Because these voters do not have an allegiance to a party, they are more likely to vote based upon the individual candidates, without regard to party affiliation. The result is more ticket splitting (*American Government*, 8th ed., pages 211-212 / 9th ed., pages 161-162).

SCORING This essay is worth 5 points. Part (a) is worth 1 point for defining ticket splitting (voting for a president of one party and a member of Congress from a different party). Part (b) is worth 2 points—1 point for identifying a trend (increase in ticket splitting since 1920) and 1 point for an explanation (parties no longer print ballots). Points would be awarded for identifying other trends, such as a drop in ticket splitting during popular presidencies—for example, the Roosevelt administration. Part (c) is worth 2 points—1 point for identifying a reason for ticket splitting (more independent voters) and 1 point for an explanation (independent voters have no party allegiance and vote for the candidate instead of the party). Points would be awarded for other reasons for ticket splitting, such as southern Democrats who voted for Reagan while voting for Democratic members of Congress.

Calculating your score on the AP Exam

SECTION 1: MULTIPLE-CHOICE QUESTIONS

_____ Minus (1/4 X _____) Equals _____
correct   wrong   score

Rounded to nearest whole number _____
                                          **adjusted
score**

SECTION II: FREE-RESPONSE QUESTIONS

Question 1 _____ X 1.875 equals _____
           Out of 8   do not round

Question 2 _____ X 2.5   equals _____
           Out of 6   do not round

Question 3 _____ X 3.0   equals _____
           Out of 5   do not round

Question 4 _____ X 2.5   equals _____
           Out of 6   do not round

TOTAL FOR SECTION II   _____

COMPOSITE SCORE:

_____ + _____ = _____
Section I   Section II   Composite Score

Student scores are weighted a differently each year to determine the final AP score. The conversion chart below is according to the weighing on the 2002 exam:

COMPOSITE SCORE RANGE	AP GRADE
94-120	5
79-93	4
61-78	3
35-60	2
0-34	1